Contents

KU-132-074

Scenic
Driving
FLORIDA

Jan Godown

FALCON®

HELENA, MONTANA

A FALCON GUIDE ®

Falcon® Publishing is continually expanding its list of recreational guidebooks. All books include detailed descriptions, accurate maps, and all the information necessary for enjoyable trips. You can order extra copies of this book and get information and prices for other Falcon guidebooks by writing Falcon, P.O. Box 1718, Helena, MT 59624 or calling toll-free 1-800-582-2665. Also, please ask for a free copy of our current catalog. To contact us via e-mail, visit our website at www.FalconOutdoors.com.

© 1998 by Falcon® Publishing, Inc., Helena, Montana.
Printed in the United States of America.

2 3 4 5 6 7 8 9 0 MG 03 02 01 00 99

All photos by author unless otherwise noted.
Cover photo by James Valentine
Back cover photo by Andy Newman / Silver Image
Color section by Jeff Ripple, James Valentine, and Richard Shock / Silver Image
Black-and-white photos courtesy Florida Tourism Marketing Association,
except where noted.

Library of Congress Cataloging-in-Publication Data
Godown, Jan, 1952-
      Scenic Driving Florida / Jan Godown.
         p.   cm.
      "A FalconGuide"--T.p. verso.
      Includes bibliographical references and index.
      ISBN 1-56044-487-8
        1. Florida--Tours. 2. Automobile travel–Florida--Guidebooks.
  I. Title.
  F309.3.G63   1998
  917.5904'63--dc21   98-10982
                                        CIP

CAUTION

All participants in the recreational activities suggested by this book must assume the responsibility for their own actions and safety. The information contained in this guidebook cannot replace sound judgment and good decision-making skills, which help reduce risk exposure; nor does the scope of this book allow for disclosure of all the potential hazards and risks involved in such activities.

Learn as much as possible about the recreational activities in which you participate, prepare for the unexpected, and be cautious. The reward will be a safer and more enjoyable experience.

♻ Text pages printed on recycled paper.

Dedication

Lovingly dedicated to the sweet memory of Albert W. Godown, with whom I took my first scenic drives and saw a Jersey Pine Barrens black bear, and to his bride, Marian Bailey Godown, still thinking scenically in Tallahassee.

Acknowledgments

Here's a tip of the sun visor to those who labor in Florida parks, preserves, museums, and historic sites. To them and to the public agency staffers, business owners, strangers, and friends along each drive route, who helped in the adventure of producing this FalconGuide, I am grateful.

I specifically thank Captain Mike Fuery, Henry Bonebrake Baker, and Myra Forsberg for research and writing lessons shared in years past in southwest Florida, at the *Fort Myers News-Press*. I am grateful to Sarah Lazin in New York for help with a postponed book project that set a foundation for this one. I salute author, editor, and biologist Susan Cerulean, named by Governor Lawton Chiles as Florida Environmental Educator of the Year. As Falcon Press Southeast Regional Editor she nurtured the project in innumerable ways, took the wheel for a memorable drive in the woods as she identified birds by song, fed me, suggested places to stay on the drives, and twice found my family beautiful temporary lodgings on short notice during the project. Also at Falcon Publishing I applaud Megan Hiller, content editor, for so ably bringing this book to production; production editors Arik Ohnstad and Larissa Berry; copy editor Virginia Hoffman; proofreader Erica Olsen; Randall Green, who oversaw early phases, and Erin Turner, who oversaw later ones. James Valentine and Jeff Ripple deserve the accolades due a talented artist for interpreting the text in compelling color photographs. I thank Dana Kim-Wincapaw for laying out the book, and cartographer Sue Murray for the well-rendered chapter maps.

I also thank chapter readers, who include Captain Mike Fuery, Sanibel Island; Richard Cook, Everglades National Park; Vernita Alexander, National Forests of Florida; Susan Cerulean; Lee Tiger and Bea Moreno, Seminole Tribal Tourism; Dr. Patricia R. Wickman, Seminole Tribe of Florida; Tom Gallaher, Seminole Tribal Ah-Tah-Thi-Ki Museum; and Daniel R. Tardona, Timucuan Ecological and Historic Preserve.

Some others (but not all) who assisted in important ways include: Dixie Nims, media librarian with the Florida Tourism Marketing Corporation, and her colleagues Katharine Morrison and Robin Knight; Kevin McGorty, Red Hills Conservation Association, for research materials including his Red Hills Case Study later published in *Views from the Road*; Dr. Joe Knetsch, consummate Florida scholar and former Florida Historical Society leader whose journal articles illuminate overlooked aspects of Florida's story; Florida Recreation and Parks Director and national ecotourism leader Fran Mainella; Bert Chares, Guana River State Park; Burkett S. Neeley, Jr., Hobe Sound National Wildlife Refuge; and author Gerald Grow, who provided a copy of his excellent guide, *Florida Parks*.

I also thank: Larry Barfield, Florida Department of Transportation State Scenic Highways Coordinator; Nadine Waslosky of State Representative Evelyn Lynn's office; staff of the State Library and Archives; Marnie George and Kevin Bakewell, AAA auto club; Ron Hartung, for providing me a muse, a canopy road greeting card from Fields of Vision in Tallahassee; and Andrea Brunais, editorial page editor, *Tallahassee Democrat*, for scheduling flexibility.

When my van refused to budge one day at the Seminole Tribe of Florida Hollywood headquarters, Osceola scholar Dr. Patricia R. Wickman, who is Tribal Director of Anthropology and Genealogy, former tribe chairman Dr. Betty Mae Jumper, and Geneva Shore met me at the repair shop and whisked me away for dinner on Miami Beach. Then Dr. Jumper, dressed in exquisite floor-length Seminole patchwork, mesmerized the audience assembled at the Sanford L. Ziff Jewish Museum of Florida as part of a tribute to women in Florida history. We told tall tales on the ride back, Pat lodged me, then brought me to my repaired van the next day so I could continue my scenic driving. Every mechanical breakdown should be so serendipitous.

Thanks are also due to Minorcan descendant Elizabeth Masters and her family, Marc Tolzman and Jack Tolzman, in St. Augustine. I also thank David Nolan; Nelson and Mary Smelker; Amy Rankin; Nancy Hamilton; Dee Pomarico; Betty Katz; Susan Marger; Martha Lanier; Camilla and Wes Donnelly; Lorri Trinka; Michelle Brent; Dawn Wilson; Jennifer Crusoe; Frank James; Dean Fowler; Mike Deming; Carolyn Yoss; Harry Hogan; and Julie and Jono Miller, for lodging in an uncommon Florida heritage house of cypress wood in Sarasota.

I thank Mary Fears in Daytona Beach, for prayers and much support; Susie Shaeffer; Julie Smith; Sylvia Starbuck; Brynn Newton; Dorothy Hillman and Jane Harmon; historian Alice Strickland, who remembers watching a Florida panther in the Astor area and once watched sea horses fluttering in the clear lagoon waters of the Halifax River; author Audrey Parente, who told me of rural places I hadn't known; Ed Wilkes; Calvin Horvath; Karen Brillante; Jan Milner; Bill Egan; and Steve Brooks. Susan Mirowski, who sent research materials, deserves much credit and at least a case of Gatorade as driver of the Native American Everglades route in 95-degree weather while the van's air conditioning went into meltdown. I also thank Mary Jo Tierney for help since our Gainesville college days, for driving a route, for mangrove-fringed accommodations in Fort Pierce, and for her car care after the van broke down; Bud Meyer for route suggestions, a picturesque *Miami Herald* Everglades calendar, and Robert Frost material; James Abraham for an inspiring Florida calendar; Jim Eggert and Phil Pollock for old Florida postcards; Elizabeth Morgan for a poolside respite; and Beverly Merchant, Frank Davies, and Kevin Davies for a tropical stay in Coral Gables.

It's also a pleasure to thank Falcon Publishing and *Tallahassee Democrat* colleague Ann Morrow, who found right whale material, listened to progress reports, and kept track of my newspaper, cat, mail, and house during some trips; Deborah Ibert Hiltzik in California, who surprised me with a vital out-of-print Florida book that had eluded me here; Sandra Hyldburg; Velma Frye, who asked good questions and supplied a key phrase; Janie and Ron Nelson; Wendy and Mike Durant; Betsy and Bernie Daley; and Sandee Coulter and Chris Coulter. Richard Drew and daughter Heather deserve a field of Florida wildflowers for sharing 10 acres of northern Florida woods, with pool and cottage, at the end of a rolling red clay road, where much of the book took shape.

Top praise is showered upon Paolo Annino for everything, but especially for keeping his sense of humor as we traveled down scenic but washboard roads that shook us up, and other sandy or mucky roads that almost got us stuck, in the process of eliminating drives from this guide. Our daughter Anna Annino spotted quiet deer in Kissimmee woods when we hadn't seen them, and quietly found wary wild turkey, coyote, and other species. Salvatore and Nellie Annino played with Anna on some occasions when she stayed behind, including one industrious week in the Everglades. Rebecca Towers, Denise King, and Melissa Lilavois also creatively occupied Anna at home when this project required uninterrupted time. Marian Bailey Godown generously offered her library of Florida books, articles, and materials, and shared a wealth of zestful Florida knowledge. Joanna Godown kept me company on several drives.

I am particularly thankful for the work of historian Michael Gannon, editor of *The New History of Florida*, author of acclaimed Florida histories and novels, and enthusiastic professor whom it was my good fortune to study with at the University of Florida. One Florida novel I especially appreciated on the road became a spiritual guide, *River of Hidden Dreams*, by Connie Mae Fowler. Finally, I loudly applaud advocates who work hard to preserve natural and historic Florida. Without them this book wouldn't exist because Florida would be without scenic drives.

Jan Godown
Tallahassee, Florida

Locator Map

Map Legend

Scenic Drive (paved)

Scenic Drive (gravel)

Interstate

Other Roads (paved)

Other Roads (gravel)

Freeway Exit

Bridge

Building

Point of Interest

Campground

Hiking Trail

River/Creek

Waterfall

Lake

Marsh

Interstate

U.S. Highway

State and
County Roads

Forest Service
Roads

Wilderness Area,
National/State Park

National Forest
Boundary

Indian Reservation
Boundary

State Boundary

FLORIDA

Map Orientation

N

Scale of Miles

0   0.5   1

Miles

Scenic Drive
Location

Introduction

One of Earth's features visible from space is a skinny finger of land that points the way from the mainland United States to the tropics. No place on this slender sand pile is more than about 65 miles from saltwater. Yet this famous, historic peninsula stretches about 1,350 curving coastal miles, from the hilly red clay border in the Panhandle to the Florida Keys' coral rock. Its complete meandering shoreline—including bays, islands, and inlets—is, after Alaska's, the longest in the United States, at about 8,400 miles. The shiploads of postcards that have been mailed around the world from the Sunshine State show off Florida's glistening Atlantic Ocean and Gulf of Mexico waterfronts.

Florida is more than just impressive ocean views. The peninsula's freshwater shores sparkle too; Florida contains at least 1,690 rivers and streams. The state's 7,700 lakes are dwarfed by comparison with the second-largest lake found within one state's border, Florida's shallow Lake Okeechobee. (The largest is found in Alaska.) Although most of the state sits close to sea level (the highest point in Florida is 342 feet), small hills found in central and northern Florida surprise visitors. The presence of 300 springs bubbling with clear water makes Florida the top springs state in the United States. Florida's impressive wetlands serve as vital water purification areas and are nurseries teeming with plant, bird, mammal, amphibian, insect, and aquatic life. An acre of Florida estuary, where freshwater mixes with saltwater, creates more food—for plants, animals, and humans—than an acre of midwestern wheat field.

Scenic Regions

Florida's Panhandle, including the curve of the Big Bend along the Gulf of Mexico, is a surprising stretch of red clay hills, river ravines with rare Appalachian mountain laurel, sandhills, and flat pine forests where black bear roam. Here ancient Native American footpaths have been converted into nationally acclaimed oak-lined country roads that pass cotton fields and cornfields. Nearby are limestone caves, rivers rippled by subtle shoals, small coastal fishing communities and interior villages with blossoming magnolia trees, eclectic museums, popular Gulf of Mexico beaches, and remote saltwater marshes—coastal zones that are stopovers for raptors and other migrating birds.

Northeast Florida, to the east of the Panhandle, holds a breezy historic savannah where buffalo and eagles thrive. The region has clear-water springs, stunning rivers, a great pine forest, legendary swamps, and wide potato fields. A string of Atlantic Ocean sea islands marches along the shore to the northern border, protecting towers of dunes and sheltering marshy

The Ten Thousand Islands region of Everglades National Park is home to mangrove islands of many shapes and sizes.

backcountry coves where winter birds, including flotillas of ducks, feed.

Central Florida is cloaked by a pine forest in the sand and filled with clear springs and rivers and visited by road-crossing black bear. Citrus groves and cattle pastures roll across the hilly landscape. To the west, where the terrain is characterized by marshes and isolated out-island preserves, the land melts into the Gulf of Mexico. Along its east coast the region offers an Atlantic Ocean seascape of dunes, ancient Native American mounds, and offshore shipwrecks. A winter bird marsh shelters the snouted, prehistoric-looking manatee, or sea cow.

South Florida is the inscrutable last stronghold of the Florida panther. Here, the Everglades and the Big Cypress Swamp dominate. The famous Everglades, a "river of grass" dotted with cypress tree islands and orchid gardens, slopes gently to the mangrove coast of Florida's Ten Thousand Islands, a twisted jungle that edges an aqua subtropical sea.

Geology

Florida's land is geologically the youngest in the United States, emerging from the sea for the last time about 6,000 years ago. The Florida peninsula is primarily a limestone base full of holes; shelly sand, clay-filled sand, and ancient Appalachian quartz sand; crushed shell beds; silt; and rich peat. Caverns slowly carved by water that drips through the soft limestone make Florida a prime state for underwater caves. This same process creates geological surprises, sinkholes that open up under a thin crust of earth. Robert Frost, the New England poet-farmer, tended mango and avocado plants at his winter place near Miami. He took a few of Florida's roads less traveled and told a reporter for the *Miami Herald* that his adopted state had "funny land." He was right.

Natural Florida

Florida mothers more species of plants and animals than any other continental state except California and Texas. Florida shelters a natural menagerie of federally listed endangered species, including the right whale, sturgeon, manatee, Florida panther, snail kite, peregrine falcon, crocodile, wood stork, red-cockaded woodpecker, indigo snake, and loggerhead and green sea turtles. Other creatures, such as bald eagle, black bear, sandhill crane, caracara, and scrub jay, are listed as threatened. Still other famous Florida symbols not listed as threatened, such as alligator, porpoise, the leaping manta ray, the silver tarpon, river otter, snowy egret, and osprey, will thrive only if Florida's waters remain clean.

Many of Florida's trees and plants are endangered or threatened. This includes rare orchids, other delicate wildflowers, and the torreya tree. The Florida hothouse sprouts 314 species of trees (compared to about 160 along the Pacific Coast) and 3,500 other plant species, and shelters about 425

Sea oats anchor sand on Florida beaches, allowing it to form dunes.

birds (more than half of all species in the United States). Florida waters are home to more than 200 freshwater fish species and more than 70 saltwater species, and 150 kinds of amphibians and reptiles live near the shores. The land also supports about 80 mammal species. These creatures compete for space with people and pavement in an urban state where about 700 new residents unpack their swimsuits and sandals every day. Because Florida is like no other place most newcomers are understandably unschooled in the ways of natural Florida. This guide is an invitation to learn and to begin to preserve the mysteries of natural and historic Florida.

Historic Florida

The first people to inhabit Florida walked onto the peninsula about 12,000 years ago. The region stretched about twice as far then as it does today, and was drier and carpeted with grassy prairies. These Paleo-Indians wandered a west coast shoreline jutting out as far as 100 miles into the present-day Gulf of Mexico. They traveled across Florida, camping at scarce freshwater sources, and hunted mammoth, camel, bison, and other big game. They left chipped-stone implements and bone and antler tools as evidence of a successful hunting and gathering society that has been uncovered by archaeologists at ancient campsites.

About 9,500 years ago the Paleo-Indians had to adapt to a changing Florida as glacial melt altered the shoreline. These peoples, called the Archaic culture, evolved a more settled existence and used a wider variety of tools, woven fabrics, bone hairpins, throwing sticks, decorated antlers, and other fascinating items that are reflected in Florida museum exhibits today. From about 1000 B.C. to A.D. 1492, Florida's residents built burial mounds, created temple mounds, lived in communal villages, and cultivated corn and other food. They also crafted cooking pots and ceremonial pottery. Eventually they enhanced their lives by trading with native people as far away as Illinois, sending Florida shells and shark teeth north in exchange for copper, stone, and other items unavailable in Florida. In southern Florida organized villagers dug integrated canal systems and paddled large canoes on oceangoing trips to Caribbean islands.

By the late 1400s, Spanish explorers had already reached islands to the south of Florida, such as Puerto Rico and Cuba. These explorers believed Florida to be an island, but a much larger one than the nearby tropical shores they had already visited. On some early maps the peninsula was labeled *Insula Florida*, "Island of Flowers."

Historians can only guess when Florida's native coastal villagers first saw Europeans. But imagine the scene one day in about 1510 when a native

Scenic Florida is a land of small, unexpected charms.

of southern Florida looked offshore to see bearded men in thick metal clothes standing on a giant sailing canoe, a Spanish slave ship. In 1513, when Juan Ponce de León took his first famous voyage to Florida, there may have been 350,000 natives prospering here. Historians studying the documents of his voyage think he landed on the Atlantic coast just south of Cape Canaveral. He called the "island" *La Florida*, because it was pretty and because he arrived in April, the time of his faith's *Pascua Florida*, or Flowery Easter.

In 1519 Alonzo Alvarez de Pineda learned that Florida was not an island, but a peninsula of a much larger land mass. Florida was the name given to the new continent by the Spanish.

In 1539 the governor of Cuba, Hernando de Soto, made landfall on Florida's west coast, probably near present-day Tampa. For four years he trekked with 600 soldiers, slaves, and others through the forests of the Florida Panhandle into Georgia and eventually to the Mississippi River, a journey of about 4,000 miles. His expedition of conquest is infamous for its atrocities, including the unleashing of Spanish war dogs on the Florida natives who resisted subjugation in de Soto's search for gold. As escaping native runners spread the news of the invading war party through Florida, thousands of villagers fled from the peninsula.

Spain continued sending explorers to Florida in hopes of extracting riches from its wilderness. But France also coveted the flowery land, which it called *Nouvelle France*, New France. French sea captain Jean Ribaut landed near present-day St. Augustine in 1562, leaving behind a marble column engraved with the French coat of arms. Two years later French explorer Rene de Laudonniere and a group of soldiers, artisans, nobles, women, and children arrived east of present-day Jacksonville with the intention of starting a colony. Laudonniere's colony, Fort Caroline, ended in mutiny. In 1564 Jean Ribaut, now the "viceroy" of New France, returned to revive Fort Caroline. Instead, he lost battles with an ambitious Spanish commander and future Florida governor, Pedro Menendez de Aviles, who began his own colony. In 1565 Menendez built a fort around a native longhouse, naming it San Augustin, which we now know as St. Augustine, the first permanent European settlement in North America. San Augustin was served by a hospital 55 years before the Pilgrims would land at Plymouth Bay.

In the 1600s the Spanish expanded their colonization of Florida, setting up a string of missions among the natives, with whom they intermarried. By the early 1700s the Spanish had introduced wagon and ox-cart travel to the peninsula, and stagecoaches bumped along over rough roads, which were often expanded native footpaths. The Spanish were stymied in their attempt to hold the region permanently by frequent raids by the British from bases in their American colonies. After 1763, following the French and Indian War, Spain yielded *La Florida* to Great Britain.

Horseback riding on the beach at Amelia Island State Recreation Area.

During the next 21 years, the white population of Florida grew as hopeful British entrepreneurs arrived in the wilderness, intending to set up sugar cane, rice, and indigo plantations using slaves and indentured servants of various nationalities. However, the British mainly found hardship in the wilderness, especially in the form of yellow fever. After the American Revolution and the Treaty of Paris, the British yielded the peninsula back to Spain. After a second attempt to flourish in Florida, in 1821 Spain traded its North American colony to the United States for payment of debt to U.S. citizens. In 1845 Florida became a state. By then travelers could reach the peninsula by river steamboat; railroads brought visitors beginning in the 1880s.

In the first half of the nineteenth century, white settlement of the peninsula advanced through the waging of three wars against natives, which cost about $40 million. These Native American residents lived in villages, fished, kept chickens and other farm animals, built log and clapboard houses, tended successful gardens, and raised herds of up to 10,000 cattle. They were considered to be without tribal allegiance, and came to be called Seminoles, a corruption of *shim-i-no-les*, a Caribbean word meaning "living free." During these wars about 3,000 Seminoles were removed to the West and about 1,500 were killed. About 200 to 300 native survivors of the wars refused to leave Florida. They retreated to a hidden life in the Everglades, never signing a peace treaty. Four decades later, in the 1890s, their descendants began peaceful trade with settlers on the Everglades' borders. The state's proud and prosperous Seminole and Miccosukee cultures survived, and about 3,000 people living in Florida today are directly descended from these survivors of war.

During the Civil War, Florida's capital, Tallahassee, didn't fall to Union control, although Key West and Pensacola, with their strategic coastal forts, remained in Union hands throughout the war. Florida next had a role in war when its leaders and business owners helped Cuban patriots buy and ship guns from Florida to the island during Cuba's war for independence. In 1898, when war broke out between the United States and Spain, Florida hosted troops and war followers—including Teddy Roosevelt and his Rough Riders—en route to Cuba. During the 1920s, Florida experienced the "land boom," the largest internal migration of people in the history of the United States up to the 1960s.

Today's visitors to Florida travel on modern roads along the same routes that ancient natives; Spanish, French, and British explorers; early settlers; and more recent native residents walked. Now the world watches as a select group of Florida visitors, space shuttle astronauts, hurtle into space from Cape Canaveral, near where Juan Ponce de León landed and named what he thought was an island—the sand pile peninsula visible from space.

How to Use This FalconGuide

Each chapter offers one drive, accompanied by photographs and a map. Use a current Florida highway map and local maps for other road information. Some chapters include side trips, discussed under a separate heading at the end of the main drive description. Postal and e-mail addresses, telephone numbers, and web sites can be found in Appendix A, at the back of the book. These will help you find more detailed information on the areas described in *Scenic Driving Florida*. Florida public agencies and selected groups that deal with natural and historic Florida are listed in Appendix B. Recommended further reading and a detailed index conclude the book.

At the start of each chapter, "at a glance" material offers a recommended travel season or a specific time to avoid, often linked to wildlife events or blooming plants, or to difficulties, such as excessive summer heat and humidity. Here, too, look for a summary of route numbers, significant sites, preserves, and general camping information.

Because many, many people from all over the world take vacations in Florida, it is wise to make reservations when possible, both for public campgrounds and private facilities, especially in the busy winter season. Drive routes are numbered as they appear on Florida road maps. Most of the drives are paved—any unpaved portions and any expected rough conditions are noted. Chapters may mention a WARNING, such as cautions about a dirt road that may become temporarily impassable after heavy rain, and they also may include a NOTE, for example, about odd hours at points of interest, such as the midweek closing of a museum.

What to Avoid

Generally, these scenic drives are open year-round, but newcomers may want to avoid a summer visit on a first trip. Summer weather is, to be honest, inhospitable for all but the toughest visitor. As author Zora Neale Hurston wrote of her native state, "I love the way the sun shines in Florida, the rain too, in great slews or not at all." While the great slews of sun are welcome in winter, they irritate when collected into a week of 95-degree F days, aggravated by dense slews of rain and 70 percent humidity that pumps up the 95-degree-F temperatures to a heat index of 124 degrees F. Temperatures inside a car parked in the sun at a museum or a trailhead, with windows closed and air conditioning off, can easily reach 110 degrees F and higher. If you overexert yourself in hot weather, you risk dehydration, heatstroke, and worse, sunstroke. Heavy summer and early fall rains make some roads and footpaths temporarily impassable. Storms can produce severe lightning; Florida is the national leader in deaths and injuries from lightning strikes. Mosquitoes, horse flies, biting midges, and other biting bugs are a plague of the long summer, which can last from April through early October. June through November is hurricane season. Pay attention to news bulletins about the progress of tropical storms toward Florida if your vacation coincides with hurricane season. If you must come in summer, and some do to watch a great sea turtle mother lay eggs or to hike into preserves for a glimpse of summer-blooming orchids, wear light-colored, loose, cotton clothes and full-brimmed hats, use insect repellent, and reapply sunscreen frequently during daylight hours. (Hats and sunscreen are prudent in other seasons too.) Take along lots of water or Gatorade. For best wildlife viewing, rise early or venture out in the late afternoon and early evening, but also be aware that biting bugs are busiest at dawn and dusk.

As for winter, while central and southern drives will be benign, visitors to northern Florida may want coats and long pants. Temperatures can reach 80 degrees F in February in northern Florida, but visitors are generally surprised to find winter highs of 40 to 50 degrees F in the north, with nighttimes in the 30s, and an occasional freeze or flurries.

Boating is fun, but it can be a dangerous activity in Florida. According to the Florida Marine Patrol, deaths usually occur when a boater falls overboard; most victims weren't wearing mandated life jackets or personal flotation devices. Frequently, alcohol is a factor. You shouldn't operate a boat without basic driving lessons and complete equipment, especially life jackets. Popular personal watercraft are an irritant to wildlife; I don't recommend using them. Tidewater salt marshes are shallow and difficult to motor through and are Florida's nurseries for a host of life. They should be left alone by boat except for a careful visit in a kayak or canoe. Learn what the water speed limits are locally and the location of posted manatee movement zones, areas of strictly limited speed or access.

Creatures

Be alert. Rural roads are used by resident animals as well as motorists. I have seen fiddler crabs marching across them in platoons in coastal zones; take care not to crunch our inch-long fiddlers. Snakes—most in Florida are nonpoisonous—crawl onto roads to warm themselves. Land turtles too cross roads, usually to reach a source of water. If you help a stalled land turtle, move it to where it's headed or it will begin to cross the road again. Alligators bask in sun on isolated road shoulders and, to the surprise of new visitors, in the middle of human footpaths that are near water. While some visitors find it tempting to toss them food, this is illegal and foolish. Even if you escape unharmed, think about the next person, especially a child, who comes along when a bold alligator taught to associate people with food expects a handout. Respect their wild nature: don't feed wild animals.

Licenses for freshwater fishing are sold in most bait shops. For complete information about saltwater and freshwater fishing and licenses, contact the agencies listed in Appendix B, or ask your wildlife guide about limits and rules. Watch out for some sea creatures: catfish have barbs, and jellyfish and Portuguese man-of-war drift inshore to some beaches and can sting even if beached on the sand. Others, such as horseshoe crabs, prehistoric creatures with brown armor and a pointed spike, are mean-looking, but harmless—unless you step on their hard shells.

At busy fishing piers accidentally hooked pelicans or line-entangled sea gulls are, sadly, a frequent emergency. In many areas wildlife rehabilitation centers, or designated veterinarians, try hard to rescue wounded animals.

Watch for wildlife bounding onto the road; signs aren't posted everywhere creatures are likely to roam. Every year black bears are killed on Florida roads. This occurs mostly at night, mostly during the spring and fall in central Florida, especially near and in the Ocala National Forest, so be alert there, too.

Unlike bears outside the state, Florida's bears have not learned to forage in park campgrounds. It is always wise to make food inaccessible to animals when camping because of other foraging creatures, such as raccoons. If you do see a bear, make noise, quit approaching, and give it a wide berth. It is unlikely you will spy a Florida panther in the wild so you have no need to fear them. Most panther sightings turn out to be bobcat, and also, in northern and central Florida, coyote.

If you see wildlife harassment or suspect violations, report the incident (you can remain anonymous) by telephone; phone numbers are in Appendix B.

Use Caution

Plan ahead. Don't expect to rely on the kindness of park rangers or strangers. Join an emergency road service, but always start out by checking the oil, fluid levels, and tires of your automobile. The remote roads that make up these scenic drives are not convenient roads on which to break down. The modern traveler in remote regions would be wise to take along a cellular telephone. In most areas, 911 is the emergency response number; otherwise dial "0." To increase security (and preserve the land) camp only in designated camping areas.

Take Home Snapshots

Visitors can take home a sample of soft sugar sand, an unoccupied sea-shell, a photograph of a green palmetto frond, or a glistening stream-polished stone. Don't snitch other souvenirs from nature. It is illegal to pick stately sea oats, because their long, tough roots anchor drifting sands. It is also illegal to disturb Indian burial sites and other archaeological sites. All parks and preserves restrict the taking of plants and most animals. In some areas, such as Sanibel Island, it is illegal to take live shells (shells still inhabited by an animal). Today, everywhere in the state, it is customary to leave live shells so they can reproduce.

Enjoy

After experiencing a scenic drive, you may have a better opinion of Florida than wildlife painter and hunter John James Audubon once recorded. During a trip here in 1831, when shallow but rough and cold water forced him and his companions out of rowboats to slog about uncomfortably by foot, he wrote disgustedly of Florida: "... all that is not mud, mud, mud, is sand, sand, sand ..." You may feel instead, in the words of the character Mrs. Aaronson from Maxwell Anderson's play (later a famous movie) *Key Largo:* "I want to stay here all the rest of the time!" If you do stay, Welcome! Pick a favorite conservation group and support it, to help increase the chances that what remains of natural Florida will endure.

1

Canoe Capital
Blackwater River Region

General description: This out-of-the-way trip is a 10-mile meander through red hills in the far northwest of Florida. The drive rolls through the longleaf pine–wiregrass habitat that Florida shares with neighboring Alabama. It also crosses and recrosses a winding woodland river.

Special features: Blackwater River State Forest, Blackwater River State Park, Blackwater River and Canoe Trail, canoeing, tubing, swimming, freshwater fishing, hiking, camping.

Location: Northwestern Panhandle, about 7 miles from the Alabama border.

Drive route numbers: U.S. Highway 90, Main Street and Second Street in Holt, Johns Road, Bryant Bridge Road, Bob Pitts Road, Deaton Bridge Road.

Travel season: Year-round. In spring and summer—the rainy season—call ahead and ask about water levels, as local flooding can make canoeing temporarily difficult to impossible, and can even make some bridges impassable. Like most of the drives in this book, this one can be sweltering in summer. Fall and winter bring seasonal hunts, so take commonsense precautions when hiking and be sure to wear fluorescent orange. Some river outfitters close in winter due to reduced demand.

Camping: Blackwater River State Park has a lovely wooded campground. The surrounding Blackwater River State Forest also has several popular campgrounds, including Krul Recreation Area, reachable via SR 4 about a quarter of a mile east of the forest crossroads and forest headquarters of Munson. The forest's Bear Lake, about a quarter of a mile east of Krul Recreation Area via SR 4, is another improved campground. There are several private campgrounds and fish camps in the area.

Services: There is a small wayside grocery and gas station in Holt. Milton, a riverfront village about 12 miles southwest of this drive, has all other services. There is a canoe outfitter (summer to fall) on the drive itself who also rents inner tubes, has restrooms, and sells supplies such as sunscreen and cold drinks. There are other canoe rentals in the region.

Nearby points of interest: Coldwater Creek, a designated canoe trail, is a popular canoeing stream located west of this drive (via SR 4) in the Blackwater River State Forest. Sweetwater and Juniper creeks in the state forest are also designated canoe trails. Milton offers a small village square of shops and cafes directly on the Blackwater River as it winds through town. DeFuniak Springs, east of this drive on US 90, is an old village with many restored buildings. There are two state parks with unusual features for Florida nearby: Falling Waters State Recreation Area (via Chipley and SR 77A) and Florida Caverns State Park (via Marianna and SR 167). **Time zone:** Central.

 # The drive

Few visitors to Florida see its largest state forest or one of its most famous rivers. These treasures are tucked away in the far northwestern corner of the Panhandle, just a few miles from Alabama. But for those visiting northern Florida who can take a trip farther northwest, this drive offers excellent canoeing opportunities including the chance to glide where river otter fish, and to visit a longleaf pine and wiregrass ecosystem that shelters turkey, bobcat, eastern bluebird, and red-cockaded woodpecker.

Begin this drive at the intersection of US 90 and Main Street in the tiny crossroads of Holt. The intersection sits between CR 189 and the Holt First Baptist Church. Drive north from US 90 on Main Street, which is marked with a street sign, one block across the railroad tracks and immediately turn left (west) on Second Street, the first street after the railroad tracks. Continue west on Second Street past village homes. After about half a mile the street enters pastureland and becomes Johns Road. Soon Johns Road enters the boundary of Blackwater River State Forest, a 183,000-acre woodland. Continue north on the road, now called Bryant Bridge Road, through pine forest and occasional private, residential inholdings. The road is two-lane, narrow, and has frequent patched potholes and rough areas, but it is totally paved. It winds through the increasingly wooded landscape, with red clay state forest service roads leading off from it to the remote forest interior. Because of the narrowness of the road and its uneven surface, most posted speed limits are 30 or 35 miles per hour, though signs at some curves call for slower speed. During hunting season, this region is busy with hunters, so wear fluorescent orange when hiking and use common sense. The road winds over gently rolling hills past pine woods dotted with seasonal wildflowers, such as the native orange flowering azalea in spring.

About 3 miles from the Second Street turn, on Bryant Bridge Road, just before small, level Bryant Bridge, slow down to turn right into the first Blackwater River overlook and canoe put-in on this drive, right at roadside. The view from the overlook includes the river as well as the adjacent forest and the cedar- and magnolia-dotted floodplain. If you plan to go out on the river, please note that glass containers aren't allowed on the river and trash must be carried out. A canoe outfitter or park ranger can inform you about bringing litter bags to help keep the river clean, and about standard disposal

Drive 1: Canoe Capital
Blackwater River Region

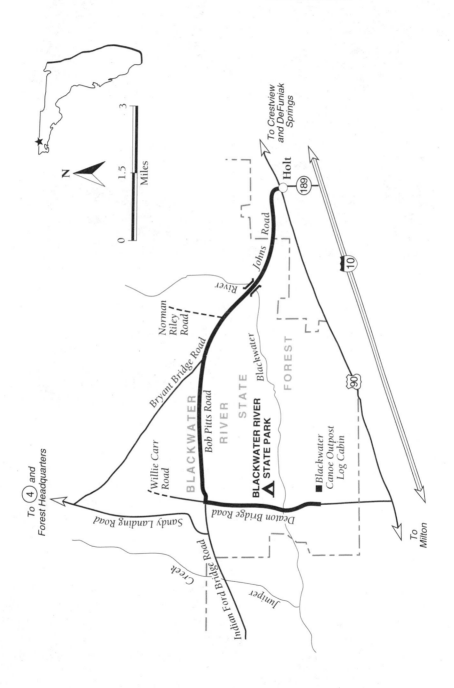

The meandering Blackwater River is a canoe trail with ancient sand beaches.

of human waste if you are traveling the river for any distance.

Continue the drive by turning right from the overlook on Bryant Bridge Road and proceeding over the Blackwater River across the short, narrow Bryant Bridge. Experts consider the Blackwater one of the world's purest sand-bottomed rivers. It originates in Alabama and flows about 45 miles to Blackwater Bay and then on into historic Pensacola Bay and the Gulf of Mexico. Continue on Bryant Bridge Road about a quarter of a mile, at which point the drive intersects an unpaved state forest access road on the right.

The forest is noted not only for the Blackwater River, but also for the unique ecological niche it occupies. The forest marches over ancient red hills north into Alabama, where it is known as the Conecuh National Forest, and this vast woodland is the largest continuous community of longleaf pine and wiregrass in the world. This ecological community once covered about 90 million acres of the southeastern United States' coastal plain. Today's remnant—less than three million acres in the southeastern United States—is home to the federally listed endangered red-cockaded woodpecker, as well as the more common bobcat, beaver, turkey, and white-tailed deer. Its wet areas also produce bogs of rare, carnivorous plants, including six species of pitcher plants. You may see these pipelike species sprouting in wet woodlands in spring through early summer.

About 1.4 miles after Bryant Bridge the curving road crosses a forest intersection known as Riley's Corner. An informal collection of old tractors is arrayed at the right, on the edge of a field. Immediately after, look in the field for a stand of short cypress trees, a small island of beauty in a forest of many beauties. Soon after Riley's Corner, Bryant Bridge Road comes to a Y intersection. The drive veers left at the Y, onto Bob Pitts Road (signed, though sign is hard to see). After turning left onto Bob Pitts Road, travel about 3 miles through more rolling hills until you come to a four-way stop. This is the intersection with Deaton Bridge Road, on the left, and Indian Ford Bridge Road, which leads to Juniper Creek, straight ahead. The drive turns left on Deaton Bridge Road, continuing about 1 mile to the boundary of 590-acre Blackwater River State Park. About a quarter of a mile farther, you will come to the first park entrance, on the left. This entrance leads to the campground, a picnic area, and a half-mile-long nature trail near the river. If you continue another quarter of a mile on Deaton Bridge Road, you reach low Deaton Bridge, which crosses the Blackwater River. Two public parking areas (fee required) on either side of the river provide overlooks on the river. The first parking area accommodates only a few cars, but it has picnic tables and a nearby beach. The second parking area, directly across the bridge, is large. You can park there and walk back across the bridge for a mid-river view. WARNING: The bridge is a narrow bridge of wooden planks, without high guard rails or sidewalks, so be exceptionally alert if there is road traffic. On popular weekends this bridge and road can be busy with pickup trucks, cars, and canoe outfitters hauling racks of canoes. But at other times you can have this small Eden of wonderland over flowing water to yourself.

If you continue along the drive on Deaton Bridge Road, you will see a log cabin on your left in about 1.3 miles. This is a seasonal canoe outfitter, as well as a place to find supplies. It is also the end of this short drive. To reach US 90, continue south on Deaton Bridge Road past the canoe outfitter and about 7.5 miles through the woods to the railroad tracks, where Deaton Bridge Road intersects US 90. A right turn on US 90 will take you directly into Milton, a riverfront town, in about 12 miles.

2

Bay Delta, Gulf Villages, and Drifting Dunes

Choctawhatchee Bay to Eden State Gardens

General description: This drive, the book's first coastal meander, covers about 15 miles of bay and gulf shore in Florida's Panhandle.

Special features: Choctawhatchee Bay; Grayton Beach village; Grayton Beach State Recreation Area and Western Lake, with an unusual dune nature trail; Seaside village; Seagrove Beach village; Point Washington Wildlife Management Area; the Wesley Mansion at Eden State Gardens; birding; beachcombing; camping; hiking; fishing; crabbing; boating; swimming.

Location: Coastal Panhandle Florida, about 140 miles west of Tallahassee.

Drive route numbers: U.S. Highway 331, U.S. Highway 98/State Road 30, County Road 283, County Road 30A, County Road 395.

Travel season: Summer in the Panhandle is the busiest season, with crowded beaches. Expect temperatures in the 90s, high humidity, lightning storms, and occasional hurricane threats. Better times to visit are November to December and March to April. If you enjoy bundling for blustery beachcombing, with temperatures in the 40s and 50s, January and February allow you to feel the beach is your own. The off-seasons are also best to see migrating birds and butterflies and wintering birds.

Camping: Grayton Beach State Recreation Area has a campground, away from the beach. Public camping is also available about 20 miles northeast of this drive on State Road 79 at Pine Log State Forest. There are several private campgrounds west and east of this drive along CR 30A and US 98.

Services: Most services can be found in the coastal villages along CR 30A, including Grayton Beach, Seaside, and Seagrove Beach. Medical care can be found in Destin.

Nearby points of interest: Choctawhatchee River tours (Black Creek Lodge); DeFuniak Springs Historic Village; Pine Log State Forest; Ponce De Leon Springs State Recreation Area; Topsail State Park; Indian Temple Mound and Camp Walton Schoolhouse, Fort Walton Beach.

Time zone: Central.

Drive 2: Bay Delta, Gulf Villages, and Drifting Dunes

Choctawhatchee Bay to Eden State Gardens

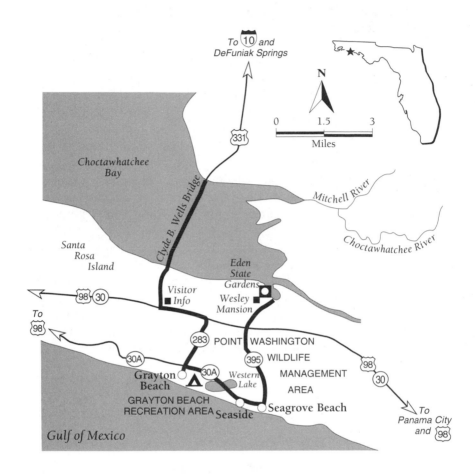

 # The drive

This drive begins by spanning a seafood-rich bay on which aboriginal Indians built villages as early as 3,000 years ago. The drive continues past Gulf of Mexico beaches interspersed with cottage villages that are long on charm, with no franchise intrusion—a sharp contrast to much of Florida's condominium-dotted shoreline. At Grayton Beach State Recreation Area, a small marsh attracts feeding birds and 40-foot-tall dunes drift powerfully over magnolia and oak trees. The drive transects Point Washington Wildlife Management Area and finishes at the bay delta. Here, in a remote live oak woods, the stately 1897 Wesley Mansion plantation home sits near its historic ornamental garden, the grounds sweeping down to a hidden delta cove of wild bay shore.

Begin this drive on US 331 as it enters Choctawhatchee Bay on the Clyde B. Wells Bridge, about 13 miles south of the US 331 junction on Interstate 10.

The long bay is a popular recreational boating and fishing resource. As you cross the water look left (east) to see the vast, marshy delta where the Choctawhatchee River, after winding 150 miles from southeastern Alabama, flows into Choctawhatchee Bay. This is a brackish marine nursery, or estuary, which supports both freshwater and saltwater species as part of Florida's fishing industry. The delta's mud flats, marsh grasses, and sedges not only help anchor a home for marine life, but also provide food and shelter for birds, insects, reptiles, and mammals. Before overfishing ruined it, the region also supported a sturgeon fishery.

After about 2.5 miles on the bay bridge, US 331 enters Santa Rosa Island, a coastal barrier that serves to buffer the mainland from hurricanes and other storms. Drive another 2 miles to the roadside Walton County Welcome Center (on the left just before the flashing yellow traffic light at the intersection of US 331 and US 98/SR 30), where you can get maps and information on availability of camping, restaurants, lodging, fishing guides, boat trips, preserves, historic sites, and wildlife, in addition to cold water and restrooms.

Continue the drive by turning left (east) on US 98/SR 30. This road is known as the Emerald Coast Parkway, for the frequent color of nearby gulf water. Drive about 1.5 miles and turn right, heading south, on CR 283. You will travel through the sandy coastal scrub of pines and palmettoes in Point Washington Wildlife Management Area, part of a 104,267-acre managed-hunting region supporting fox, deer, raccoon, bobcat, rabbit, dove, and turkey. In about 1.5 miles CR 283 intersects CR 30A at the old village of Grayton Beach. You've reached the Gulf of Mexico coast.

Crossing CR 30A, drive about a quarter of a mile on CR 283 (DeFuniak Avenue), which is lined with cafes, small inns, cottage shops, and homes. Potsherds and other evidence uncovered by archaeologists date human activity here back to at least 1000 B.C. Much later, in the 1700s and 1800s, the Euchee and Choctaw tribes fished and swam here. In about 1880, a retired New England sea captain named Gray built a wood-frame house in the dunes, lending his name to the community. At least one original home stands, a feat considering the more than 100 intervening years of winds, saltwater floods, rains, and humidity. The village experienced a flurry of

Western Lake at Grayton Beach is a feeding ground for wading birds,
including the great white heron.

The Wesley Mansion recalls the period when Point Washington was still a company town.

expansion in the 1920s, when houses were built from local cypress on sandy, tree-shaded streets, setting the tone for the village you see today.

From Grayton Beach village retrace your path to the DeFuniak/CR 30A intersection and turn right (east) on CR 30A, locally known as Beach Highway. NOTE: County Road 30A is a winding two-lane road, a paved ribbon that can accommodate small RVs. Parking at coastal restaurants, inns, and shops is extremely limited, and in many cases drivers of larger RVs will have difficulty parking. Be alert for people and wildlife crossing this road, as well as adjoining CR 283 and CR 395.

After about half a mile you will see the entrance to Grayton Beach State Recreation Area on the right. This park is one of the smallest in the state system, yet its dunes and pristine quality helped it win honors as the top beach in the nation in a 1994 ranking by the University of Maryland. The 1-mile-long beach is an ancient geological feature of glistening, snow-white quartz sand, washed down from the northern Appalachian Mountains eons ago. This ancient sand is found at other Panhandle coastal preserves, which have longer coasts but aren't as easily accessible.

Another feature in this park is the dune nature trail—a rare opportunity since walking on sand dunes is prohibited in Florida's preserves. Grayton's dune trail meanders up and down the soft sand for 0.75 mile, and features 15 numbered markers corresponding to nature notes provided in a free trail pamphlet, available from a trailhead self-service box at the beach parking lot. At times the path reaches treetop level, where visitors can look down on stunted magnolia trees. The wind-driven sand also piles up against live oak, palmetto, and slash pine, at times nearly smothering them. In these and other tree branches, keen observers will notice flitting songbirds, such as the vireo, cardinal, towhee, and white-throated sparrow. Other markers along the way point to native plants and views of the park's Western Lake and marsh—prime feeding ground for wading birds such as the great blue heron, and wintering grounds for various ducks, including the blue-winged teal, red-breasted merganser, and lesser scaup.

Upon exiting the park, turn right (east) on CR 30A, the Beach Highway, and travel for about 1 mile. Past Western Lake and across a cove of the small lake is the community of Seaside. This village, begun in 1981, won national honors for designs that include an updated version of metal-roofed steep-sloped cottages on stilts, close clustering of buildings, creative use of community areas, and little need for cars. With white picket fences, brick streets, sand paths, vest-pocket gardens, hidden walkways, scattered arbors, and attractive cottages and shops that have front porches, second and third-story screened balconies, and white gingerbread trim, Seaside is an intrusion, but a soft-style one, in this fragile coastal zone. Well-staged events, such as storytelling, lectures, festivals, and musical performances at the village green amphitheater are frequently scheduled.

NOTE: Driving isn't allowed on the streets of Seaside except to reach lodging destinations; streets are reserved for walkers and bicyclists. Vacant parking spots at Seaside are scarce in the busy summer season and on some weekends.

Continuing east along CR 30A about half a mile past Seaside, the drive visits the village of Seagrove Beach, which was homesteaded by a retired Union Army captain from Ohio. About half a mile past the T intersection of CR 30A and CR 395, look for walking access to a small, local beachfront park that has stunning 40-foot sand bluffs above the gulf shore. The corner grocery in Seagrove Beach, the two-story Sugar Beach Inn with its profusion of wildflowers, and the bookmobile set up on schedule on CR 395 are simple features of this small crossroad community.

At the intersection of CR 30A and CR 395, this drive leaves the gulf shore. Travel inland (north) on CR 395, through another portion of Point Washington Wildlife Management Area. After about 3 miles the drive intersects US 98/SR 30. At the stop sign, continue across the highway on CR 395, and go straight ahead about 1 mile to a dead end at an old bayou community called Point Washington, which is today home to a small number of rural residents. This area developed in the 1890s as a lumber company town, with a company store, worker cottages, sawmill, and busy wharf on Tucker Bayou, where timber was floated away on barges to be loaded on gulf steamboats and shipped to customers in Europe and South America.

About a block before CR 395 dead-ends at Tucker Bayou, look on the left for the entrance to Eden State Gardens, the end of this drive. Go about half a mile through a tunnel of palmetto and live oak woods to emerge into an open, manicured expanse of park. A white, two-story columned mansion dominates the scene, sheltered under massive live oak trees fringed with silver-gray Spanish moss. The Wesley Mansion and grounds are closed Tuesday and Wednesday. The gardens no longer boast 35 workers laboring over them at one time. But with secluded benches and curving paths they are still a lovely place of quiet.

3

Apalachicola Bay Ramble

Apalachicola to St. George Island State Park

General description: This 23-mile coastal Panhandle drive begins at a former Native American village that later became a cotton plantation port. The drive climbs across two bridge and causeway systems over sparkling marine nurseries famous for oysters, to arrive at St. George Island, a Gulf of Mexico resort island renowned for its nesting shorebird colonies, seasonal raptor migration, drifting sand, and a 4.5-mile drive along undeveloped gulf shore.

Special features: Apalachicola Historic District, including John Gorrie State Museum; Apalachicola Maritime Museum and rides on 1877 *Governor Stone* schooner; the Raney House; Chapman Botanical Garden; St. Vincent National Wildlife Refuge headquarters; Apalachicola National Estuarine Research Reserve visitor center; private guided wildlife trips; Dr. Julian G. Bruce St. George Island State Park; beachcombing; bay, surf, and deep-sea fishing; snorkeling; birding; summer crabbing; swimming; camping; canoeing.

Location: Coastal Panhandle.

Drive route numbers: U.S. Highway 98, State Road 300.

Travel season: Late fall through early spring (November through April) is the best time to enjoy the island park's prime position as a stopover for migratory birds, especially raptors, and to beachcomb in cooler weather. Summer is the high season, popular with sun worshippers and crabbers, who can expect daily temperatures in the 90s or higher, aggravated by high humidity, thunderstorms, hurricane threats, and biting bugs. NOTE: Sunscreen is a must year-round, and on warm fall and spring days without breezes, insect repellent is usually necessary on the barrier islands.

Camping: Dr. Julian G. Bruce St. George Island State Park offers a popular campground, a reservation-only youth camp, and primitive camping. There are private campgrounds at Eastpoint and Apalachicola. T. H. Stone Memorial St. Joseph Peninsula State Park, a recommended side trip (see below), has a public campground.

Services: Apalachicola has charming bed and breakfast inns, restaurants, cafes, shops, and other services. There are also some services in Eastpoint and on St. George Island.

Nearby points of interest: T. H. Stone Memorial St. Joseph Peninsula State Park, the Carrabelle village waterfront, Dead Lakes State Recreation Area, Ochlockonee River State Park.

Time zone: Eastern.

 # The drive

This drive introduces an out-of-the-way fishing village and Florida maritime history. The village of Apalachicola sits next to a delta preserve of the Apalachicola River, whose floodplain supports the tupelo trees which provide the nectar for the region's pure tupelo honey. Many restored buildings date to the bustling 1840s riverport days. The drive also includes St. George Island State Park, a coastal barrier beach offering excellent beachcombing. You can depart from the village of Apalachicola to both the St. Vincent National Wildlife Refuge and the T. H. Stone Memorial St. Joseph Peninsula State Park; see the side trip description at the end of this drive for details.

Start the drive in downtown Apalachicola, at 268 Water Street, the Maritime Museum office. This exhibit center is the administrative headquarters for the *Governor Stone* sailing ship, a grand two-masted schooner built in 1877, honored as a National Historic Landmark and probably the oldest operating vessel in the South. The ship, which is docked nearby, is open for rides to benefit the fledgling Apalachicola Maritime Museum.

During its boom days in the mid-1800s, Apalachicola's 43 warehouses, each three stories tall, held piles of cotton bales. The cotton arrived by churning steamboat from slave-owning plantations upriver in Alabama, Georgia, and northern Florida. The port stayed so busy that Apalachicola challenged New Orleans as a top gulf seaport.

About this same time, 80 to 120 deep-sea divers, with the earliest of diving equipment, collected natural sponges from the sea floor, helping the village to open the state's first sponge exchange. Giant cypress and other trees from inland forests were felled for valuable timber and also brought to port here. The prosperity of the times financed many large wood-framed homes featuring wide verandas and gingerbread trim. An unrestored sponge warehouse built about 1840 and two cotton warehouses built about 1838 still stand, two blocks east of Market Street, along the waterfront. The success of railway systems in Georgia and northern Florida, and other factors, led to the decline of Apalachicola's port.

In later years, oyster harvesting from the bay and nearby St. George Sound became the primary cash crop of the region, and oysters are still considered king here, along with "pink gold," fresh Gulf of Mexico shrimp. The first weekend in November Apalachicola attracts thousands of visitors for a seafood festival that features an oyster-shucking contest. There are usually no vacant rooms during festival time. The event attests to Apalachicola's continuing and crucial ties to the area's fragile waterway systems and marine produce. Visitors are asked to observe good environmental practices on and around the water; contain waste onboard and dispose of it properly once on shore.

Drive 3: Apalachicola Bay Ramble

Apalachicola to St. George Island State Park

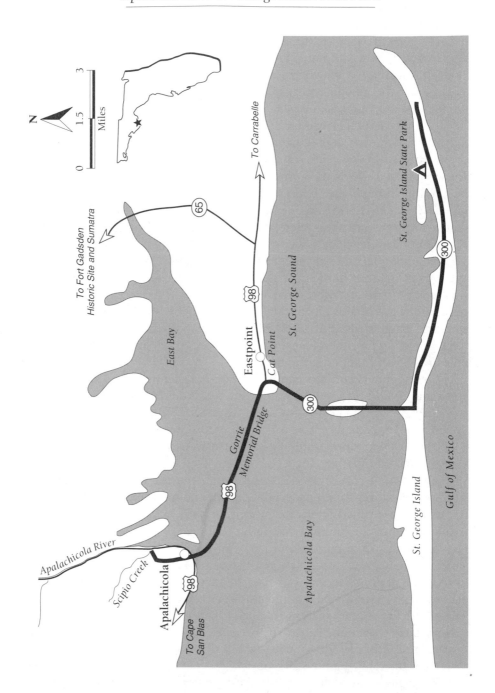

After the Maritime Museum office, the next stop is the Apalachicola Chamber of Commerce, tucked inside the Apalachicola State Bank building on the corner of Market Street and Avenue E. Ask for the self-guided tour brochure. The village was started about 1821 and incorporated as West Point in 1827. Later it received the more lyrical Apalachicola. As often occurs with words of Native American derivation, historians can only speculate about the meaning. It may be an interpretation of a native phrase, possibly *apalachi okli*, for "people on the other side," or it may be from a native term for allies. Before the Maskoki people, also called Creeks, had a village here, the earlier natives of this region were the Apalachi, Apalachen, or Apalachees.

After orientation at the Chamber, continue north one block to 45 Market Street, a two-story Greek Revival home with four Doric columns. The Raney House, built in 1838, is the former home of a cotton merchant who moved the building from nearby St. Joseph when an epidemic of yellow fever wiped out that town. Included on the National Register of Historic Places, the Raney House is sometimes open for special events.

Continue a few blocks along Market Street to the Chapman Botanical Garden (on the left side of the street). A small public park with Victorian-style street lights, it honors the internationally acclaimed naturalist Alva Wentworth Chapman, whose name was given to a rhododendron species found in the mountains and also in the Apalachicola River region. A physician, Dr. Chapman used Apalachicola as a base in the mid- to late 1800s for plant-collecting journeys. Just south of the garden is stately Magnolia Hall, built in 1838 and today a guest house.

Market Street continues another quarter-mile before ending at the Scipio Creek marina and park, on the waterfront. Across the narrow canal note the two-story pile of shucked oyster shells, used for road pavement and development fill. Immediately to your right as you enter the park sits the two-story, gray, wood-frame headquarters (open weekdays) of the St. Vincent National Wildlife Refuge. The island refuge itself is about 20 miles west of Apalachicola and part of a side trip mentioned at the end of this chapter. Interpretive exhibits here explain the human and natural history of the refuge, which was formerly a private hunting preserve for exotic species owned by the creator of the Pierce-Arrow luxury car.

Adjacent to the marina and park, on the left (west), sits the visitor center of the Apalachicola National Estuarine Research Reserve. The reserve is the nation's largest, with 240,000 acres, most of it wetlands. The visitor center (open weekdays) explains the reserve's role as a national study center, with the region's shallow waters and shoreline, a fragile marine nursery, serving as classroom. At the visitor center, you can learn about topics of ongoing research, including marine mollusks, the endangered loggerhead turtle, and the rare Atlantic sturgeon.

Retracing your path along Market Street, go a block past the Raney

Apalachicola, an 1840s riverport on the Gulf of Mexico, is home to a number of restored mansions.

House and turn right at the blinking traffic light onto Avenue E/US 98. Travel west a few blocks to Sixth Street (also called Broad Street) and turn left, going one block to the John Gorrie State Museum, which overlooks Gorrie Square. Working with yellow fever victims in 1841, Dr. John Gorrie considered that the mysterious—and deadly—illness, whose cause was yet unknown, didn't occur in cold or dry climates. Theorizing that cooled air could reduce the chance of disease, and would certainly make the fever sufferers feel better, he attempted to keep his patients' rooms cooled. He is now considered the grandfather of ice making and air conditioning, and the air-cooling machinery he designed is owned by the Smithsonian Institution.

To continue this drive, retrace the few blocks to Market Street and turn right (south) onto it, traveling about one block, noting on the right the balconied Gibson Hotel, built about 1907. Now redecorated, with shops, a restaurant, meeting space, and inn-style lodging, the hotel sits at the foot of the towering Gorrie Memorial Bridge (US 98), which takes you across the bay.

As you climb Gorrie Bridge heading east, look far left toward the mouth of the Apalachicola River, where its 112-mile journey comes to an end. The high bridge affords a bird's-eye view of the river, which carries the biggest volume of water of any Florida river. After the bridge arches past a small island on the left, the water on the left is part of East Bay, within the research reserve. East Bay is a strategic nursery ground for shrimp, oysters, and other aquatic life, and is part of a plan to restore water quality to the region. Look for fish-catching ospreys, also called sea hawks, returning to nests in the tall transmission towers on the left. Porpoise often surface in these waters.

In 5 miles the causeway reaches the mainland at Godley's Bluff in Eastpoint, an oyster processing and fishhouse community. Travel about three-quarters of a mile ahead on US 98 and turn right (south) onto SR 300, marked by a small brown park sign for St. George Island State Park. Travel south just under 1 mile to Cat Point and the beginning of a bridge and causeway system that replaced the ferry around 1965, connecting the mainland to the fragile barrier island. To the right is Apalachicola Bay and to the left is St. George Sound. Out on the water the gray flat-bottomed boats, about 9 feet long, are anchored to collect oysters. Giant hand-held tongs are used to pull the oysters up from the oyster beds.

The 4-mile bridge and causeway system to St. George Island is a restricted-access nesting area from April through summer, for the protection of shorebirds, black skimmers, and least terns. Heed No Trespass signs, and park and fish only in designated areas.

Shrimp boats bring "pink gold" to port at Apalachicola's working waterfront.

18

As the drive enters St. George Island, continue traveling about two blocks straight ahead, taking a left turn at the sign for St. George Island State Park, as SR 300 turns left and is now also called East Gulf Beach Drive.

This island's service center area is a commercial intersection with little evidence of habitat preservation efforts, but stick with the drive, continuing east on East Gulf Beach Drive, past shops and homes built on stilts to minimize damage from hurricane and storm-driven floodwaters. As the drive continues away from the service center, protective dunes gradually appear along the gulf shore. In 8.5 miles East Gulf Beach Drive (SR 300) empties directly into St. George Island State Park.

WARNING: Stay on roadbeds and park only in designated areas anywhere on the sandy island, including the park. Cars frequently become stuck in the soft sand, providing steady business for tow trucks.

The park was once famous for towering dunes, but cycles of storms and hurricanes have washed across this fragile spit of sand. The narrow park is a good example of how coastal barrier island shores aren't geologically suited for construction. Unrelenting tides, winds, storms, and hurricanes continually rearrange the sand, swiping land from one location to deposit it in another. Barrier islands such as this one serve to absorb the brunt of this natural rhythm and help protect the mainland.

The state park, which ranks high on national lists of top public beaches, is busy in summer, sometimes filling to capacity on weekends with sunbathers and crabbers who stalk blue crabs with dip nets along gulf shore beaches. Visitors in late fall through early spring will likely see migrating birds. They will also avoid the crowds, intense heat, humidity, thunderstorms, and biting bugs of summer.

Any time of year waves toss up a variety of shells and flotsam onto the park shore; look for cockles, whelks, and scallops. Today it's understood that live shells are left behind to reproduce; take only shell skeletons. The state park covers 1,962 acres, including 9 miles of beach shoreline. Sandy secluded coves, marshes, and oak forests characterize the park's St. George Sound shoreline. In fall the park is a prime area to spot migrating raptors. It is also a favorite place to observe warbler and vireo species. Resident ospreys, which are a sight to behold as they fly overhead carrying freshly caught fish in their talons, build nests here high in pine trees.

The park, which is the end of this drive, offers a popular campground in pine forest. Boat launching ramps are at East Slough and the youth camp area. From the main campground a 2.5-mile trail follows an old logging path through the inland pine forest to Gap Point on the St. George Sound shore, where you may observe nesting bald eagles.

Beach side trips

Two coastal beaches deserve attention, the first about 20 miles west and the second about 27 miles west of Apalachicola. To see the first, St. Vincent National Wildlife Refuge, it's best to hire a boat and guide in Apalachicola. You can drive to the second beach park, at T. H. Stone Memorial St. Joseph Peninsula State Park, via US 98, then SR 30 and SR 30E.

St. Vincent National Wildlife Refuge was a site of early human occupation. Island pottery shards have been dated to A.D. 240, and occupation likely began much earlier. Franciscan friars named the island when visiting the region's aboriginal natives in 1633. Today the refuge's 12,358 acres offer undisturbed nesting beaches for federally listed endangered loggerhead turtles, nesting trees for bald eagles, and freshwater lakes for migrating endangered wood storks. The refuge is also the site of a red wolf breeding program. Wild wolf pups born here are weaned and then reintroduced into original range, such as Great Smoky Mountains National Park. The island is located at the convergence of Apalachicola Bay, St. Vincent Sound, and the Gulf of Mexico. Access is by boat only, and Apalachicola-based guides offer day trips to the refuge.

NOTE: There are no facilities at the refuge so water and food must be taken over by boat, and trash, of course, must be taken out. All native plants, Native American sites, and wildlife are strictly protected. A deer and hog-hunting season is observed, and this is the only time overnight primitive camping is allowed.

Farther west of the national refuge sits the T. H. Stone Memorial St. Joseph Peninsula State Park, about 27 miles from Apalachicola via US 98, SR 30, and SR 30E. This park is on the fall migration route of the federally listed endangered peregrine falcon. The park features towering coastal dunes and sand scrub habitat of wind-stunted trees. You may also be fortunate enough to glimpse coyotes, deer, great blue herons, stingrays, horseshoe crabs, blue crabs, jellyfish, and other wildlife. Raccoons travel in marauding troops of three or more, even in daytime, and skunks are frequent campground visitors at night. The park's eastern shore hugs a bay famous for scallop beds; the mollusks are harvested fresh in the summer.

4

Oyster Coast and Forest Pines
Eastpoint to Fort Gadsden Historic Site

General description: This 68-mile drive begins in Eastpoint, a coastal center for oyster and seafood processing, then proceeds inland to Fort Gadsden Historic Site, and returns to Eastpoint, taking in a few miles of sheltered shoreline and the pine flatlands of Apalachicola National Forest along the way.

Special features: Oyster-processing district, coastal highway, Fort Gadsden Historic Site, Apalachicola National Forest, Apalachee Savannahs National Forest Scenic Byway.

Location: Panhandle coast and inland.

Drive route numbers: U.S. Highway 98, State Road 65, Brickyard Road and Fort Gadsden Road (Forest Service), County Road 379.

Travel season: November through April is recommended to avoid summer temperatures of 95 and higher, biting bugs, swarms of gnats, and heavy rains which can make travel on unpaved Forest Service roads difficult. November, March, and April are the best times to see wildflowers in bloom along roadsides.

Camping: Apalachicola National Forest campsites are located on Owl Creek at Hickory Landing and on a small lake in the pines at Wright Lake, about 4.5 miles north of the turnoff to Fort Gadsden Historic Site, via unpaved Forest Roads 101 and then 101B (Hickory) and 101C (Wright). There is private camping in Eastpoint along the Apalachicola River, and along the stretch of US 98 from Eastpoint east to Carrabelle. About 26 miles northeast of this drive, Ochlockonee River State Park, on US 318 near Sopchoppy, has a popular campground. Torreya State Park, a recommended side trip (see end of this drive), also has a public campground.

Services: Gas, groceries, restaurants, private campgrounds, and lodging are available in Eastpoint; other services, such as bed and breakfast inns and medical care, can be found in Apalachicola. WARNING: Once the route turns north onto SR 65, there are no services. Sumatra, on a side trip of this drive, has a gas station/convenience store/bait shop.

Time zone: Eastern.

Drive 4: Oyster Coast and Forest Pines

Eastpoint to Fort Gadsden Historic Site

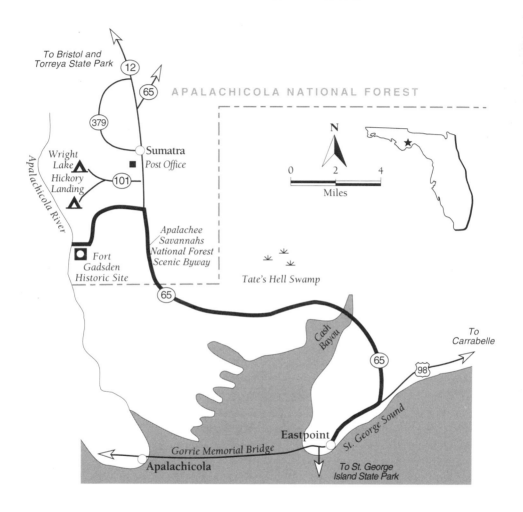

 # The drive

You'll begin and end this drive in coastal Eastpoint. It is recommended that you start out not long after dawn in hopes of glimpsing forest wildlife, such as wild turkeys, the federally listed endangered red-cockaded woodpecker, deer, and fox squirrel, so called because of its big, bushy tail. This will also enable you to be back in Eastpoint for lunch and a chance to sample some of the freshest seafood in the state.

Begin in Eastpoint on US 98, about 5 miles east of the village of Apalachicola, on the east side of Apalachicola Bay. Eastpoint is a little-known coastal community, an unpretentious seafood-processing center with rectangular, single-story oyster houses lining the two-lane highway. The community hugs a flat inland coast along narrow St. George Sound, a shallow bay where oysters grow between Eastpoint and St. George Island. As you travel east along US 98, you will see boats tied up at small piers behind the oyster houses. Beyond the boats lies St. George Sound, with St. George Island beyond. The flat-bottomed boats here are primarily used for oyster harvesting. Giant hand-held tongs are used to pluck the oysters up from the bottom of the sand in the sound; the oysters are then moved to the processing houses, sprayed with water to loosen grit and silt, and shucked by workers wielding special shucking knives. Most oyster processing houses are closed to the public, but some occasionally allow visitors to take a peek at the processing work, and some have retail counters for oysters and other seafood.

After passing through about a mile of this commercial district, the drive continues along the open shore, hugging the water. The broken pilings and tree snags in the water are evidence of destruction from storm-driven waves. Portions of this highway are often washed out after hurricanes, forcing temporary closing and emergency repairs.

About 3 miles from the oyster processing district on US 98, make a left turn onto SR 65, the James Gadsden Highway. The highway is named for Lieutenant James Gadsden, who served with General Andrew Jackson in this region after the War of 1812. Continue north on SR 65, and in about 4.8 miles the drive crosses Rake Creek with its freshwater marsh system. Look here for wading birds such as the great blue heron.

In another 2.6 miles the drive skirts the western border of a vast 100,000-acre swamp region known as Tate's Hell. This little-traveled area between Carrabelle and Sumatra is celebrated in Florida folklore; as once sung by Florida troubadour Will McClean, Tate's Hell received its name after a pioneer called Tate was discovered after crawling through the swamp, snakebit and feverish, for 12 days. The dying Tate told his rescuers his name and said, "I've just been in hell."

Tate's Hell does not have marked canoe trails or developed recreational areas. The best way to visit Tate's Hell is with someone experienced with its features. A wildlife guide based in Apalachicola offers canoe trips into the swamp, and Tallahassee chapters of national conservation groups sponsor occasional journeys.

Continuing north, the drive ambles through reforested pinewoods. In 9.5 miles, SR 65 becomes the Apalachee Savannahs National Forest Scenic Byway, and the drive enters the Apalachicola National Forest. This is the

Insect-eating pitcher plants poke up from the bogs of the Apalachicola National Forest in the spring. Vernita Alexander, National Forests of Florida photo

largest national forest in Florida—569,014 acres of flat terrain featuring pines, cypress swamps, and wet prairie savannahs. This western section is frequented more by fishers and hunters than by tourists. Some sections of the forest are managed to protect the endangered red-cockaded woodpecker. Other woodpeckers native to this area include the pileated (which is crow-sized), the red-bellied, and the small downy.

This region is known for its tupelo honey, made by bees that collect nectar from the tupelo gum tree. Beekeepers here in northern Florida produce the only certified-pure tupelo honey in the world. This beekeeping tradition is the backdrop for a thoughtful 1997 film called *Ulee's Gold*, which makes a good introduction to the Apalachicola region.

About 4 miles into the national forest (or 20.8 miles from the drive's turnoff from US 98), look for a brown sign for Fort Gadsden Historic Site. Turn left from SR 65 onto Brickyard Road and follow this unpaved Forest Service road about 1 mile through the woods. Make another left turn, onto Fort Gadsden Road, and you will find the entrance to the historic site in about a quarter of a mile. A tall row of wooden posts, called pickets, can be seen as you approach this memorial.

Overlooking the Apalachicola River about 15 miles from its mouth, the site is an elevated area of thickly wooded ravines called Prospect Bluff.

The river served as transportation from Georgia into the Florida Panhandle, and upriver from Apalachicola into the interior, during the 1800s, before railway systems became widely established. For centuries before that, Native Americans paddled and poled along this waterway in hand-built, cypress-log canoes.

During the War of 1812 British Marines arrived here and built a log fort, from which they recruited Seminole Indians and escaped slaves to fight with them against the United States. When the British left their outpost in 1814 under pressure from Spain (which owned Florida at the time), they turned the fort over to the Indians and escaped slaves, leaving them fortified with artillery and gunpowder. Native American families moved near the protective fort, creating a village. The fort was called Negro Fort by U.S. military leaders, who were incensed that Spain was not policing the natives and escaped slaves to their satisfaction. Sharpshooters from within the fort regularly fired on U.S. military boats traveling from Apalachicola to Fort Scott, Georgia. In an exchange of volley in 1816, the munitions area inside the fort was hit, resulting in an explosion that killed 277 men, women, and children. Only 33 people survived the destruction of the fort.

Two years later, General Andrew Jackson sent Lieutenant James Gadsden to build a new fort here as part of his campaign to remove Semi-nole Indians from the region. The fort again came to prominence in the Civil War, when Confederate troops occupied it to control the river corri-dor. After that it went largely unused. The log structure gradually blended into the forest that grew up around it.

The site is listed on the National Register of Historic Places. It is also a stop on Florida's Black Heritage Trail. There is a miniature fort replica and interpretive exhibits. You can also visit the cemetery site and steamboat landing nearby.

From here you can take the recommended side trip (described at the end of the chapter) or return to Eastpoint by retracing your path to SR 65 and turning right (south).

If you are delighted by unusual plant life, you can make a short diver-sion here before returning to Eastpoint. Turn left on SR 65 and travel north about 3 miles to Sumatra. Just north of Sumatra take the angled left turn from SR 65 onto CR 379, a two-lane paved continuation of the Apalachee Savannahs National Forest Scenic Byway. (For a side trip to Torreya State Park from Sumatra, see the Torreya-Apalachicola Ravines side trip descrip-tion at the end of this drive.) In about 2 miles, begin looking on the right for pitcher plants—lime green trumpets sticking out of the black, boggy ground—readily visible from the road if your timing is right (mid-March into April). Don't walk into the bogs—you might sink. These unique, car-nivorous plants also boast teacup-sized flowers that grow on separate stalks.

Oysters are taken from the waters near Eastpoint with giant tongs.

Torreya-Apalachicola Ravines side trip

If you are taking the side trip, continue about 20 more miles on CR 379 until it makes a Y intersection with SR 12. Turn left (north) onto SR 12, and proceed toward Bristol. At Bristol continue about 13 more miles via SR 12 and CR 271 to Torreya State Park. This is a riverfront preserve with a popular campground and attractive 1849 plantation home, the Gregory House. The park is renowned for its federally listed endangered torreya tree. The unusual botany of the region is a result of plants that thrived here during the glacial age when this area was cool and wet. After temperatures rose, the plants survived in river ravines and steepheads—deep wooded cuts along the river—which are cooler and wetter than surrounding terrain. Near the park, The Nature Conservancy's Apalachicola Bluffs and Ravines Preserve protects a rare ecosystem of ancient flora. Although linked by trails to the state park, the preserve itself is private. Contact the manager first (address listed in Appendix A) for access information for the self-guided trails.

5

Mysteries of Strange Waters
Wakulla Springs State Park to
St. Marks National Wildlife Refuge

General description: This 20-mile drive begins at one of the largest springs in the world, continues through pine forest to nearby St. Marks National Wildlife Refuge, then follows the refuge's 7-mile wildlife drive past pools of feeding birds on stilt-like legs to the historic St. Marks Lighthouse.

Special features: Edward Ball Wakulla Springs State Park and Lodge, guided boat tours, swimming and snorkeling, nature trails and park events, Wakulla River and Canoe Trail, Tallahassee–St. Marks Historic Railroad State Trail, St. Marks National Wildlife Refuge and visitor center, Florida National Scenic Trail, St. Marks Lighthouse, observation tower, refuge events, excellent birding, alligator sighting, hiking, and fishing.

Location: Florida Panhandle, inland and coast.

Drive route numbers: State Road 61, County Road 267, County Road 59, U.S. Highway 98.

Travel season: All year. December through March is best, being the prime birding season for migrating and wintering waterfowl. October is monarch season at the refuge, when the butterflies flutter around coastal wildflowers before their long journey to Mexico. Spring and summer are busy seasons for the state park, with reunions and picnics held on the lawn and at the park lodge.

Camping: There are no campgrounds in the state park or the national wildlife refuge. (Primitive, remote campsites in the refuge are for registered backcountry hikers only.) A public campground at Ochlockonee River State Park is located southwest of the drive on US 319 about four miles south of Sopchoppy. Silver Lake campground is located in the Apalachicola National Forest west of Tallahassee off SR 20 via CR 260. There are private campgrounds on US 98 at Panacea.

Services: All services are available in Tallahassee, and Woodville has gas and food. The state park lodge offers lodging, a dining room, and an old-fashioned soda fountain in the gift shop. Bed and breakfast inns operate at St. Marks and at Saint Teresa along US 98.

Nearby points of interest: San Marcos de Apalache State Historic Site; Natural Bridge State Historic Site; village of St. Marks; Wakulla River; Otter Lake Recreation Area of St. Marks National Wildlife Refuge and Gulf Specimen Marine Laboratories in Panacea; Ochlockonee River State Park; Leon Sinks Geological Area, Trout Pond, Lost Lake, and Silver Lake in Apalachicola National Forest.
Time zone: Eastern.

 # The drive

This 20-mile drive begins in a hardwood forest that parts to reveal the Wakulla Springs State Park Lodge, located at the edge of a clear, 72-degree spring basin, with the mighty Wakulla Springs below. The drive continues through pinewoods to the coastal St. Marks National Wildlife Refuge, a prime habitat for alligators, fishing birds, and other wildlife. The journey ends in a coastal fishing area dominated by a working lighthouse.

Begin the drive about 10 miles south of Tallahassee, at the intersection of SR 61 and CR 267, at the entrance to the 2,860-acre Edward Ball Wakulla Springs State Park.

Enter the state park to the south and meander along its main road, Spring Drive, past the Sally Ward Spring (near the entrance). You may want to return later on foot and investigate this spring via its 0.75-mile trail. The 1.25-mile Hammock Trail, which crosses the main drive a little farther south, is also worth exploring. About 1.8 miles from the park entrance there will be signs to a parking area, which serves the lodge as well as Wakulla Springs and the bathhouse, boat dock, and wooded picnic area.

The park is named for the financier and DuPont estate trustee who purchased the longtime birding mecca about 1928 and built the lodge in 1937. Because this spot was known in birding circles from the earliest conservation days, records exist for sightings of now extinct species, such as the majestic ivory-billed woodpecker. Today park visitors may glimpse wild turkey, white-tailed deer, limpkin, alligators, and other wildlife. The magnificent hardwood forest shelters the state's largest sassafras, beech, and basswood trees.

The waters of Wakulla Springs maintain a temperature of about 72 degrees year-round. Perhaps this explains the interpretation of the Native American term *Wakulla* as "mysteries of strange waters"—the spring sends up spiraling, wraithlike mists of steam in the winter. During the Ice Age, when polar ice caps lowered the ocean level about 250 feet, early residents here hunted the region's big game—mastodon, giant armadillo, giant ground sloth, bear, and camel. When the water is clear, bones of some of these giant

Drive 5: Mysteries of Strange Waters
Wakulla Springs to St. Marks National Wildlife Refuge

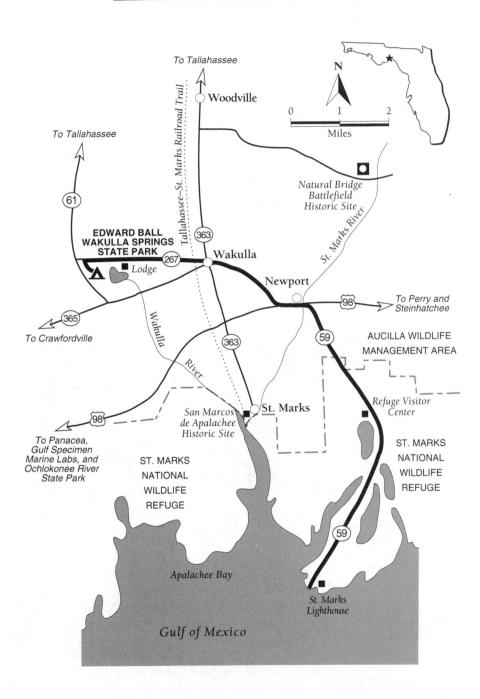

prehistoric beasts can be seen in the bottom of the spring basin. Divers have retrieved some of the fossils; a mastodon skeleton taken from here is displayed at the Museum of Florida History in Tallahassee.

Under the lodge and park road is the springs' famous companion, the massive underwater Wakulla Cave, which extends at least 11,000 feet back and 300 feet deep. It can be reached only through the spring. Although public diving and fishing are prohibited, snorkeling and swimming are allowed in a roped-off area of the spring bowl.

WARNING: As in other parts of Florida, use common sense around alligators. It is illegal to feed them and foolish to approach them.

The Apalachen or Apalachee Indians who were farming in the region when European explorers arrived considered this water to be a source of good health. The Spanish explorer Hernando de Soto, who bivouacked at present-day Tallahassee in the winter of 1539–1540, is said to have ridden in on horseback to taste the Wakulla elixir.

Glass-bottomed boat tours are available, conditions permitting, and afford spectacular views into the spring, which spews forth about 350 million gallons of water per day. A 3-mile float on about half of the park's riverfront is another option, one that allows the visitor to see the many turtles, alligators, large swimming fish, and waving eelgrass. In winter, as

Wakulla Springs, fed by a deep spring, is a wildlife wonderland.

many as 2,000 waterfowl can carpet the river. The old-growth bald cypress trees in this water are a species related to the giant redwoods. For its outstanding features, this park is known as the Wakulla Springs Archaeological and Historic District on the National Register of Historic Places.

After your park visit, return to CR 267 and turn right, traveling about 4.8 miles east through swampland, over McBride Slough, and then through woods approaching the intersection of CR 267 and SR 363, at the crossroads known as Wakulla. About a quarter of a block before the intersection, look on the left and right of CR 267 for signs marking the Tallahassee–St. Marks Historic Railroad State Trail—a 16-mile paved path built on top of an 1837 railbed, running from Tallahassee south to the historic coastal village of St. Marks. To visit the nearby Natural Bridge Battlefield from Wakulla, see the Natural Bridge Battlefield side trip at the end of this drive. Three other nearby side trips depart from here as well; they are also described at the end of this drive.

To continue this drive, stay on CR 267, crossing SR 363 and going on about 2 miles through rural timberland, to the intersection with US 98. (A side trip to Panacea departs from this point; see the description at the end of this drive.) To continue this drive, turn left on US 98 and cross the narrow St. Marks River, at a former cotton port called Newport. Just beyond the bridge on the left is the Newport wayside park. Across the highway, on the right, look for SR 59, which continues this drive. Turn south on SR 59, locally known as Lighthouse Road, and travel about 2.5 miles through the state-managed Aucilla Wildlife Management Area. SR 59 then enters St. Marks National Wildlife Refuge, a state-managed 96,500-acre federal preserve. The gate and visitor center are about 2 miles farther.

The visitor center offers excellent exhibits about the animals, insects, and trees that are native here, and also interprets the area's human history. Many birders make the trek to see some of the 270 species of birds found in this area. Guides from Tallahassee offer individual or group trips, and the refuge sponsors bird walks and occasional rides through areas usually closed to vehicles. There is an observation deck over the pond by the visitor center, with several trails nearby. There are 75 miles of trail in the refuge, and information is available at the visitor center. Be sure to buy the interpretive guide for the 7-mile wildlife drive, which is the continuation of SR 59/Lighthouse Road to the coast.

Return to the main park road, Lighthouse Road, and turn right (south). December through February is an excellent time to view waterfowl by the · thousands, along with wading birds and raptors. Alligators cruise the waters all year long, and the refuge is home to more than 50 species of mammals, including black bears, beavers, bobcats, and feral hogs. Ospreys, bald eagles, and more than 100 species of reptiles and amphibians also make their homes here.

An 1841 lighthouse watches over the Gulf at St. Marks National Wildlife Refuge.

About five miles past the refuge's visitor center along Lighthouse Road, look on the left for parking for the mile-long Mounds Pool Interpretive Trail, which features an observation tower overlooking managed refuge pools. A self-service box contains interpretive trail pamphlets. The path passes an ancient Native American mound known as a kitchen midden, or trash heap. This coastal region was home to natives from about 10,000 B.C. to the end of the 18th century, when Spanish explorers arrived here. The ancient mounds left in the refuge contain discards from generations of meals. It is illegal to disturb these sites.

Returning to Lighthouse Road and continuing south, you will soon arrive at the coast and a small parking area. A quarter-mile-long path here, Levee Trail, introduces coastal plants (pamphlets are available from a self-service box). Although state maps show that you are at the Gulf of Mexico, don't expect a pile of sandy beach. This section of gulf shore, known as the Big Bend, has a marshy shoreline due to extensive shallowness and low waves.

October is an ideal time to visit this part of the refuge; monarch butterflies flutter over wildflowers, preparing for their journey across the Gulf to winter in Mexico. To fully appreciate this seasonal sight, park farther inland along Lighthouse Road at a designated pullover and walk the last portion of the road. Drive slowly to avoid colliding with any of the winged beauties.

At the water's edge, an 80-foot-high white tower commands the coast. This working lighthouse attracts fans of maritime history not only for its stark, simple beauty, but also for its stories, which include Paris of 1829, where its glass light was crafted, the Civil War, and hurricane tragedy. Several families, including some brave women, have kept this lighthouse over the years. It was built for the U.S. government in 1829, was rebuilt in 1831, and again in 1841. In 1843, walls of water from a hurricane roared through, sweeping away all coastal buildings except this tower. Water flooded into the lighthouse, where several families had fled, hoping to save their lives, and 15 drowned. Except for an annual open house, St. Marks Lighthouse is closed to the public, although you can drive right up to it.

This is as far as you can go by car. To finish this drive, trace your route back to the refuge entrance. Five nearby side trips are detailed below.

Natural Bridge Battlefield side trip

To visit the Natural Bridge State Historic Site, the site of a Civil War skirmish, retrace your path back to the intersection of CR 267 and SR 363 at Wakulla, then turn right (north) onto SR 363, traveling about 3 miles to Woodville. The access to this geological and Civil War park is reached by taking a right turn off SR 363 in Woodville, directly onto Natural Bridge Road, then driving about 5.5 miles to the narrow natural bridge. Ten hours of skirmishing here on March 6, 1865, kept Tallahassee the only Confederate capital that didn't fall to Union control. This park, with picnic area and restrooms, is busy every March when the event, which killed 24 men and wounded 111, is re-enacted.

Tallahassee–St. Marks Rail Trail side trip

You may want to hike or bicycle the entire 16-mile Tallahassee–St. Marks Historic Railroad State Trail. Return to SR 363 at Wakulla and drive north along SR 363 to Tallahassee, about 10 miles. You will find the trailhead on Capital Circle Southwest in Tallahassee. Skates and bicycles can be rented here. The 16-mile rail trail ends in coastal St. Marks.

Village of St. Marks side trip

Back at the intersection of SR 59 and US 98, turn left on US 98. In about 2 miles, it intersects SR 363. Turn south (left) on SR 363 about 2 more miles to the end of the road in the St. Marks River village of St. Marks. You can rent bicycles or canoes, walk or bike on the rail trail, enjoy restaurants, and visit the San Marcos de Apalache State Historic Site. This site's museum and ruins interpret the riveting Native American, Territorial, and Civil War history that evolved here at the confluence of two strategic waterways, the St. Marks River and the Wakulla River. In May the village hosts a manatee and conservation festival.

Canoeing the Wakulla River side trip

Returning to SR 363 in St. Marks, travel north, back to the intersection with US 98. Turn left on US 98 and travel to its bridge over the Wakulla River, downstream about 4 miles from the spring bowl at the state park visited earlier on this drive. There is no designated parking area except at a tiny boat ramp on the southwest side of the bridge. A safer and more enjoyable way to see this water wonderland is to park at the canoe rental outpost here on US 98 at river's edge, rent a canoe, and paddle up and down the Wakulla.

Panacea side trip

Continue west on US 98 about 13 miles to Panacea, an old resort community that attracted early tourists who visited a nearby spring. Although the 1902 wooden, two-story Panacea Hotel is gone, visitors today can see several sites. The small Otter Lake Recreation Area of the St. Marks Wildlife Refuge (via Otter Lake Road off US 98) is marked with a federal sign. On the east side of US 98 in Panacea, look for the large white sign directing visitors to acclaimed nature author Jack Rudloe's Gulf Specimen Marine Laboratories, at the intersection of Palm Street and Clark Drive. Visitors here can enjoy the saltwater touch tanks, picking up live starfish, seashells, sea squirts, and other species, as well as marine specimen observation tanks, which hold live octopuses, rays, sharks, sea horses, and eels. Nearby, about 5 miles south of Panacea at Ochlockonee and Apalachee bays, the Mashes Sand County Park offers a sheltered, sandy beach, restrooms, and picnic area, via CR 372.

6

Red Hills at the Roof of the State
Havana to Thomasville to Tallahassee

General description: This 48.5-mile drive in northern Florida and south-western Georgia begins in the village of Havana, known for its antiques district, before ambling up and down the region's red clay hills through farm fields and pinewoods, past rural homes and churches, to a world-famous nature center of simple beauty. The drive ends at Alfred B. Maclay State Gardens, located on a small lake.

Special features: Village of Havana, Meridian Road, Birdsong Nature Center, Pebble Hill Plantation, De Soto Trail, Alfred B. Maclay State Gardens, birding, wildlife watching, hiking.

Location: Northern Florida and southwestern Georgia.

Drive route numbers: State Road 12; County Road 12; County Road 155, also known as Meridian Road; Georgia Road GA 93S; U.S. Highway 319/Thomasville Road.

Travel season: You can drive this route year-round, but summer brings temperatures of 95 degrees and higher, high humidity, biting bugs, and intense thunderstorms. Try November and December, when dropping temperatures elsewhere send migratory and wintering birds to the region, and hardwood trees dress in autumn leaves. January and February can be cool, with 40- to 50-degree daily temperatures, and sometimes frost or a dusting of snow. March and April are ideal, with daily temperatures of 65 to 80, and an abundance of spring wildflowers in bloom. Room reservations need to be made well in advance if travel falls on a fall football weekend (when Tallahassee's two universities have home games), on a graduation weekend, during the 60-day session of the Florida Legislature in March and April, or during Springtime Tallahassee, a family festival held in April.

Camping: There are no campgrounds along this route. There is a public campground in the Apalachicola National Forest, which borders the western edge of the Tallahassee area, at Silver Lake via SR 20. There is a private campground in the eastern Tallahassee area on US 90, locally called Mahan Drive, between Tallahassee and the US 90–Interstate 10 interchange.

Services: In addition to antique district shops, galleries, and cafes, Havana has limited services, such as gas stations and banks. The Nicolson Farm House Restaurant (open for dinner Tuesday through Saturday) on SR 12 West is worth the stop. Thomasville and Tallahassee have full services, including medical care. There are bed and breakfast inns in Havana, Tallahassee, and Thomasville, a town known for charming restored mansions.

Nearby points of interest: As Florida's capital, Tallahassee has the Old Capitol; the new Capitol; a host of other state government buildings, including Florida's Supreme Court; the Museum of Florida History; the 1841 Union Bank Building; the Florida A&M Black Archives; and the Florida State University Fine Arts Gallery. The downtown district has the circa 1895 John G. Riley House, the circa 1843 Knott House Museum, the LeMoyne Art Gallery in the 1854 McGinnis-Munroe House, the Park Avenue Historic District, the 1903 David S. Walker Library building, the 1856 Brokaw-McDougall House, and the Odyssey Science Center and Art Museum, debuting in late 1998. The nearby Governor's Mansion on North Adams Street is open for scheduled tours during the legislative session and December holiday season. Other places of interest in Tallahassee are Goodwood Plantation and three significant archaeological and historic sites: the Lake Jackson Mounds State Archaeological Site; the Mission San Luis de Apalachee, with weekend re-enactments; De Soto Historic Site, where Hernando de Soto camped in the winter of 1539–1540; and an unusual zoo of native animal species, Tallahassee Museum of History and Natural Sciences.
Time zone: Eastern.

 # The drive

This 48.5-mile drive begins in northern Florida in the country village of Havana and its charming antiques and art district. The drive meanders from Havana northeast through fields and woods over gently rolling hills into Georgia and an acclaimed private nature center in the woods. The drive continues up and down red clay hills, for a visit to a quail-hunting plantation, now a museum and private park. The drive returns to northern Florida, ending at a Florida state park famed for seasonal shows of blooms.

Begin this drive about 12 miles north of Tallahassee in the village of Havana, directly on US 27. Havana is a former tobacco farming center. Its old brick buildings and wood-frame homes combine with antique shops, an out-of-print bookshop, art galleries, cafes, and craft shops that attract visitors from far away.

After exploring Havana drive north on US 27, locally named Main Street, two short blocks past the Havana intersection at Seventh Street. From US 27 turn right onto Fifth Street, also called SR 12 East. NOTE: Do not confuse this with SR 12 West, which turns left off US 27 a few blocks *before* you get to SR 12 East.

Continue on SR 12 East through rural areas and woods, noting the reddish-orange, iron-rich soil. In about 4.5 miles, look on the left for a large rectangular building of weathered wood. It is an old tobacco barn, the sort

Drive 6: Red Hills at the Roof of the State

Havana to Thomasville to Tallahassee

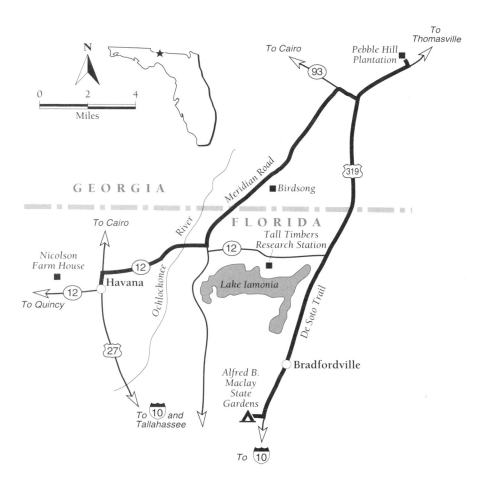

of structure that once characterized this rural region. About three-quarters of a mile farther, SR 12 intersects with CR 157 at a blinking yellow light. Continue on SR 12 across CR 157 for another 4 miles through rural landscape dotted with small residences and country churches, across the short, flat bridge over the winding Ochlockonee River. CR 12 is now locally known as Fairbanks Ferry Road. In 2.3 miles it meets at a T intersection with CR 155 (Meridian Road).

Turn left (north) onto Meridian Road from CR 12. Meridian is a narrow road that winds beneath large oak trees, its shaded beauty and long history earning it a place in United States travel lore. Watch for bobwhite quail feeding and walking in nearby ground cover. In just 1.3 miles, Meridian Road crosses the border into Georgia. On the left along Meridian, immediately after crossing into Georgia, some of the buildings of Mistletoe Plantation are visible, along with sleek horses grazing in roadside pasture. There are about 65 plantations still in existence in the region, many of them now operating as private quail-hunting estates. Much earlier they produced crops such as cotton and sugar cane with slave labor. All but three of this drive's plantations—Birdsong, Pebble Hill, and Susina Inn—are closed to the public.

In about 3 miles Meridian Road meets Hadley Ferry Road at a crossroads known as Rocky Hill. On the left is the white, wood-frame Rocky Hill African Methodist Church. Two miles beyond that, and not prominently marked, is the turnoff on the right to the Birdsong Nature Center—formerly a part of a plantation and today a private, nonprofit education center devoted to native plant and animal species and environmental study. The center is famed for its "bird window," which looks out from the living room onto the sheltered yard, an inviting place for birds to drink, bathe, and feed. At Birdsong, you can also walk to the Listening Place, near the swamp, to hear banjo frogs and wood ducks, and visit the Birdsong pond where native nocturnal beaver make their home. The center is usually open Wednesday and Friday 9 A.M.–noon, Saturday 9 A.M.–2 P.M., and Sunday 1 A.M.–5 P.M.

After a Birdsong sojourn, return to Meridian Road and turn right, heading north, traveling 1 mile to the entrance of Susina Plantation, on the left, a bed and breakfast inn in an 1840s plantation house. Although not open to the public on a drop-in basis, expected guests have the opportunity to appreciate this architectural landmark amid blooming magnolias.

Continue about 2 miles farther on Meridian Road to the intersection of Georgia Road GA 93S. Turn right on GA 93S and travel east about three-quarters of a mile to the intersection of US 319, also called Thomasville Road. Turn left onto US 319 and travel another three-quarters of a mile to Pebble Hill Plantation, on the left behind the gatehouse. This is a unique chance to peek into 150 years of wealthy plantation life, not duplicated at all area plantations, but abundant here. The last owner, who died in 1978, fortuitously decided that the 3,000-acre estate, once with its own dairy, Baptist Church, and schoolhouse for workers and their families, shouldn't be carved into housing lots but should become a private park and museum. During its active social years guests on the estate included the Duke and Duchess of Windsor and presidents Dwight D. Eisenhower and Jimmy Carter. NOTE: Only children in first grade and older can tour the main house, where fragile treasures are displayed. Younger children can visit public areas of the plantation grounds.

After a tour of Pebble Hill, return to US 319. If you are taking a side trip to the 1880s and 1890s winter resort of Thomasville, described at the

Tallahassee's network of canopy roads, roofed by arching live oaks,
is one of America's top scenic byways.

end of this drive, turn left and travel about 4 miles on US 319 into Thomasville. Otherwise this drive continues by turning right on US 319 to travel 2.7 miles through plantation country to the Georgia state border, with the remainder of the drive in Florida. About a mile after the border, CR 12 turns to the right off US 319. This drive continues on US 319 (now called De Soto Trail), but it's worth noting that CR 12 leads west about 3 miles to the 4,000-acre Tall Timbers Research Station on Lake Iamonia, a world-renowned private conservation association.

About 19 miles from the Georgia-Florida border is Bradfordville, and about 4 miles beyond that you approach the I-10/US 319 interchange. Look on the right for a large sign marking the entrance to Alfred B. Maclay State Gardens, the end of this drive. This enclosed green Eden on Lake Hall in Tallahassee offers an excellent place to launch a canoe, sail, and enjoy lake swimming and nature trails, including those under development in the park's Lake Overstreet Addition. It is known for a stunning manicured expanse of garden that adjoins pools. It has the rare torreya tree, 150 kinds of camellias, 50 kinds of azaleas, and a native garden along Lake Hall. The park's Maclay House is open January through April.

Thomasville side trip

Thomasville has an 18-acre city park, as well as restored mansions on tree-lined streets, gourmet restaurants, and a downtown shopping district with old-fashioned lamps and no parking meters. Sites here include the Thomasville Rose Garden at Cherokee Lake; the Lapman-Patterson House State Historic Site; the Big Oak, a landmark grandmother tree more than 300 years old; and the Thomas County Historical Society Museum. The town is a former cotton plantation center that became an 1880s and 1890s winter resort for wealthy northern visitors, including many of the country's major industrialists. This is also the hometown of Lieutenant Henry O. Flipper, who became the first black man to attend West Point. Thomasville hosts an annual rose festival every April.

7

The Canopy Roads
Pisgah Church Road to
Lake Miccosukee to Monticello

General description: This 20-mile drive, partly unpaved, in the Red Hills region near Tallahassee, meanders on roads that are old trading paths, some dating to stagecoach and mule-drawn wagon days. This drive visits an 1858 country church, a 1927 country store, and a historic, cypress-edged lake, then it meanders on an unpaved red clay plantation road shaded by old live oak trees, little changed from the days it was a route to a busy 1820s riverport. The drive ends in a rural county seat.

Special features: Centerville Road, Pisgah Church Road, Old Pisgah Church, Bradley's Country Store, Reeves Landing/Lake Miccosukee, Old Magnolia Road, village of Monticello, birding, fishing.

Location: Northern Florida.

Drive route numbers: County Road 151/Centerville Road, Pisgah Church Road, Moccasin Gap Road, Cromartie Road, Reeves Landing Road, Old Magnolia Road, U.S. Highway 90.

Travel season: Open year-round, but November through April are best to avoid summer temperatures of 95 and higher, high humidity and intense summer storms. Spring storms may also make travel on unpaved portions of this route difficult. Old Magnolia Road is hard-packed and graded, passable at low speed with mild washboard in places. The generally dry fall weather in November and December is ideal, although this is hunting season on the private plantations.

Camping: There is no public campground on this route.

Services: Services are available in Tallahassee. Bradley's Country Store has gas, groceries, and some supplies. Reeves Landing has fish camps and snacks. Monticello has some services, including a bed and breakfast inn directly on this route.

Nearby points of interest: Tallahassee has abundant sites, some of which are listed in "Nearby points of interest" for Drive 6.

Time zone: Eastern.

Drive 7: The Canopy Roads
Pisgah Church Road to Lake Miccosukee to Monticello

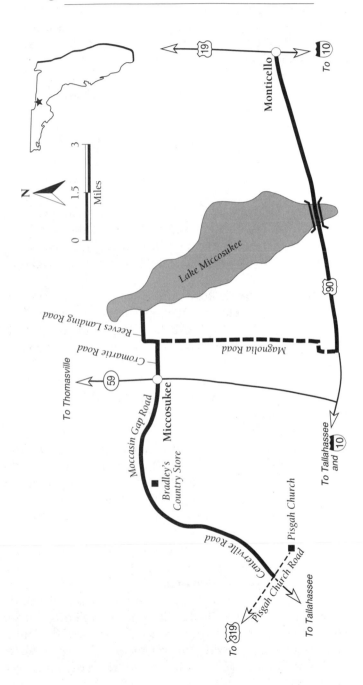

 # The drive

The drive begins in a reverent green grove sheltering an 1858 country church, and follows one of the Tallahassee area's famed, meandering, two-lane canopy roads. At a curve in shaded pasture, the drive visits a 1927 country store that is long on local character. The tour then visits a nearby historic lake region, once the home of aboriginal mound builders and, later, Native American farmers living in a complex village culture. Today the panoramic lake, covered with pond lilies and other vegetation, is known for lunker bass and abundant alligators. Wander away from the lake on a historic, red clay road that rolls through two private hunting plantations to emerge at a scenic federal highway. The last portion of the ride is across gently rolling hills, and across a swampy edge of Lake Miccosukee, to Monticello, county seat of Jefferson County.

Begin by taking SR 151 East (called Centerville Road locally) 7 miles north from downtown Tallahassee, to the middle of the woods where it intersects CR 0340 (Pisgah Church Road). Centerville Road is a narrow, winding, two-lane paved road, where many local drivers tend to ignore posted speed limits.

Turn right from Centerville Road onto Pisgah Church Road, a red clay road that dead-ends one block later at the Old Pisgah United Methodist Church. This stunning white clapboard building, built in 1858 and still used today, is one of the oldest churches in Florida. It has hand-hewn wooden pews and towering clerestory windows with green shutters. Slaves were required to worship in the upstairs galleries, while white women were seated on one side of the main aisle and white men on the other. The church cemetery contains the unmarked graves of some of the victims of the region's 1841 yellow fever epidemic.

Return to Centerville Road and turn right, heading northeast. Continue on Centerville Road, winding through pastureland. Note how the horizontal branches of live oak trees reach across the road in places to form a green canopy. The dead-looking, singed brown plants attached to these branches turn lime green after a rain, earning them the name "resurrection fern."

In 4.3 miles, you will notice a large field on the right and a pond on the left. This is the crossroad where Bradley's Country Store (closed Sundays) serves local residents and workers. Grandma Mary Bradley began selling kitchen sausage in 1910, and today her grandson Frank Bradley and family members continue the tradition. The family store also offers country-milled grits, corn meal, honey, preserves, cold drinks, groceries, and supplies. The outbuildings feature a mule-powered sugar cane press and a kettle for boiling syrup, both used during an annual November festival that attracts a

Anglers at Lake Miccosukee.

thousand visitors or more. The syrup always sells out.

After a visit to Bradley's, continue northeast on Centerville Road, now called Moccasin Gap Road, for another 4.3 miles to the crossroads community of Miccosukee.

By 1778, this village, then known as Mikasuki, had 28 Native American farming families, at least 60 houses, and a village square. But in 1818 General Andrew Jackson brought an army of 3,000 through the area, burning the prosperous village and slaughtering its people. Survivors were pushed on into central and southern Florida, and white settlers took over the area, helping pave the way for Spanish Florida to become a U.S. territory in 1821.

Crossing CR 59 on Moccasin Gap Road, which is now called Cromartie Road, continue east through rolling pasture for 1.9 miles, where Cromartie forms a T intersection with Magnolia Road. Turn left on Magnolia and travel about a half-mile, then turn right on Reeves Landing Road, which dead-ends at the lapping shore of expansive Lake Miccosukee.

This lake offers rustic fish camps for anglers, and boat rentals for anyone who might want to get out on the breezy lake. Narrow boat trails wind through rafts of floating lake plants. Ring-necked duck are sighted here, along with great white heron and other long-legged wading birds. The alligators are so abundant here the Florida Game and Fresh Water Fish

A charming rural store northeast of Tallahassee. JAN GODOWN PHOTO

Commission holds a yearly lottery for the coveted opportunity to hunt them. This area was home to aboriginal mound builders, who developed a highly organized social, religious, and political society. From about A.D. 1000 to about A.D. 1500, trading paths linked Lake Miccosukee residents with Native Americans as far away as the Great Lakes region.

From the lake, retrace your path on Reeves Landing Road to Magnolia Road, then south the half-mile to the intersection with Cromartie Road. The next 6.9 miles of Magnolia is rough, unpaved road that can be almost impassable after a heavy rain. There are two possible drive routes from here: If you choose not to explore Magnolia, turn right onto Cromartie, then at the Miccosukee crossroads turn left on CR 59. Travel south about 6 miles to US 90 and turn left (east). This will take you all the way to Monticello, about 9 miles away. If you like roads less traveled, continue south on Magnolia for a Florida drive unlike any other public route in the state.

In addition to its leafy overhead canopy of live oak branches, Magnolia Road also features steep, red clay banks on either side, forming another tunnel of sorts from centuries of travel that has worn down the roadbed. Exposed tree roots and layers of iron-rich clay help drivers to see this 22-foot-wide path almost as it was in the days of mule-drawn wagons, when

46

it served as a primitive highway for plantation commerce from Georgia and northern Florida south to the busy port of Magnolia.

The last quarter-mile of the road is paved, alerting you to the upcoming intersection with US 90. Turn left onto this two-lane highway and proceed past rural homes and businesses for about 3 miles, where it crosses the swampy southern edge of Lake Miccosukee. In about 5 miles US 90 enters Monticello. Its historic district centers on the silver-domed, white courthouse. As you approach the courthouse, you will notice the Clarke House Bed and Breakfast—a perky yellow Victorian mansion on the left, on the corner of Hickory Street. Across from the courthouse, the 1890 Perkins Opera House is still open occasionally for special events.

8

Magnificent Mud Flats and Marsh Coast

Scenic Road 361 to Steinhatchee

General description: A 52.5-mile rural drive through pinewoods to a remote coastal mud flat and marsh preserve, and to an inland river region known for saltwater and freshwater fishing, hunting, and abundant wildlife. This is one of the least developed of Florida's coastal areas, and the seclusion creates prime winter shelter for nesting bald eagles, and for osprey and brown pelicans year-round. The drive ends at the site of a former Seminole Wars outpost, today an unpretentious river fishing community and crabbing and scalloping center.

Special features: Keaton Beach, Hagen's Cove of Big Bend Wildlife Management Area, Steinhatchee River and village of Steinhatchee, excellent migratory and winter birding, summer birding, mud flat walking, summer scalloping, excellent saltwater and freshwater fishing, canoeing and river rafting.

Location: Coastal Big Bend Florida.

Drive route numbers: State Road 361, Hagen's Cove Road, State Road 51.

Travel season: October through March for best migratory and winter birding, and to avoid summer heat and lightning storms. However, July 1 through August 31 is the popular scalloping season, and summer is tarpon season in offshore areas. Sections of the Big Bend Wildlife Management Area along the drive attract hunters of deer, quail, duck, turkey, and wild boar during hunting seasons.

Camping: No public campgrounds are along this drive. There is a very open roadside commercial campsite at Keaton Beach. In Steinhatchee there are several small fish camps with campsites, and motels with a few campsites.

Services: Dekle Beach has a cottage resort on the water, with a small marina. Keaton Beach has a gas station, restaurant, marina, motel, apartments, fishing guide services, and also public restrooms and picnic shelters at Hodges Park overlooking the Gulf of Mexico. Steinhatchee has gas stations, a small grocery and bank, restaurants, traditional fish camps, guide services, an excellent creekside resort, and efficiency motels. There are full services in Perry, about 27 miles northwest of this drive via SR 51 and US 19/98.

Nearby points of interest: Steinhatchee Falls; Forest Capital State Museum and Cracker Homestead, Perry.
Time zone: Eastern.

 # The drive

This isolated drive takes you into a flat area of pines and live oaks, favored by families all over the Southeast who retreat here to fish and hunt. More recently it has been discovered by those who simply want to explore nature. The drive follows a narrow, two-lane, paved road, through planted pine forest and occasional cypress swamps, to a tiny coastal marsh community, then through a state wildlife management area to Hagen's Cove, a magnificent mud flat preserve. This is a natural outdoor observatory for birds and tidal marine life. The drive continues on to a crabbing and scalloping center.

NOTE: This drive is very remote and shouldn't be driven at night. The first gas station and public telephone along this drive are at Keaton Beach, about 22 miles from our starting point. The next such assistance is about 28 miles farther, at Steinhatchee.

The drive begins at the intersection of US 19/98 and SR 361, about 22.5 miles southeast of Perry. (There is an interesting homesteading museum at Perry; see the Perry Museum side trip description at the end of this drive.) Go southwest from US 19/98 onto two-lane SR 361, toward Adams Beach. The drive goes through wide pastureland, past live oaks, planted pines, and an occasional longleaf pine, a towering Florida native that is most easily distinguished from other pines by the large (5-inch and longer) cones it drops.

After 12.3 miles, SR 361 makes a sharp curve left, and the drive follows it. At this curve a spur about 1 mile long goes to Adams Beach, a former resort washed away by years of storms. Adams Beach is a beautiful section of coast, but its small parking area and inadequate turnaround make a visit impossible for large RVs. But if you are in a car or small camper, and are alert for glass shards at this nighttime lover's lane, you will enjoy the view of the marsh, flats, and gulf. Otherwise, at this curve, follow SR 361 for the next 9.5 miles, looking for soaring birds overhead, such as kites in the spring and summer. Their scissorlike tails and black-and-white forms slice the sky with sharp beauty.

The drive along scenic 361 is blessedly free of franchises and shopping strips. It continues through coastal scrubland, punctuated by low palmettoes at ground level and scrub oak on sandy ridges. As SR 361, which residents informally call the beach highway, dips close to the coast, you will

Drive 8: Magnificent Mud Flats and Marsh Coast
Scenic Road 361 to Steinhatchee

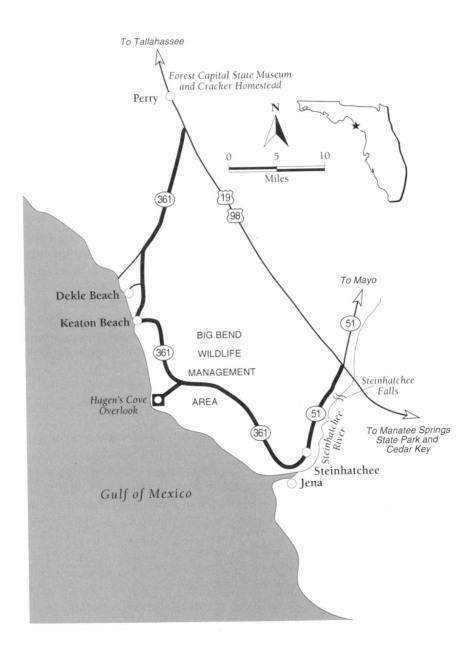

To Tallahassee

Forest Capital State Museum
and Cracker Homestead

Perry

N

0   5   10
Miles

361

19

98

Dekle Beach

Keaton Beach

361

BIG BEND

WILDLIFE

MANAGEMENT

AREA

Hagen's Cove
Overlook

361

To Mayo

51

Steinhatchee
Falls

51

Steinhatchee River

To Manatee Springs
State Park and
Cedar Key

Steinhatchee

Jena

Gulf of Mexico

see scattered collections of homes built on the marshy waterfront, elevated on stilts to allow floodwaters to roll through beneath.

In 9.5 miles the drive comes to a T intersection. This drive takes the short spur straight ahead to Keaton Beach, another community directly on the Gulf of Mexico. Hodges Park, with parking, restrooms, and picnic shelters, is at the end of the spur, about a mile ahead. As you look out across the water here you might think you are standing on the shore of the largest lake in North America. The tea-colored water is clear and shallow, and the sand under the water is soft, almost muddy feeling, resulting from low wave action over the extensive shallows of the Big Bend. Some consider this to be part of the Apalachee Bay system. Keaton Beach was a coastal residence and fishing community as early as the late 1800s and early 1900s. Today it is still a base for fishing, from sea trout to tarpon. Artificial reefs near the shore, as well as natural, rock-based reefs, attract fish; they are best explored with a wildlife guide. The miles of grass beds are a lush marine nursery. To stay in the area without getting out in a boat is to miss much of what the region offers.

The Steinhatchee marsh region is part of Florida's Big Bend. JAN GODOWN PHOTO

After visiting Keaton Beach, trace your path back to the T intersection and turn right, continuing on SR 361 toward Steinhatchee. The drive continues for almost 16 miles through pines and coastal scrub of the Big Bend Wildlife Management Area, 56,673 acres of woodland and wetlands purchased and held by The Nature Conservancy until Florida could buy it under the state's Save Our Coast program. The management area shelters such wildlife as the federally listed endangered black bear, as well as numerous wading birds, among them the great white heron.

About 15 miles after rejoining SR 361 at Keaton Beach, slow down and watch for a small green sign on the right side of the road, announcing Hagen's Cove Recreation Area coming up in 500 feet. Turn right at the next Hagen's Cove sign, off SR 361. This 1.5-mile access road begins in pinewoods and crosses marsh twice, via narrow, one-lane, flat culvert bridges with no railings. Watch for soft shoulders on this graded-sand road, which ends at a wide, V-shaped, hard-packed public parking area. To the right are an interpretive kiosk, picnic tables under longleaf pines, and access to the mud flats. Look here for native redwood cedars growing along the shore. The left arm of the parking area is slightly more developed, with portable toilet, grassy area, picnic tables under roofs, more mud flat access, and a quarter-mile walk to the 25-step observation tower, offering a bird's-eye view of coastal flats and pine-covered islands. There is no fresh water source here.

Fiddler crabs are abundant here, and in fall and spring look for migrations of a great variety of shore and wading birds such as American oystercatchers, sandpipers, plovers, and willets. Soaring osprey, brown pelicans, and bald eagles are found year-round. Many waterfowl winter here, including the red-breasted merganser.

After visiting Hagen's Cove, trace your path back to SR 361 and turn right, continuing east about 13 miles toward Steinhatchee, beside the dark and winding Steinhatchee River.

You have arrived in Steinhatchee as SR 361 bends along the eastern end of Deadman's Bay, where the river empties into the Gulf. The road winds along the riverside, past docks, seafood restaurants, fish camps, homes, marine repair shops, and other small businesses. Across the river is the tiny crabbing and fishing community of Jena. As SR 361 bends sharply left, our drive curves north to parallel the Steinhatchee River, and the road becomes SR 51.

Local commerce began here in the late 1880s, with the harvesting and selling of the then-abundant and large cedar trees for lumber, to be shipped south by raft to Cedar Key. Sponge collecting offshore was also an early source of income, as well as oystering, which continues today. The name (pronounced "STEEN-hat-chee") possibly comes from *isteen hatchee—hatchee* is a Creek-Seminole word for river, and *isti* can be interpreted as meaning man.

Rapids like these on the Steinhatchee River are rarely seen in Florida. JAN GODOWN PHOTO

President Zachary Taylor spent time here during the Seminole Wars in the 1830s. Steinhatchee was at that time Fort Frank Brooke, which served as a way station and malaria treatment center for troops. Taylor was a brevet general in the U.S. Army and stayed at the fort with his aides for several weeks in 1838. The exact location of the fort and its cemetery remain an archaeological mystery and a topic of considerable interest in the region, where several artifacts, including old glass bottles, have been recovered. A natural river feature uncommon in Florida, Steinhatchee Falls is described in military correspondence as being 10 miles upriver from the fort. See the Steinhatchee Falls side trip description below for information on visiting the falls.

Steinhatchee Falls side trip

While visiting Steinhatchee, try to see the small rapids on the river, called Steinhatchee Falls, located off SR 51 about 6 miles north of Steinhatchee Landing. The falls, or rapids, are on the right side of the road, not visible from SR 51, and reached by driving on a hard-packed sand road through private timber ground that allows public access. From SR 51, about 6 miles north of Steinhatchee Landing resort and about 5.5 miles after Palm Grove Fishing Lodge, turn right at the small, yellow sign that says, "Public River Access." Since there are several of these similarly marked accesses to the river off SR 51, the best way to find it is with an area wildlife guide. If the water is high, you may be able to arrange for a raft trip through the rapids. If you go without a guide, turn right off SR 51 and travel about 1.4 miles on the sand road to the Y. Take the right fork into isolated woods for about 1 mile until you come to a picnic area with concrete tables under spreading live oaks on the riverbank. Walking upriver and downriver a few yards from the rapids, you will notice cuts in the riverbanks on each side, which may be the scars of an old pioneer bridge built here or the site of an even earlier Native American footpath. Early frontier correspondence indicates that Native Americans, the U.S. Army, and settlers forded the river near these rapids on an old ox and horseback route.

Perry Museum side trip

Via US 19/98 North, you can visit Perry, the Taylor County seat, site of the 13-acre Forest Capital State Museum and Florida Cracker Homestead Park. The museum interprets the state's lumber industry. Don't skip the adjoining wooden farm home, the Whiddon House. It has a wide covered porch from which you can peer into three dark rooms and see mosquito netting draped over the bed and a kerosene lamp on the hand-hewn table. This house is not a re-creation, but a real homestead built in

1864 at another location and then moved here. It is constructed in classic Florida Cracker "dogtrot" style, using a breezeway to separate two single cabin rooms. The wide porch added shade, the wedge-shaped piers, or stilts, kept the house off the damp ground, and a north-south exposure allowed sunlight on three sides, which is one reason the untreated logs didn't decay.

Every October, the town of Perry hosts a festival celebrating the timber industry, with crosscut and chain saw tree-cutting contests and a free fish fry, usually serving 3.5 tons of fried mullet, a Steinhatchee specialty.

9

Suwannee River Ramble

White Springs to Suwannee River State Park

General description: This 35-mile northern Florida drive celebrates Florida's eclectic folk culture at the Stephen Foster State Folk Culture Center, and tours a region of country roads that wind through pastures and woods by the steep banks of the Suwannee River. The area is popular with campers, hikers, bicyclists, and canoeists.

Special features: Big Shoals State Recreation Area, Suwannee River Canoe Trail, two segments of the Florida National Scenic Trail, Stephen Foster State Folk Culture Center, Suwannee River, Suwannee River State Park, Withlacoochee River, swimming, canoeing, hiking, fishing, and bicycling.

Location: North-central Florida.

Drive route numbers: County Road 135, U.S. Highway 41, County Road 136, County Road 136A, U.S. Highway 129, County Road 132.

Travel season: Year-round. Winter is low-water time on the Suwannee River and portages may be more frequent. Spring brings occasional seasonal flooding along the river and summer delivers intense lightning storms. One of the best times here is the cool days of November and December.

Camping: There is a youth campground at Stephen Foster State Folk Culture Center, and a full campground at the Suwannee River State Park at the end of the drive. The drive is near the Spirit of the Suwanee, a private camping resort that holds festivals and has a canoe outfitter available. There are other private campgrounds in the region.

Services: A bed and breakfast inn, gas station, convenience food stores, and craft shop are located in White Springs. Other services are clustered at the intersection of Interstate 75 and CR 136; still other services, including a grocery store, are available in Live Oak, about 14 miles west of White Springs via CR 136. Canoe outfitters are available in Live Oak and on this drive at Spirit of the Suwannee Park.

Nearby points of interest: Falmouth Springs; Peacock Spring State Recreation Area; Suwannee County Historical Museum; Ichetucknee Springs State Park; Okefenokee Swamp, Georgia.

Time zone: Eastern.

Drive 9: Suwannee River Ramble

White Springs to Suwannee River State Park

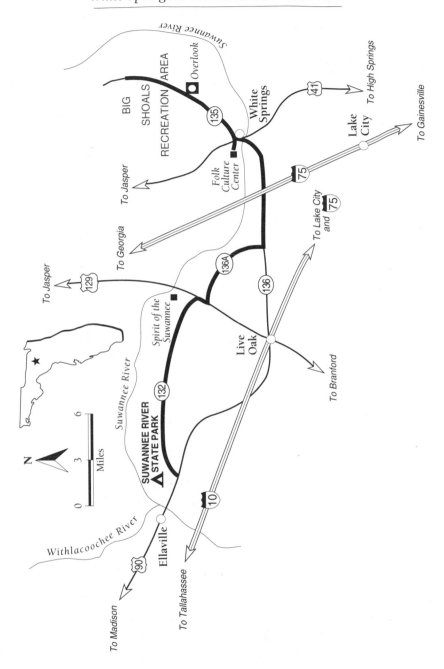

 # The drive

This drive visits a region sometimes called the Original Florida, both for what it has—woodlands and pastures, hills, winding rivers with rapids and steep riverbanks—and for what it lacks—coastline, condominiums, and hectic development. The whitewater rapids on the Suwannee River at Big Shoals State Recreation Area add to the impression that you are in the Carolina mountains, not Florida.

The drive takes a short trip down the road to a park dedicated to Florida folk culture, nestled on the Suwannee River. The rest of the drive is a rural ramble to a state park and campground on a different, but equally stunning, stretch of the river.

Begin this drive about 3 miles north of White Springs on CR 135, at Big Shoals State Recreation Area, a 3,495-acre preserve managed by three agencies. It stretches to the banks of the meandering, tea-colored Suwannee River, which flows 245 miles from its headwaters nearby in the Okefenokee Swamp in Georgia, past these shoals and on to the Gulf of Mexico. Canoe outfitters can advise you on overall river conditions; generally the difficult shoals are portaged, even by experienced canoeists.

Return to CR 135 from the recreation area, turn left, and travel about 3 miles to the crossroads of CR 135, US 41, and CR 136, at White Springs. The entrance to Stephen Foster State Folk Culture Center is one block beyond this intersection, on the left side of US 41.

This park is known for its celebration of Florida folk culture, including Seminole and Miccosukee traditions as well as pioneer-settler traditions, and African-American, Cuban, Caribbean, Jewish, Greek, Minorcan, Spanish, Central American, South American, Italian, Asian, and other cultures. The center also recognizes regional traditions and longtime Florida occupations, such as the state's maritime and cattle industries. There is a craft shop, a small interpretive center, and a 4-mile section of the Florida National Scenic Trail. Several times during the year special events are staged, such as Rural Folklife Days in November and the annual Florida Folk Festival on Memorial Day weekend.

The park area, including the town of White Springs, was a busy resort in the early 1900s. Called White Sulphur Springs, the village attracted visitors who believed the springs at the edge of the Suwannee River held curative powers. Those tourists followed a long tradition established by Native Americans, who referred to the springs as Medicine Waters. Several tribes peacefully shared use of the springs, and the region was considered sacred ground. Today an old springs bathhouse (inoperative) is within the Stephen Foster State Folk Culture Center.

The Suwannee River flows from its headwaters in Georgia's Okefenokee Swamp to the Gulf of Mexico.

After a park visit turn right at the park entrance and trace your path back one block to the intersection of CR 135 and US 41. Turn right (south) on US 41 and take the first right (west) onto CR 136. Go 3.5 miles on CR 136, as it travels over I-75 and then on through farmland.

At this point CR 136 makes a sharp right curve, and in another third of a mile intersects with CR 136A on the right. Turn here and follow this winding drive through more farmland for almost 7 miles until it reaches an unmarked T intersection with US 129. Turn right (north) on US 129, toward Jasper, and travel 2.4 miles to the T intersection on the left with CR 132. If you want to visit the riverfront Spirit of the Suwannee Park, a private camping resort that holds festivals, with music, storytelling, and crafts, continue ahead one block on US 129 to the park entrance on the left.

Otherwise, where US 129 meets CR 132, turn left on CR 132 and travel west past cornfields and grazing cattle. In about 8 miles, CR 132 crosses CR 249. Travel another 8 miles, and CR 132 makes a sharp left curve, then in 1.3 miles ends at an unmarked T intersection. Immediately on the right you will see the large sign and gate for the Suwannee River State Park.

This park is a longtime local favorite. It preserves the site of the old community of Columbus, which grew up at the confluence of the

Withlacoochee and Suwannee rivers. (This Withlacoochee River is not the same Withlacoochee River that flows through central Florida.) The entire village is gone today, except for the cemetery, which is within the park borders and can be reached by a footpath. The park offers a beautiful view overlooking the rivers, it preserves an earthwork built for the Civil War, and it has a landing for steamboats that once cruised the river. A 4.6-mile portion of the Florida National Scenic Trail is also part of the park. Wildlife here includes red-tailed hawks, turkeys, otters, beavers, alligators, and gopher tortoises.

This park is the end of our drive. To find Interstate 10 you can leave the park the way you came in and continue straight, half a block, driving over the railroad tracks, to the T intersection of the park entrance road and US 90. If you turn left (east) onto US 90, access to the interstate is in about 7 miles.

10

The Forest of Civil War History
Olustee Battlefield Loop

General description: This 15-mile loop in northern Florida's Osceola National Forest begins at a Civil War battle site and circles around a popular recreational lake, through forested swamps and pine-covered ridges that are home to the endangered red-cockaded woodpecker. NOTE: About 5 miles of this drive, unpaved and narrow, aren't suited for large recreational vehicles.

Special features: Osceola National Forest office, Olustee Battlefield State Historic Site, Ocean Pond, Olustee Beach, Florida National Scenic Trail, fishing, lake swimming, hiking, birding.

Drive route numbers: U.S. Highway 90, County Road 250A, Forest Road 241, County Road 231.

Location: North-central Florida.

Travel season: Summer is locally popular at forest recreation areas, but brings with it extreme heat, biting bugs, and intense summer storms that can cause temporary flooding of forest roads. November through January is hunting season in the forest so expect campgrounds to be at capacity. The annual reenactment of the Olustee Battle is held during the second weekend in February. The battlefield visitor center is open 8 A.M.–5 P.M. Thursday through Monday. The Forest Service information office is open 7:30 A.M.–4 P.M. on weekdays. So if you want to stop at both, a Thursday, Friday, or Monday visit is best.

Camping: The forest has lakeside campsites at Ocean Pond Campground and primitive campsites at Hog Pen Landing, also on this drive. Other Forest Service campgrounds nearby, but not directly on the drive, include Cobb and Wiggins, both with primitive campsites. A Forest Service map for sale at the office on this drive points the way to area campgrounds.

Services: All services, such as franchise motels and restaurants, are in Lake City, about 11 miles west of the drive at an intersection with Interstate 75, about 3 miles south of Interstate 10. Lake City also has an attractive downtown shopping district. There is a gas station with convenience store and bait shop in Olustee.

Nearby points of interest: Mount Carrie Wayside Park and Trail; Florida Sports Hall of Fame, Florida Tourist Welcome Center, and Columbia County Historical Museum, all in Lake City.

Time zone: Eastern.

Drive 10: The Forest of Civil War History
Olustee Battlefield Loop

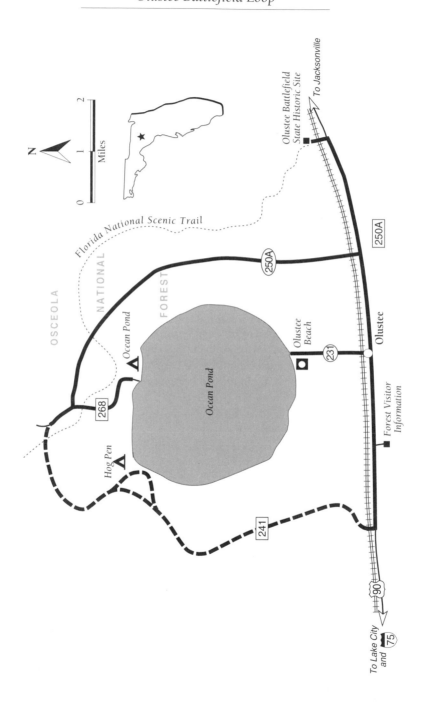

The drive

This drive is ideal for those who like to probe into Civil War history and get away from the city at the same time. This is a 15-mile loop through lush, flat, wooded country, with the opportunity to see federally listed endangered red-cockaded woodpeckers, white-tailed deer, and other wildlife, to fish at a lovely lake, and to walk through still woods and small cypress swamps on a path featuring numerous wooden boardwalks over the wetlands.

Begin this drive about 11 miles east of Lake City, at the Osceola National Forest office on the south side of US 90. It has a well-stocked rack of forest and nature brochures, a selection of nature and history books for both children and adults, Forest Service Smokey Bear items, and a few interpretive exhibits. Ask the staff about recent sightings of turkey, federally listed threatened black bear, coyote, otter, beaver, and bobcat.

After a visit to this office, turn right on US 90, toward the tiny forest community of Olustee. Drive east toward Olustee on US 90, past Forest Service signs for Olustee Beach and Ocean Pond campground (visited later in the drive). After 3.4 miles, turn left at the gray, carved-wood sign for the Civil War battlefield and memorial.

At the Olustee Battlefield State Historic Site, visit the small interpretive center for orientation about the battle. Stroll the battleground, through woods and open field, to contemplate the events of February 20, 1864, which resulted in the deaths of 2,807 Union and Confederate soldiers. If you arrive for the battle reenactment in February, shuttle buses can bring you here from off-site parking locations. At the annual reenactment, re-created camps of Union and Confederate soldiers are set up, as are supply camps of sutlers and camp followers. Participants dress, talk, cook, eat, clean, and otherwise approximate the primitive camp conditions of Civil War times. The story of this death day unfolds like the sad drama it was. The five-hour fight included cavalry, cannons, men bearing colors, a drummer, an African-American unit (the Union's Eighth Colored Troops), and a lack of supplies. During the afternoon engagement momentum shifted back and forth between the sides, until the Union forces retreated at dusk.

From the battlefield, turn right onto US 90 and travel 1.3 miles, then take a right turn onto paved, two-lane CR 250A. This will follow an 11.8-mile loop through the 187,000-acre Osceola National Forest. Listen and look for flitting songbirds, such as towhees and pine warblers, along this route. You may also see a fox squirrel with its big, bushy tail. In 3.3 miles, look for a path on either side of the road, and signs indicating that this forest walkway is part of the Florida National Scenic Trail, which eventually connects with the Appalachian Trail. You can park on the wide grassy

Osceola National Forest's cypress swamps are places of still beauty.

shoulder of the road and walk a portion of this path, here called Osceola Trail. If you enter the path on the left side of the road, you can walk a short spur trail several hundred yards across flatland to a cypress swamp board-walk, an easy way to visit these cool, dark wetlands. When future pur-chases are complete, this forest will provide a wildlife corridor stretching north into the Okefenokee Swamp, on the Florida-Georgia border.

Retracing your path to the road, continue on CR 250A and in just 0.8 mile, you can turn left onto FR 268 for the 1-mile drive to Ocean Pond campground. Although this is an ideal spot in the pines by the lakeside, this campsite is reserved for registered campers only.

Continue on CR 250A to a T intersection a quarter of a mile ahead, where unpaved, hard-graded FR 241 turns left. This is a 5-mile route that will return to US 90. FR 241 is narrow and bumpy in places, and has mild washboard, but is passable—for all but the largest RVs—unless a strong storm has covered the road with rainwater and swamp overflow. NOTE: If you are in a large recreational vehicle—more than 20 feet long—it is rec-ommended that you turn around here and trace your path back on paved CR 250A to US 90. If you turn back, then you will want to turn right on US 90 and travel about three-quarters of a mile to the right turn onto CR 231. This takes you to the Olustee Beach area of the forest, ending at Ocean

Pond. Otherwise, turn left from paved CR 250A onto unpaved FR 241. In about 1 mile you'll want to pause as the road carries you over a small cypress pond, with sunning turtles and feeding birds on either side of the road. In 0.8 mile, FR 241A takes a half-mile loop on the left to the Hog Pen Landing primitive campsite on the lake.

FR 241 continues on through quiet forest another 3.3 miles before it connects with US 90. Turn left onto US 90 and drive 1.6 miles to the left turn on CR 231, which takes you to the Olustee Beach area of the forest. This is a locally popular recreational spot at the edge of 1,700-acre Ocean Pond, featuring swings, a fishing pier, sandy beach, restrooms, picnic shelters, wide grassy lawn, a reserved-group area, and a boardwalk among cypress trees at the edge of the lake.

Olustee Beach is the end of this drive. To return to Lake City or one of the interstates, take CR 231 back from Olustee Beach to US 90, turn right (west), and drive about 11 miles to reach Lake City.

11

The Sea Islands
Kingsley Plantation to Fernandina Beach

General description: This 35-mile drive through sea islands on curving two-lane and one-lane roads meanders through tidal salt marsh to reach a national historic site, and past Atlantic Ocean dunes to a historic fishing village on the Florida-Georgia border.

Special features: Kingsley Plantation and slave cabin ruins in a national park called Timucuan Ecological and Historic Preserve, Saturiwa Trail scenic drive at Fort George Island State Cultural Site, Huguenot Memorial Park, Talbot Islands geopark, Amelia Island State Recreation Area, National Historic District in Fernandina Beach, Fort Clinch State Park, Amelia Island Lighthouse, fishing, canoeing, birding, beachcombing, hiking, and camping.

Location: Northeast Florida, near the Georgia border.

Drive route numbers: State Road 105, Palmetto Avenue, U.S. Highway A1A, Atlantic Avenue, Centre Street.

Travel season: November through April is best to see migratory and wintering birds. Fall and winter is when right whales migrate into area waters to calve. Summer is sea turtle nesting season, but brings with it temperatures of 95 degrees and higher, biting bugs, high humidity, and lightning storms.

Camping: Public campgrounds on this drive are at Little Talbot Island State Park, the regional Huguenot Memorial Park, and Fort Clinch State Park.

Services: Full services are available in Fernandina Beach on Amelia Island, in Jacksonville, and also in Mayport, a side trip to this drive. Some snack shops, bait shops, and gasoline stations are located along SR 105 on Fort George Island. There are restrooms but no food at Kingsley Plantation.

Nearby points of interest: Cedar Point Area, Timucuan Ecological and Historic Preserve; Fort Caroline National Memorial and the Theodore Roosevelt Area, both part of the Timucuan Preserve and located on the south side of the St. Johns River; Mayport Historic District and Mayport ferry ride across the St. Johns River; Jacksonville Zoological Gardens; Museum of Science and History in Jacksonville.

Time zone: Eastern.

 # The drive

Just 15 miles east of Jacksonville, historic sea islands sit in a vast marsh at the mouth of Florida's stately St. Johns River. A winding rural road and narrow bridges through tidal zones link this low country ramble. The drive continues across several islands, to end at the historic district of Fernandina.

This drive has two recommended side trips, mentioned at the end of this chapter, and their access is at the start of this drive.

This drive begins at Fort George Island on SR 105/US A1A, about 15 miles east of Jacksonville. Continuing east, look for the unmarked intersection of SR 105 and Palmetto Avenue, and a sign directing you to Kingsley Plantation. Turn left (north) on unmarked Palmetto Avenue. The first half-mile twists through tidal marsh. At low tide thumb-sized pink fiddler crabs can be seen scurrying across the mud flats. WARNING: At extreme high tide or after heavy rain, water runs across this low road.

After the first half-mile, look in a clearing on the left for the gnarled walls of a ruin. Although many assume this is the ruin of a slave cabin, it was most likely a mid-1800s pioneer house. The construction material is called tabby, a concrete made of shell developed by Spanish colonists in the 1580s. Visitors are welcome to walk around the base of the ruin.

Just ahead, the road climbs a slight rise to a Y intersection. Continue straight to enter a 4.4-mile road loop called the Saturiwa Trail, which leads into the Fort George Island State Cultural Site at trail's end, and the national park service's Kingsley Plantation on the Fort George River. If instead you go left at the Y intersection, onto unpaved road, this continuation of Palmetto Avenue takes you 2 miles directly to the plantation, a national historic site. Either way is scenic.

The Saturiwa Trail is named for the Timucua chief, Saturiwa. The Timucua (also Timuguana) predated Florida's better-known and contemporary Seminole and Miccosukee tribes. The first part of the Saturiwa Trail is paved; later the raod becomes unpaved and narrow. The route skirts the island's eastern side, thick with marsh grasses, passing the Rollins Bird and Plant Sanctuary (no developed facilities).

Longleaf pine and live oak dominate the forests here, known as hammocks. The swaying scarlet wildflowers along the road in late spring are native coral bean. The clumps of curly silver strings hanging from oak trees are Spanish moss. In the late 1800s, island workers picked Spanish moss for mattress stuffing and to pack oranges and grapes for shipment north. Much earlier, in the 1500s, it had been collected by native women to make skirts. After a heavy rain look on the tree limbs for a burst of color as resurrection ferns turn from brown to vivid green.

A booklet, available from a self-service box halfway around the loop, explains 28 historic and natural sites you'll see along the way. The booklet

Drive 11: The Sea Islands
Kingsley Plantation to Fernandina Beach

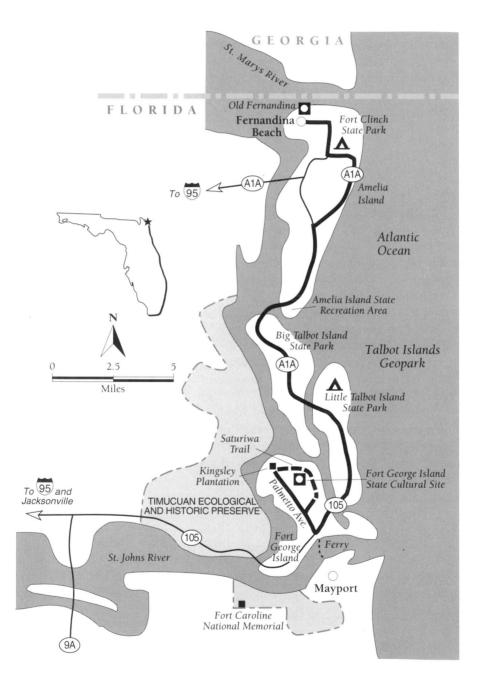

also outlines a brief history of human occupation of the island, including aboriginal Indians; French, Spanish, and British attempts at colonization (from about 1562 to 1812); nineteenth-century cotton plantations; and hunting clubs in the 1920s. One notable stop on the Saturiwa Trail is Mount Cornelia, a 65-foot promontory said to be the highest point along the Atlantic seacoast south of North Carolina. Elsewhere, look for opossums at dusk, and gopher tortoises in the daytime.

The loop finally intersects with Palmetto Avenue, where a right turn will take you through the entrance to Kingsley Plantation. Across an expanse of manicured lawn, Zephaniah Kingsley's riverfront house stands in sharp contrast with the nearby slave quarters. Most slave shacks across the South vanished because they were made of unprotected wood, but here portions of the tabby walls of 23 cabins remain, helping visitors imagine the cramped family life under the cruel slave system. Built around 1800, the Kingsley house may be the oldest remaining plantation house in Florida.

After Kingsley Plantation, exit the same gate you entered and travel straight ahead on Palmetto Avenue. About half a mile after leaving the plantation grounds, you may want to stop at the pullover on the left and walk 1.25 miles to Blue's Pond. Look for wood storks, marsh rabbits, and ducks. Continue on Palmetto Avenue to its intersection with SR 105, where this drive began. At this point you might want to take a side trip to Fort Caroline or to the Mayport ferry and village; see the descriptions at the end of this drive. To continue the main drive, turn left (north) on SR 105 and follow the road across the marshes of Fort George Island. Soon SR 105 curves east and becomes US A1A, the coastal highway. This section of highway is noted for its wide salt marsh vistas and casual 1940s fishhouse-style development, compared to the more developed areas along Florida's East Coast. The drive on A1A continues across a series of low, narrow bridges that are popular fishing spots.

After 1.5 miles, you'll see Huguenot Memorial Park on the right. This is prime winter shorebird territory, holding thousands of gulls, terns, oyster-catchers, and other species. The busy regional park has campsites, an observation tower, restrooms, and picnic shelters.

This drive along A1A crosses the Fort George River after Huguenot Park, to get to the next two islands on this drive, Little Talbot and Big Talbot. These islands are family-friendly, offering hiking, fishing, beachcombing, birding, and swimming at the ocean's edge. The entire island of Little Talbot is a state park. Enjoy ranger-led walks, camping, a bathhouse, picnic tables, and canoe rentals. Fish for speckled trout, striped bass, bluefish, redfish, flounder, sheepshead, and whiting here. Shells are not abundant on every Florida beach, so take advantage of the empty whelks, banded tulips, pen shells, and olives that wash up along the 5.5 miles of white sand.

An 1899 railway depot in Fernandina Beach's historic district is now a visitor center.

From the park's observation deck look for brown pelicans, laughing and ring-billed gulls, and royal terns. In summer you may see federally listed endangered loggerhead turtles digging nests at night, or the hatchlings struggling to get to the ocean. In fall and winter ask park rangers to show you the best places offshore to glimpse the rare right whale as it migrates into this region to calve. Further inland, enjoy hiking trails through the thick forest of Southern magnolia, live oak, and American holly, watching for bobcat tracks, migratory warblers, painted buntings, and river otters.

Returning to A1A, take a right turn and head north, leaving Little Talbot Island State Park. You will cross a bridge and then enter the next large island, Big Talbot Island, which is home to a less-developed facility, Big Talbot Island State Park. Here canoe paths wind through protected salt marsh, and there are pullovers to reach hiking trails, such as the Blackrock Trail, and a popular promontory, the Bluffs, but there are no developed facilities. Ask rangers at Little Talbot for hiking and canoe trail recommendations at Big Talbot.

Continue on A1A across Nassau Sound onto Amelia Island, the last island of this drive. Here the route is known as Buccaneer Trail. There are no facilities, but horses can be reserved at Sea Horse Stable, for a trot along the Amelia Island State Recreation Area beach.

Amelia Island is at the roof of the state, on the Georgia border, and is a legendary pirate hangout. The island was named for Princess Amelia, daughter of England's King George II, in 1735. In 5 miles you will come to a blinking light. Turn right and continue on A1A (now South Fletcher) to Fernandina Beach, following the coast. In 6 miles you will reach the intersection of A1A and Atlantic Avenue. Turn left on Atlantic. A quick jog right brings you to Fort Clinch State Park, a federal Civil War outpost and now a popular camping place. The 1,100-acre park has a fishing pier and offers excellent beachcombing opportunities. Inland, alligators and turtles can be seen at the park's Willow Pond. On the first weekend of each month, rangers re-enact life as Union soldiers in 1864.

To reach downtown after visiting the park, turn right onto Atlantic Avenue, which turns into Centre Street and enters the Fernandina Historic District, where this drive ends. This 50-block district of wood-frame buildings, circa 1857–1900, is listed on the National Register of Historic Places. It borders the bustling waterfront, where you'll see shrimp boats tied up next to restaurants on the docks.

The Amelia Island Museum of History on Third Street (closed Sundays) is a good introduction to the island's history. Museum guides lead walking tours of Centre Street, and of private historic homes. Numerous historic sites, including the stunning Fairbanks House (built 1885), a still-working lighthouse, Florida's oldest surviving tourist hotel (built 1857),

Kingsley Plantation's idyllic setting on the Fort George River belies the cruelties of slavery once practiced here.

and (what is possibly) Florida's oldest bar, make it worthwhile to spend some time touring this area. At Fernandina Beach, you can choose among restaurants, boat rides, horse-and-buggy rides, or just watching the sun set beyond the shrimp boats on St. Marys River.

Fort Caroline side trip

This is a side trip to a portion of the Timucuan Ecological and Historic Preserve, a national park preserve that straddles both the north and south shores of the St. Johns River and includes the Kingsley Plantation. Fort Caroline National Memorial has a model of the fort established here by French Huguenots in 1564. There are also several marked nature trails and a visitor's center. To take this side trip, start about 7 miles west of the starting point of this drive, at the intersection of SR 105/ US A1A and SR 9A. Take the SR 9A bridge south across the St. Johns River, then take the first exit off SR 9A, marked with a sign for Fort Caroline Road and the Fort Caroline National Memorial. Go left (east) on Fort Caroline Road and travel about 5 miles, where you will see the entrance to the memorial on the left. Trace your path back across the river to return to the main drive.

Mayport ferry and village side trip

The second side trip, perhaps Florida's only major car ferry ride, begins 2.5 miles before the drive's actual starting point. Pull into the large roadside parking lot marked with a Mayport Ferry sign, on the south side of A1A (SR 105) about 12.5 miles east of Jacksonville, and wait for directions to load onto the ferry. RVs are easily accommodated on this ferry. The 10-minute breezy trip south across the St. Johns River takes you to Mayport, a town that calls itself the oldest fishing village in the United States. It has a working lighthouse that is closed to the public, active fishing docks, a historic district, restaurants, shops, and a naval base. Take the ferry back across the river to return to the main drive on A1A (SR 105).

The Mayport ferry ride makes a breezy, salty side trip.

12

Guana River Marsh and Ocean Dunes
St. Augustine to Guana River State Park

General description: This 30-mile drive on two-lane paved road explores a coastal zone that stretches from river to lake to ocean. It contains some of the last towering dunes on the northeastern Florida coast. The drive visits a sheltered river marsh and dammed lake where osprey, brown pelicans, and alligators abound.

Special features: Guana River State Park and Guana River Wildlife Management Area, hiking, fishing, crabbing, birding, beachcombing, boating, canoeing, picnicking.

Location: Northeast coastal Florida. The drive starts about 2 miles northeast of historic St. Augustine at the junction of St. Augustine Inlet Bridge and U.S. A1A North.

Drive route number: U.S. Highway A1A North.

Travel season: October through April is recommended, to view migrating federally listed endangered peregrine falcons. In winter, vast flocks of ducks such as American coots and pied-billed grebes feed here, as well as white pelicans. Winter also affords a chance to glimpse the rare right whale in calving grounds. Summer is nesting season for the federally listed endangered loggerhead turtle. However, intense heat, lightning storms, and biting bugs may make summer unpleasant.

Camping: There is no camping in Guana River State Park. Public campgrounds are located about 13 miles south of the drive at Anastasia Island State Recreation Area, via State Road A1A South and the Bridge of Lions at St. Augustine Beach. There are also public campgrounds on the mainland in Faver-Dykes State Park, off U.S. 1 at its junction with Interstate 95, about 15 miles south of the St. Augustine historic district. Private campgrounds are located closer to the park off A1A and in St. Augustine and St. Augustine Beach.

Services: Services are south of the Guana River State Park on A1A and also in St. Augustine, St. Augustine Beach, and north of the park on A1A in the golf resort of Ponte Vedra Beach. St. Augustine has many historic bed and breakfast inns.

Nearby points of interest: Historic St. Augustine, including Spanish Quarter Museum Village, Spanish Military Hospital, Historic St. Augustine Government House and Castillo de San Marcos National Monument, Fort Mose site, Lighthouse Tower and Museum, Lightner Museum, Anastasia

State Recreation Area; Fort Matanzas National Monument with guided ferry to Rattlesnake Island; Marineland, a national historic site; and Washington Oaks State Gardens.

Time zone: Eastern.

 # The drive

This ocean drive along the northeastern Florida coast offers what many people hope to find in the Sunshine State, access to an unspoiled beach. The beach is significant not only for its panoramic views of the Atlantic, but also because of its tall barrier dunes, anchored by long-rooted plants and trees. This type of towering dune has largely disappeared from Florida's beaches—flattened for development, or for better ocean views, or by storms. This drive also visits an adjacent manmade lake that offers excellent fishing and birding opportunities in a little-known state park that shelters bobcat and osprey.

Begin this drive at the junction of A1A North (May Street) and CR 5 (San Marco Avenue), about 2 miles north of the downtown St. Augustine Historic District. (For a side trip to the St. Augustine Historic District, see the description at the end of this drive.) Take A1A North about 2 miles from the downtown district. Just after the Old City Jail, turn right, headed east on A1A North, over the Vilano Bridge across the North River. On the right is St. Augustine Inlet.

At the end of the bridge turn left and travel north along the coast on A1A. You will pass oceanfront homes built on stilts so floodwater can run underneath. There are several public beaches along A1A, where you can stop and visit the ocean. After 11 miles, there will be a sign on the left side of A1A designating Guana River State Park.

This 2,400-acre state park has 5 miles of beach and borders a 9,600-acre state wildlife management area. Pick up a park brochure from the self-service box at the entrance gate, then follow the hard-packed, sandy road about half a mile through low palmettoes to the small dam and unpaved parking area. Here you'll see a sweeping view of the Guana River tidal marsh and adjoining Guana Lake. Check on the information board at the dam for maps of backcountry roads and ranger-led events.

The best times to view wildlife are early morning or late afternoon. The osprey is one of about 185 bird species found in this area, along with migrating birds. Falcons and hawks can be spotted in fall and winter, and sometimes the rare peregrine falcon as well.

At the dam look for brown pelicans paddling on the water and squatting on the shore. Oyster beds—which look like grayish-black clumps in the muck on the south side of the dam—are exposed at low tide. Look in

Drive 12: Guana River Marsh and Ocean Dunes

St. Augustine to Guana River State Park

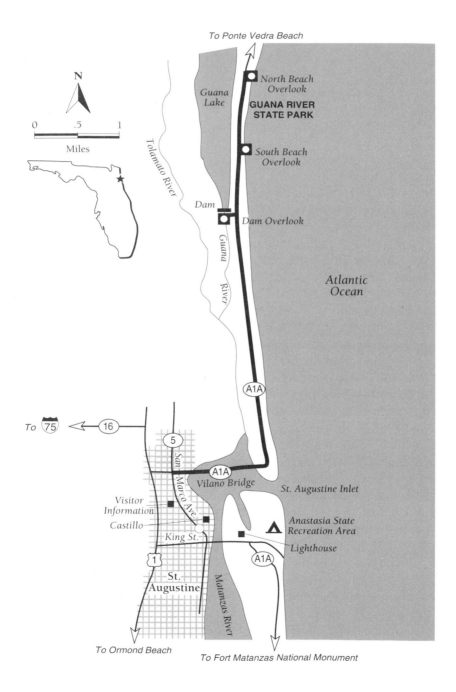

To Ponte Vedra Beach

N

0   .5   1

Miles

North Beach
Overlook

Guana
Lake

GUANA RIVER
STATE PARK

Tolamato River

South Beach
Overlook

Dam

Guana River

Dam Overlook

*Atlantic
Ocean*

A1A

To (75)   (16)

(5)

San Marco Ave.

A1A

Vilano Bridge

St. Augustine Inlet

Visitor
Information

Castillo

King St.

Anastasia State
Recreation Area

Lighthouse

(1)

A1A

St.
Augustine

Matanzas River

To Ormond Beach

To Fort Matanzas National Monument

the marsh here for large wading birds, such as great blue heron and great white heron. On the north side of the dam, the narrow, 10-mile-long Guana Lake is a manmade impoundment teeming with waterfowl, shorebirds, and wading birds, as well as alligators and otters. In winter up to 4,000 migratory ducks, American coots, common moorhens, and common gallinules blanket the lake. You may even be lucky enough to see visiting white pelicans.

From the dam parking area you can explore the Guana Peninsula along the 10-mile Hammock Road, a narrow service trail. Other walks include the 1-mile Shell Bluff Road to the Tolomato River (which forms the western edge of the park), the 3-mile Timucua Trail and, beyond it, the 2.8-mile South Peninsula Loop. These are good places to spot white-tailed deer, gopher tortoises, raccoons, and elusive bobcats. The lake and inland trails are popular during hunting seasons. The region's fish, shellfish, sea turtles, and abundant mammals were hunted by the aboriginal Timucua Indians, who piled up mounds of shells and other remains. Some of these mounds can still be seen in the park.

After visiting the dam area, return to A1A, turn left (north), and travel 3.7 miles. You will see the parking for South Beach on the left. The beach is across the highway. This beach is often crowded, so you may choose to continue north on A1A another 1.2 miles to North Beach, where parking is also on the left. Neither beach has a fresh water source, and the restrooms are port-a-johns.

Whichever beach you choose, you'll find 30- to 40-foot sand dunes punctuating the landscape, supporting such plant life as prickly pear cactus, cabbage palm, palmetto, sea oats, and beach wildflowers such as firewheel and Indian blanket. Climb the wooden observation decks at each beach for a bird's-eye view of both the Atlantic Ocean and Guana Lake. The decks are also a good place to look for birds and migrating right whales, which calve near the shore during the winter months.

Taking the boardwalk down to the beach, you can walk along the high-tide line to examine seaweed, driftwood, starfish, sea slugs, and shells tossed up by ocean waves. (Today most beachcombers take only the shell skeletons, leaving the live ones to reproduce.)

If you are interested in visiting a golf resort, you can continue from the park beaches north about 2 miles to Ponte Vedra Beach. Otherwise, trace your path back to the start of this drive for a side trip to St. Augustine.

Historic St. Augustine side trip

About 2 miles south of this drive's starting point is the Historic District of St. Augustine, one of the most famous in America. At the intersection of A1A and San Marco Avenue, travel about a quarter of a mile south on San

The surf rolls in at Guana River State Park.

Marco Avenue to the Visitor Center Welcome Station on the right, at San Marco Avenue and Riberia Street. Stop here for orientation, recommended walking routes, tips on the best places to park and walk the historic streets where cars aren't allowed, tram and buggy ride information, and brochures on more than 20 historic buildings and sites. The narrow streets border preserved or re-created 16th- and 17th-century homes, inns, shops, and public buildings. St. Augustine is America's oldest community that has been in continuous use, founded 42 years before Jamestown and 55 years before pilgrims landed at Plymouth Rock.

A book, *The Houses of St. Augustine*, by historian David Nolan, is a good introduction to the intriguing architectural aspects of this historic city. Other attractions here include a restored 1887 hotel on King Street (now operating as Flagler College); the small but eclectic Lightner Museum; the remains of Fort Mose, which in 1738 housed the continent's first black village and militia; and the Castillo, the oldest masonry fort in the United States, a national historic landmark, built in 1695.

13

Down to Earth

Gainesville to High Springs

General description: A 20-mile drive through rolling hills of farmland, horse pastures, and hardwood forest leading from a sinkhole you can climb into to the country retreat of High Springs, a former railroad village.

Special features: Devil's Millhopper State Geological Site, San Felasco Hammock State Preserve, Alachua antiques district, High Springs Train Depot Museum and antiques district, Santa Fe River, hiking, biking, tubing, kayaking, canoeing, fishing, swimming, snorkeling, scuba diving, picnicking, birding.

Location: North-central Florida.

Drive route numbers: State Road 232 (Millhopper Road), County Road 241, County Road 235, U.S. Highway 441.

Travel season: Year-round, but expect biting insects and intense heat in summer. Fall and spring are best to see migratory birds. Rivers and springs are crowded in summer, especially on weekends. The best weather for river tubing is late spring to early fall.

Camping: O'Leno State Park has excellent public camping northeast of this drive via US 441, and there are fine private campgrounds, many of them by the river, and fish camps in nearby woods.

Services: Many services, including gas stations and bed and breakfast inns, are in High Springs and Alachua, and all services can be found in Gainesville.

Nearby points of interest: Poe Springs Park, Ginnie Springs, O'Leno State Park, Ichetucknee Springs State Park, Santa Fe Canoe Trail, Dudley Farm State Historic Site, Gainesville-Hawthorne Rail Trail, Florida Museum of Natural History, Samuel P. Harn Museum of Art, Bivens Arm Nature Park, Morningside Nature Center, Santa Fe Community College Teaching Zoo (open weekends only from 9 A.M. to 2 P.M.), Kanapaha Botanical Gardens (closed Thursdays), downtown Gainesville and Gainesville Historic District, Matheson Historical Center, the Fred Bear Museum (open Wednesday through Sunday).

Time zone: Eastern.

Drive 13: Down to Earth
Gainesville to High Springs

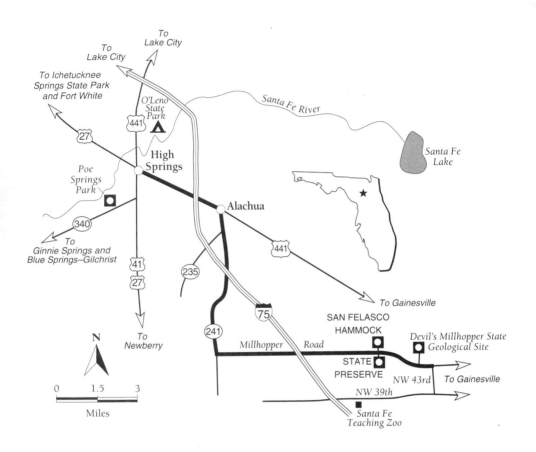

 The drive

This drive begins at the Devil's Millhopper sinkhole—located in a quiet northwestern Gainesville neighborhood of shops, homes, and small woods. Tourists have climbed down into its earthy, damp interior since the 1880s. A long weekend in Gainesville is a recommended side trip, mentioned at the end of this drive. The drive continues northwest out of town through a well-preserved woodland, crossing rolling farmland, wetlands, and uplands. The drive ends in a charming former railroad village, a popular base from which to explore area springs and rivers. The sites along this drive beg participation—walking, canoeing, swimming, snorkeling, and diving (if you are certified).

Start this drive in Gainesville at the intersection of NW 43rd Street, a main north-south route, and Millhopper Road. To reach NW 43rd Street from Interstate 75, take the NW 39th Avenue exit from I-75, heading east. (This is also the exit for the Santa Fe Community College NW Campus.) Travel east on NW 39th (SR 222) about 3 miles to its intersection with NW 43rd Street. Turn left (north) onto NW 43rd, and drive about 1 mile to its intersection with Millhopper Road (NW 53rd Avenue/SR 232). Turn left (west) on Millhopper Road and travel just about 1,000 feet before turning right at the entrance to Devil's Millhopper State Geological Site.

At Devil's Millhopper, a small open-air visitor center next to the parking lot interprets the natural and human history of the site. The sinkhole is about 500 feet across at the bottom. The bowl-shaped opening was created in the Earth's crust as rainwater dripped through porous limestone, forcing an underground cavern roof to collapse. You can walk down 221 steps, or about 120 feet, into the sinkhole. As you follow the wooden steps, listen for the sound of small waterfalls tumbling down the fern-lined slope to disappear into crevices in the sinkhole floor. Look among lush ferns for water-loving frogs and salamanders. You may notice that the temperature is slightly cooler as you descend. WARNING: The walkway down into the sinkhole is very slippery when wet.

Leaving this green glade, turn right (west) on Millhopper Road, which winds through wooded housing developments. In about 4 miles look on the left for a small, unpaved parking area and sign for San Felasco Hammock State Preserve. The parking lot is dotted with trees, making it a tight fit for large RVs on crowded weekends. This is the entrance to the 6,500-acre hammock preserve, an Eden of sinkholes, brooks, sandy hills, swamps, forests, and champion trees—meaning individual trees measured and found to be giants of their species. In Florida a hammock is a term used to refer to a dense area of trees, usually elevated above surrounding land.

A 1-mile nature trail begins at the parking lot and winds through the preserve's pine forest and hardwood hammock. Directly across Millhopper Road from the parking lot is the entrance to the preserve's footpaths and jogging trails. White-tailed deer, bobcat, wild turkey, and gray fox are common here, although bobcats are rarely seen. Nesting birds include federally listed endangered wood storks. Migratory songbirds come through in September and October, and again in April and May. Rangers can arrange group hikes with advance notice; weekend programs, by reservation only, include orienteering and overnight campouts.

Continue left on Millhopper Road through scattered development and past picturesque horse ranches—a billion-dollar Florida industry. In about

Thoroughbreds graze at a chain of farms between Gainesville and High Springs.

a mile, you will cross busy I-75, and a half-mile later turn right (north) at the T intersection of Millhopper Road and CR 241. In 1.5 miles, CR 241 again crosses I-75. In about 2 more miles at the inverted Y intersection, turn right on CR 235 to enter the country village of Alachua.

In Alachua, a two-block historic district along Main Street features inviting shops and cafes. After stopping here, return to CR 235 (NW 140th Street) and head north (left) two blocks to its intersection with US 441.

Turn left on US 441 and travel northwest about 8 miles on this divided, four-lane highway, until it enters the popular weekend retreat of High Springs. You can reach the historic downtown area a few blocks early by taking a curving left off US 441 at the sign that directs you downtown. But if you miss that entrance continue a few more blocks to the traffic light at the intersection of US 441 and Main Street. The downtown district, listed on the National Register of Historic Places, stretches out a block or so each way, so just find a parking spot (they're free) and stroll along Main Street, being sure to step inside the old High Springs Opera House, built about 1865. It served as a dance hall and old-time mercantile company, and today is a popular cafe and shop. The High Springs Chamber of Commerce, in a restored railroad building half a block off Main Street, offers information on area parks, springs, inns, and sites.

Railroad enthusiasts will want to visit the High Springs Train Depot Museum, also half a block off Main Street. This is a restored Atlantic Coastline passenger station that explains the town's significant railroad history. At the Conestoga Restaurant on Main Street you can try some distinctive Florida foods such as smoked mullet dip, frog legs, and fried alligator tail.

Two side trips depart from High Springs: O'Leno State Park and Ichetucknee Springs. They are described at the end of this drive.

There are several recreation areas close by. Just 3 miles west of High Springs on SR 340, Poe Springs, a regional public park, offers fishing, picnicking, a playground, and freshwater swimming below the bluffs of the winding Santa Fe River. A bit farther west on SR 340, a private camping resort in the woods, Ginnie Springs, is popular for its warm springs (72 degrees year-round). It is often thronged with scuba divers, inner tubers, and campers. Camp Kulaqua, a camping resort featuring Hornsby Springs, is located about 1 mile north of downtown High Springs off US 441. This retreat, popular for family reunions and youth groups, is run by a religious group and open by reservation.

This rural area of Florida, where Native Americans, Spanish colonists, and American pioneers first settled, looks so unlike the state's condominium-dotted coastline; the region is sometime called the Original Florida.

O'Leno State Park side trip

Take US 441 north out of High Springs about 5 miles to O'Leno State Park. In addition to sheltering a woodland on the banks of the Santa Fe River, this park features a river disappearing act. You can walk across a delightfully shaky 1930s suspension bridge over the winding Santa Fe, a tributary of the larger Suwannee River. Follow the path a short distance to where the river collects in a dark pool and disappears underground. O'Leno is also a popular campground.

Ichetucknee Springs side trip

Northwest of High Springs via US 27, travel about 10 miles to Fort White and then north on SR 47 to CR 238. Take a left (west) on CR 238, and drive on to Ichetucknee Springs State Park. This park protects a fast-flowing river fed by six clear springs. This preserve has been designated a national natural landmark by the U.S. Department of the Interior. Floating the river, via inner tube or raft, is a popular summer activity, so expect crowds in June through August, with strict limits on the numbers of people allowed on the river.

Gainesville side trip

The University of Florida has several attractions for visitors. The Florida Museum of Natural History (on Museum Road) has interpretive exhibits about the Timucua Indians, residents of northeastern Florida when the first Spanish explorers arrived. The museum also offers a re-created Florida limestone cavern to walk through, as well as an Object Gallery and Fossil Study Center. Also located on the campus is the expansive Samuel P. Harn Museum of Art, on Hull Road. You can easily see alligators in the wild on the western shore of the university's own preserve, Lake Alice.

Off campus, visit an outstanding collection of game trophies along with spears, shields, Native American carvings, and other artifacts, displayed at the Fred Bear Museum, on Archer Road. The Matheson Historical Center, 513 East University Avenue, offers a collection of 18,000 old Florida postcards and 1,200 stereo-view cards, along with the 1857 Matheson House and native plant garden. The Santa Fe Community College Teaching Zoo displays worldwide species and is open weekends. Morningside Nature Center, 3540 East University Avenue, holds a re-created Gainesville farm of 100 years ago, with barnyard animals, a cabin, an heirloom garden, and 7 miles of nature paths.

Kanapaha Botanical Gardens, 4625 SW 63rd Boulevard, shelters a large bamboo stand, a cluster of carnivorous plants, an herb garden, water lily pond, fern grotto, sunken garden, and palm hammock. The downtown Gainesville Historic District features the highly regarded Hippodrome Theater Company and several blocks of cafes and shops in restored brick buildings. Bivens Arm Nature Park, 3650 South Main Street, offers a nature center and 1,200-foot promenade through oak forest. The Thomas Center, 306 NE Sixth Avenue, is the city's cultural center, with garden, local history exhibits, art galleries, and 1920s period rooms in a restored hotel.

14

Crossing Creeks and Prairie
Island Grove to Paynes Prairie to Micanopy

General description: This 15-mile inland drive in north-central Florida, north of Ocala and southeast of Gainesville, visits the community of Cross Creek and the home of a Pulitzer Prize–winning author of the 1930s. The drive spans Cross Creek and other waterways of simple beauty, and meanders through pastures frequented in winter by tall cranes. The drive continues to Paynes Prairie State Preserve—featuring a habitat rarely associated with Florida. The drive ends under the shade of spreading live oaks in nearby Micanopy, an antiques center known for its specialty bookshops and cafes housed in restored buildings.

Special features: Lochloosa Wildlife Management Area, Marjorie Kinnan Rawlings State Historic Site and living history tour, Orange Lake, Cross Creek and surrounding community, Paynes Prairie State Preserve and visitor center, Micanopy, fishing, excellent birding and wildlife watching opportunities, hiking, canoeing, boating.

Location: North-central Florida.

Drive route numbers: U.S. Highway 301, County Road 325, County Road 346, U.S. Highway 441, Savannah Boulevard, and Cholokka Boulevard.

Travel season: Open all year, with October through March the recommended season to see wintering sandhill cranes and other wildlife, to take advantage of seasonal ranger-led events, and to avoid intense summer heat, biting bugs, and lightning storms. The Rawlings cottage is open Thursday through Sunday, but is closed during August and September.

Camping: Paynes Prairie State Preserve has a popular campground. Private campgrounds are located in Cross Creek, Gainesville, and Hawthorne.

Services: Micanopy has bed and breakfast inns and cafes; other services are along US 441 or in Gainesville.

Nearby points of interest: Gainesville offers a myriad of outstanding attractions to visitors, including the Gainesville-Hawthorne State Rail Trail, via Gainesville's Boulware Springs Park (see Gainesville side trip, Drive 13).

Time zone: Eastern.

 # The drive

This 15-mile inland drive takes you past rolling pastureland to a tiny fishing community nestled between two lakes, and the former home of a famous 1930s author, Marjorie Kinnan Rawlings. The drive visits Florida's most significant prairie, where North American bison once fed on prairie grasses and, later, aboriginal natives were enslaved by Spanish ranchers. The final stop is Micanopy, a small, tree-shaded village noted for its antique shops, bookshops, and cafes. This drive is rich in aboriginal, Seminole Indian, and Spanish history.

Begin this drive in Island Grove, about 19 miles north of Ocala at the intersection of US 301 and CR 325. Turn west from US 301 onto winding, two-lane CR 325. This road gently curves through pastures dotted with tall pines and ancient live oaks, and after about 1 mile passes through Lochloosa Wildlife Management Area, managed as a hunting ground. In wet sections of the pastures along this drive, look for sandhill cranes—four feet tall, gray, with black legs and a patch of red skin on their bare heads. Every October and November, up to 2,500 arrive in this region from the Great Lakes area.

Florida bison, once butchered by Florida's Native Americans, have been reintroduced and now roam at Paynes Prairie near Gainesville.

Drive 14: Crossing Creeks and Prairie

Island Grove to Paynes Prairie to Micanopy

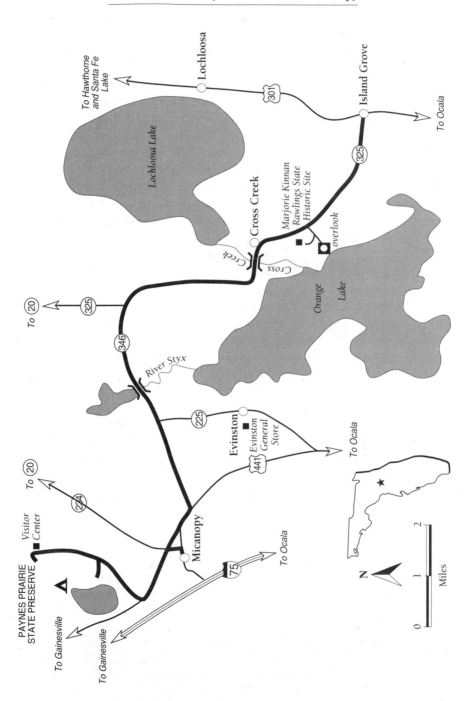

You may also see mockingbirds, red-winged blackbirds, towhees, cardinals, ground doves, and more. A little less than 3 miles into the drive, CR 325 brings you to a well-marked parking area (on the left), with access to Marjorie Kinnan Rawlings Park and adjacent state historic site. The Pulitzer Prize–winning author of *The Yearling* lived here in the 1930s, in a simple cottage surrounded by orange and pecan trees, and wrote many stories about this area of Florida that she called home.

The rambling cottage comprises three interconnected wooden buildings. Over the years Rawlings entertained a number of friends and guests on its shaded porches and breezeways, including Zora Neale Hurston, Robert Frost, Margaret Mitchell, and Dylan Thomas. The author, who died in 1958, left it to the University of Florida in nearby Gainesville, where she sometimes taught, for the benefit of creative writing students. Today, the house and grounds are maintained by the Florida Park Service, and open to the public Thursday through Sunday. There are guided tours at 10 and 11 A.M. each day, and other times, though visitors can take a self-guided tour. The house is closed to the public in August and September. Nearby, there is a nature trail in the woods. To reach it, open the author's front gate, walk across CR 325, and take the cool, dark loop path (0.5 mile) through hardwood forest.

To continue this drive, turn left from the historic site onto CR 325 and drive 0.8 mile slowly past other cottages and around a sharp left turn in the road. Before crossing the small bridge, pull into one of the fish camps near the bridge, and enjoy a view of Cross Creek, a narrow waterway lined with private docks. Cross Creek connects Lochloosa Lake, to the north, with Orange Lake, to the south. You can rent a canoe or motorboat from area fish camps, or you can hire a guide. Bird Island in Orange Lake is a good area for bird watching, as the name implies. Orange Lake is one of Florida's geological attractions. At its southwestern end is a large sinkhole, and in various spots clumps of matted plant material can be seen floating, some substantial enough to be called "floating islands." The quality of fishing in the lake depends on fluctuating water levels. Ask a local guide first.

Return to CR 325, go across the bridge and on through the Cross Creek community. In 1.4 miles on the left, the Creek Shop, a gift shop featuring ceramics and souvenirs, may particularly appeal to fans of Marjorie Kinnan Rawlings. Continue on CR 325 another 2.3 miles to a T intersection with CR 346. Turn left (west) onto CR 346, and in 2.1 miles slow your speed as CR 346 becomes a short, flat bridge over a cypress slough, a current of fresh water. This waterway is called the River Styx, and when Rawlings crossed it on horseback, she commented that she had lived to cross the River Styx.

Continuing along CR 346 another 0.4 mile, you can take a 2.5-mile spur road on the left (CR 225) to Evinston, site of a former Potano Indian village. Today there is a small country store, beautiful fields of wildflowers,

Sandhill crane flock to the fields of the Cross Creek and Paynes Prairie region every year.

The Cross Creek cottage of writer Marjorie Kinnan Rawlings, kept as she decorated it, is a tribute to the beautiful simplicity of rural life.

and excellent places to glimpse sandhill cranes from the roadside during their winter visits. From Evinston, return north on CR 225 to CR 346 and turn left (west).

In 2.8 miles, CR 346 intersects with four-lane US 441. Turn right and travel north on US 441 for 1.8 miles to the south entrance of Paynes Prairie State Preserve, named for the native leader King Payne. The park drive, Savannah Boulevard, winds about 3 miles through a lush palmetto and oak habitat and ends at the visitor center. From this main park road there is well-marked access on the left to the preserve's campground, a former University of Florida lakefront recreational park. At the end of the main park road, there is a visitor center, nature trails, and an observation tower from which it's possible to watch bald eagles soar over the waving grassland, overgrown in areas with bushes and small trees. A small but excellent museum interprets the rich and varied history of this 21,000-acre historic preserve, a region where aboriginals hunted and camped as much as 10,000 years ago, and where Native Americans and Europeans later vied for control in the early years of this nation's history.

Scattered bison roamed in northern Florida, including Paynes Prairie, as late as the early 1700s, though never in the great numbers associated with the West. Today a reintroduced herd of bison roams freely here but is seldom seen. Try looking from the observation tower, and along the 6-mile Cone's Dike Trail, which begins at the visitor center. The bison are sometimes seen from the Alachua Lake platform near the preserve's North Rim Interpretive Center (not part of this drive, located at the end of SE 15th Street, Gainesville).

To leave the preserve, trace your path back on Savannah Boulevard to US 441. If you are reluctant to end your preserve experience, you can turn right on US 441 and drive onto the prairie across US 441 about 10 miles into Gainesville, stopping at a roadside pullout about halfway across the prairie to observe the view. This wayside stop provides access to the preserve's Bolen Bluff Trail, a 1-mile walk into the woods, ending with a 0.6-mile spur walk to an observation platform on the prairie basin.

Our drive continues in the opposite direction, turning left onto US 441 at the park entrance and heading south about half a mile to the well-marked right turn to Micanopy. Micanopy is known for its excellent bookshops specializing in out-of-print volumes. Park under one of the live oak trees and walk Micanopy's blocks of restored buildings, now open as antique shops featuring furniture, collectibles, and vintage clothing and jewelry. Be sure to visit the Herlong Mansion (circa 1845) on Cholokka Boulevard, the village's main street. It is a landmark operated as a bed and breakfast inn. Another bed and breakfast inn, The Shady Oak, also on Cholokka Boulevard, offers stained glass workshops.

15

Cedar Islands Coast and Suwannee River Waterland
Cedar Key to Manatee Springs State Park

General description: This 41.5-mile drive begins just outside an 1840s island seaport where naturalist John Muir ended his noted 1,000-mile walk to the Gulf of Mexico. The drive then takes a remote back route through a national wildlife refuge of pine uplands, river wetlands, and coastal marsh. It travels the back roads to a state preserve of clear, fish-laden waters, where ancient cypress trees grow tall and manatees usually return in winter to float in warm springs near the historic Suwannee River.

Special features: Cedar Key Historic District, Cedar Key Historical Society Museum, Cedar Key State Museum, Cedar Keys National Wildlife Refuge, Cedar Key Scrub State Reserve, Lower Suwannee National Wildlife Refuge, Shell Mound Archaeological Site, River Trail, Fowler's Bluff, Manatee Springs State Park, birding, canoeing, kayaking, fishing, beachcombing, crabbing, biking.

Location: Central Gulf Coast.

Drive route numbers: State Road 24, State Road 347, State Road 326, Camp Azalea Road, State Road 320.

Travel season: October through April. The roads are open year-round but late fall through early spring is recommended to avoid biting deer flies and other biting bugs, summer temperatures of 95 or higher, and lightning storms. The first several miles of Camp Azalea Road on the way to the state park is unpaved, with mild washboard. The road is a graded, well-used route, but it can be slippery after heavy rains. (The Lower Suwannee National Wildlife Refuge office, open weekdays, can direct you to an alternate route to Manatee Springs State Park, via SR 347, SR 345, US 19/98, and SR 320.)

Camping: Private campgrounds are at Cedar Key. A remote Levy County waterfront campground operates near Shell Mound Trail in the Lower Suwannee Wildlife Refuge on SR 326. Manatee Springs State Park, at the end of this drive, is a popular campground.

Services: All services, including gas, bed and breakfast inns, a historic hotel, and resort lodging are found at Cedar Key. There are no gas stations on the second part of the drive, the back route to the park. Limited snacks and supplies are sold in a boat landing bait shop, which isn't always open, on the short side trip to the Suwannee River at Fowler's Bluff. Manatee Springs State Park has a small snack stand. Chiefland, the state park's host community on US 19/98, has all other services.

Nearby points of interest: Rosewood Massacre Historic Site; Hart Springs Park; Crystal River State Archaeological Site; Homosassa Springs State Wildlife Park; Waccasassa Bay State Preserve, via boat.

Time zone: Eastern.

 # The drive

Fans of John Muir, founder of the Sierra Club, are among those who will enjoy this visit to a collection of about 100 Florida islands, almost all of them reached only by boat, known as the Cedar Keys. Muir, then 29, spent the winter of 1867–1868 resting here after a 1,000-mile walk from Indiana to the Gulf of Mexico.

Plan to stay in this area overnight, if possible, because of the remoteness of the islands and the wealth of historic, natural, and archaeological features nearby. Access to the Cedar Keys National Wildlife Refuge is by private boat; wildlife guides are based in Cedar Key and the surrounding region. After a tranquil visit to the old island fishing village, the drive heads northwest out of town, to a tree-covered hill of oyster shells Native Americans spent 3,500 years creating. This 5-acre garbage heap, called a kitchen midden, is preserved within the 51,341-acre Lower Suwannee National Wildlife Refuge. The refuge is home to the endangered black bear and also 250 species of birds, including turkeys and ducks that are hunted in season. The route continues in pine forest uplands and has a short walking trail to overlook the historic Suwannee River. After a backwoods ramble on partly unpaved road, the drive ends at a clear spring that empties into the river, part of a state manatee preserve and campground.

Begin this drive in the village of Cedar Key, on SR 24 where it leaves mainland Florida, about 55 miles southwest of Gainesville.

A bracelet of bridges and causeways leads about 3 miles into town from the mainland. This part of the drive offers easy views of small mud flats and oyster bars, places for prime bird watching. Dots of land rise above the marsh, a nursery for saltwater fish, shellfish, and crustaceans. Early morning and evening and at low tide are the best times to see white ibis; great and snowy egrets; great blue, little blue, and tricolored herons; and abundant wintering ducks on the exposed flats, with osprey flying overhead.

The town of Cedar Key is on the island of Way Key. A collection of seafood houses on stilts, historic buildings, quaint rental cottages, restaurants, galleries, a pier, a public marina, a tiny beach, small resorts, and shops

Drive 15: Cedar Islands Coast and Suwannee River Waterland

Cedar Key to Manatee Springs State Park

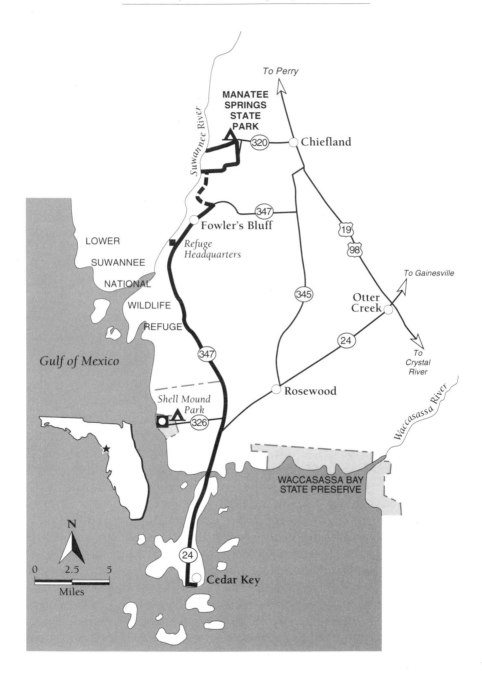

characterize the village. Most of the year, the pace is slow enough that some residents drive golf carts instead of cars for local trips, and ducks stop traffic when they waddle across downtown streets. An art fair in April and a seafood party in October attract huge numbers of visitors, as well as on holiday weekends.

Cedar Key was Florida's busiest seaport in the 1850s, with 2,000 residents. Today the population is only about 700. It has 30 original buildings, some dating to the 1840s. The Island Hotel on Second Street was built of tabby, a durable concrete made of shell, in 1849. It opened as a general store, with the second floor operating as a busy custom house. Today it is a popular lodge and restaurant.

Two small museums offer excellent orientation. The Cedar Key Historical Society Museum (downtown at the junction of SR 24 and Second Street) features exhibits on Native American life, the area's defunct cedar wood and palmetto fiber factories, the old saltworks, and marine industry including sponge and shellfish harvesting. There is a self-guided walking tour, good local history books, and island souvenirs. The Cedar Key State Museum, reached by bicycle or car on a well-marked route away from downtown, features a fascinating private shell and Native artifact collection.

Around the village, look for ancient shell mounds built by Native Americans. The most visible ones can be seen on the south side of Second Street, the west side of G Street, and the west end of Sixth Street.

At the public marina and pier, brown pelicans beg for bait and fish scraps, sometimes injuring themselves as they grab for fish that have been caught and not yet unhooked. The pier is a small business district with shops that sell citrus fudge, shells, manatee and pelican figurines, and all manner of artwork, and with fresh seafood restaurants perched on pilings.

The many coves, tidal creeks, and islands of the Cedar Keys National Wildlife Refuge and nearby Waccasassa Bay State Preserve are worth the boat trip, though there are no facilities. On the water you may be able to see porpoise, and from a quiet boat even more marine life, including sea turtles and otters.

The Cedar Key Chamber of Commerce has information on boat rentals and wildlife guides, as do lodging offices. Spend some time exploring this island group, including the stunning beach at Seahorse Key, often glistening with shell skeletons, an ideal swimming and picnicking spot. Other sites include a lighthouse built in 1855, the site of a Civil War skirmish, and the site of a prison way station, where many of Florida's Native Americans stopped as they were forced from Florida to reservations in the Midwest. While some island coasts are accessible, camping on the islands and walking into their interiors is forbidden. Some beach areas are also closed March through June, during shorebird nesting season.

In John Muir's day Cedar Key was not only an abundant wildlife area, it also served as a railroad depot, commercial port, and transfer point for travelers who wished to continue onward by steamer to southern Florida. The area's aromatic red cedar forests gave up their valuable wood for the world's pencil supply, and the forests were soon depleted. This began Cedar Key's economic decline, which continued after railroad builder Henry Plant rerouted his rail line to Tampa in the 1880s. The village's decline actually served to guard the area's pristine islands, marshes, and other natural features from development.

These islands, today unoccupied, were the main site of the first Cedar Key village. Way Key served as a federal depot from 1839 to 1842, including a detention camp for Seminole and Miccosukee Indians. About 8 miles outside Cedar Key is the site of the African-American village of Rosewood, which was torched by a white mob on New Year's Day, 1923, precipitating violence that killed six blacks and two whites. An interpretive center to be built here will explain the history.

For the second half of this drive, head north out of Cedar Key on SR 24. If you plan on camping at the end of the drive in Manatee Springs State Park, call ahead for reservations and load up on supplies in Cedar Key before leaving. Take SR 24 from the village to the mainland, then travel 0.3 mile to a left fork, SR 347. Take this left fork, heading north for 2.5 miles, where the drive borders Cedar Key Scrub State Reserve, an area of sandy ridges with no interpretive center or marked access yet, other than views along the drive. These sandy ridges are dotted with dwarf live oaks, palmettoes, and other vegetation that is suited to the parched conditions here. Look for scrub jays, swallow-tailed kites, and gopher tortoises.

After 2.5 miles on SR 347, turn left on SR 326, at the sign marking the shell mound site. Travel west through the northern boundary of Cedar Key Scrub State Reserve. After 3.2 miles, on the right, the Levy County campground (called Shell Mound Park) has a boat launch area and views into the marshes of the Lower Suwannee National Wildlife Refuge.

From the campground, return to SR 326, taking a right. In 500 yards the two-lane paved road ends and an unpaved lane continues into Lower Suwannee National Wildlife Refuge. Soon there is a sand and limestone parking area, with access to two walking paths. There are no facilities here; a self-service box offers a refuge brochure and map. The Dennis Creek Trail is a 1-mile loop to coastal creek habitat. If your time is short, take the 0.3-mile Shell Mound Trail, which climbs over a portion of a heavily wooded 5-acre shell mound built by aboriginals. Over the course of 3,500 years, they discarded the skeletons of abundant oysters and other shellfish, forming a huge garbage heap called a kitchen midden. (The region's aboriginal history is interpreted at the Crystal River State Archaeological Site, on US 19/98, at

Manatees usually visit Manatee Springs State Park in winter.

Cedar Key is a place to fish and feast on fish.

Crystal River.) At a height of 28 feet, this mound is the tallest point on the flat Big Bend Coast of Florida.

Returning to SR 326, trace your path back the 3.2 miles to SR 347 and turn left (north), traveling through scrub habitat that gradually gives way to palmetto ground cover and pine forest. In 3.6 miles a sign announces your arrival again in Lower Suwannee National Wildlife Refuge. This is a little-known preserve, one of the largest undeveloped estuarine systems in the United States It attracts hunters as well as wildlife enthusiasts. The refuge shelters federally listed threatened Florida black bear, which are rarely seen, and abundant white-tailed deer, which are frequently seen at dusk feeding along the roadside. You may see some of the 250 species of birds here, such as blue-winged and green-winged teals, wood duck, turkey, osprey, bald eagle, and swallow-tailed kite. Alligators, federally listed endangered sea turtles and manatees, frogs, and land turtles are also spotted.

Continue about 11 miles on SR 347 through the refuge to its north entrance gate for developed facilities. Here a log cabin office is open during weekday business hours, with restrooms, a water fountain, and rangers who can answer questions about recent wildlife sightings and backcountry conditions. Across from the refuge office you can picnic or walk the 0.8-mile River Trail through the woods to the Suwannee River, where you might see migrating manatees in late fall and early spring. There is no public campground in the refuge and visitors should be alert for seasonal hunters, especially on holiday weekends.

Leaving the refuge, take a left on SR 347. In 1.4 miles you can take a half-mile loop on the left, into the small community of Fowler's Bluff, perched on the banks of the Suwannee River. A public boat ramp here allows access to the river, and a small bait shop keeps irregular hours. Returning to SR 347, continue north. In 3.1 miles, when the main road curves to the right, take the unpaved, limestone road on the left called Camp Azalea Road, the route to Old Camp Landing, another public boat access on the Suwannee River.

In 2.6 miles, Camp Azalea Road takes a sharp right, becomes paved, and quickly takes a sharp left. To see the Suwannee River you can follow a boat ramp sign one block to the small, steep ramp. To continue the drive, go back toward SR 347 one block, take a left on Camp Azalea Road, and follow it as it winds 5.3 miles through the pinewoods of the Lower Suwannee Conservation Area. It ends in a T intersection with SR 320, just outside the entrance to Manatee Springs State Park. Take a left from Camp Azalea Road onto SR 320, which ends in about half a mile at the park gate.

Manatee Springs State Park is one of the oldest public state campgrounds in Florida and the site of a former aboriginal village. It is best known for sheltering federally listed endangered manatees during the winter.

Although for years manatees didn't visit this spring run, with its constant temperature of 72 degrees, in recent years they have returned.

The 2,075-acre park features a 600-foot boardwalk with interpretive signs along the edge of the spring run, past cypress trees growing in water. There are plentiful fish seen from the boardwalk in the clear run, offering a window into this natural aquarium. There are frequent sightings of the non-poisonous Florida brown snake, coiled at the base of cypress trees.

In addition to the boardwalk, which ends at a dock overlooking the river, the park has two other walks: the 0.6-mile Sink Trail, which visits an area of sinkholes, and the 8.5-mile North End Trail into sandy hills, which is suitable for walking or bicycling. A park concession offers canoe rentals and snacks during the summer months. Also seek out information on campfire programs and ranger-led events.

16

The Forest of Florida Scrub
Volusia to Alexander Springs to Wildcat Lake

General description: This 36-mile loop drive is almost entirely within the Ocala National Forest in central Florida. The forest, the first national forest designated east of the Mississippi, is a 400,000-acre timberland refreshed by rivers, lakes, and springs, and it also enfolds a group of sand islands that once dotted an ancient sea. The drive introduces this forest scrub sandscape and also visits a mammoth freshwater springs in a cypress swamp, a green glen that was inhabited about A.D. 1000.

Special features: St. Johns River, the Volusia Oak at Astor, Alexander Springs Recreation Area and Timucuan Nature Trail, Florida National Scenic Trail, Paisley Woods Bicycle Trail, Flatwoods Horse Trail, Pittman Visitor Center, Lake Dorr Recreation Area, Little Sellers Lake, Grasshopper Lake, Wildcat Lake, birding, hiking, canoeing, springs and lake swimming, snorkeling, fishing, horseback riding, wildlife watching.

Location: Inland central Florida.

Drive route numbers: State Road 40, County Road 445, State Road 19.

Travel season: Open year-round, but November through April are recommended for best wildlife watching and weather. NOTE: The Ocala National Forest is a prime deer hunting grounds, so be alert for hunters on trails from mid-November to mid-January. Although summer is popular with local residents, it can bring temperatures of 95 degrees and higher, lightning storms, and biting bugs.

Camping: There are two Ocala National Forest campgrounds directly on this route, one at Alexander Springs Recreation Area and the other at Lake Dorr Recreation Area. National forest campgrounds that are nearby include the primitive but popular Buck Lake campsite, about 3 miles west of this drive on unpaved FR 535, and the better developed, but often crowded, Juniper Springs, about 5 miles west of this drive on SR 40. NOTE: These campgrounds do not take reservations, so arriving early is the best idea, especially on weekends. There is private camping at fish camps at Astor, at a unique horse ranch south of the visitor center and Lake Dorr, and at other commercial locations on SR 40 and SR 19.

Services: Services such as restaurants and gas stations can be found in some of the forest communities, such as Altoona. Full services can be found at historic DeLand, about 17 miles southeast of the drive, and at Silver Springs and Ocala, 27 miles west of the drive.

Nearby points of interest: Barberville Pioneer Settlement for the Creative Arts; Lake Woodruff National Wildlife Refuge; Blue Spring State

Park, DeLeon Springs State Recreation Area; Hontoon Island State Park; downtown DeLand; areas of Ocala National Forest not directly on this drive, such as Clearwater Lake, Salt Springs, Silver Glen Springs, Juniper Springs, Mill Dam, and Lake Eaton Sinkhole Trail.
Time zone: Eastern.

 # The drive

This drive, through longleaf pine forest and tracts of planted pine, visits a portion of the 400,000-acre Ocala National Forest, the most popular of the state's three national forests, and introduces an unusual habitat, Florida scrub. Scrub has white sandy hills, stunted trees, low ground cover needing little moisture, and the unique sand pine, which grows only in scrub habitat. Near the forest scrub, at Alexander Springs, the terrain changes to a dark, cool hardwood forest and cypress swamp.

The Ocala National Forest, which was designated by Theodore Roosevelt in 1908, is home to abundant wildlife, including wild turkey, northern bobwhite, alligator, gopher tortoise, river otter, coyote, and black bear. On this drive I have seen bald eagle, swallow-tailed kite, limpkin, great blue heron, great white heron, woodpecker, bobcat, and several white-tailed deer. (Raccoon are taken for granted, like ants at a picnic.) WARNING: Bear are hit and injured, or even killed, by speeding traffic every year on this drive, so please be alert, especially at night or near dawn.

Begin about 17 miles northwest of the historic village of DeLand on two-lane SR 40 at the riverfront community of Volusia. This old landing is a St. Johns River village with early Native American, Spanish, and settler history. You may wish to explore the rural side streets, many of which lead to popular fish camps along the river. You may also want to stop and contemplate the large tree on SR 40, immediately on your right before the bridge across the north-flowing St. Johns River. This is the Volusia Oak, saved from the axe by the Daughters of the American Revolution (and others) in 1926, when it was slated to be cut down for road widening.

Travel west on SR 40 from Volusia across the St. Johns River, to the old community of Astor, which once had a fine hotel, a stop on the now-defunct St. Johns and Eustis Railroad line. You can find residents who remember seeing panther here in the wild. Florida's early residents carved the image of this animal in totemic figurines from about A.D. 200 to A.D. 1300, one of which is in the Smithsonian Institution.

Continue west out of Astor on SR 40 about 3 miles, past fern farms that grow greenery for the nation's florists, to the forest community of Astor Park. Here our drive veers left onto two-lane CR 445, which is marked with

Drive 16: The Forest of Florida Scrub
Volusia to Alexander Springs to Wildcat Lake

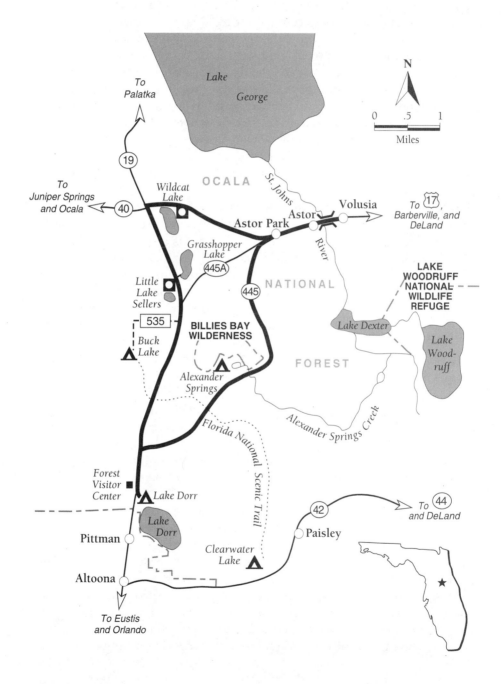

a sign to Alexander Springs, with SR 40 continuing on to the right.

After turning left onto CR 445, in about half a mile the road splits into a V. Take the left fork, which is the continuation of CR 445. The right fork, marked CR 445-A, is a local road into the forest. CR 445 now introduces the dry sandy world of Florida scrub. On either side of the road you can see white, sandy hills. Growing out of the deep, fine sand are gnarled, bent trees such as scrub hickory, scrub oak, and scrub bay. Also growing here is rosemary herb, prickly pear cactus, and the dry, silvery green lichen commonly called deer moss. Towering above this low-growing vegetation is a singular tree, the sand pine, which has learned to grow in this arid climate. The glistening white sand was once part of a desert that stretched across the country. The white quartz sand hills were made eons ago when Florida wasn't a peninsula, but instead a group of islands in an ancient sea. When the sea receded, these high sandy ridges were the first areas to support plant life again.

One species surviving only in Florida scrub is the federally listed endangered scrub jay, a fascinating family bird, with generations of birds helping to raise the young in groups. The scrub is also home to insects, lizards, and mammals that adapt by burrowing into the sand to escape the intense heat and to seek moisture. In a state with abundant rain, this area continues to be arid because the sand doesn't trap Florida's immense rainfall, but instead allows the water to quickly filter through into natural, underground water storage areas, called aquifers.

In 3.2 miles on the left, there's a small pond to watch for wading birds such as great blue heron. Shortly after this, on the right, notice signs indicating Billie's Bay Wilderness Area (no recreational facilities or drinking water). Access is allowed to backcountry visitors who register with rangers at a forest visitor center such as the one just north of Pittman. The unpaved FR 552 on the left leads about 5 miles to another remote region, the Alexander Springs Wilderness, which includes a portion of Alexander Springs Creek and borders the St. Johns River and Lake Woodruff National Wildlife Refuge. These areas also have no facilities and are accessible only to registered backcountry hikers.

In 2.5 miles, CR 445 crosses Alexander Springs Creek. You can park by the side of the road before or after the bridge to observe the wide creek. Canoeists are likely to appear around the bend from upstream, as this is a popular canoe route. Returning to CR 445, continue south and in about half a mile look for the right turn to Alexander Springs Recreation Area. On some weekends, traffic backs up for admission, so try to arrive on a weekday. Reservations are taken in advance for canoe rentals. This recreational site has a campground in the woods, a small camp store, a snorkeling and diving area in the spring, and a sandy beach for swimming. (No fishing is allowed,

Ocala National Forest is a popular camping mecca.

but the fish are a delight to watch with snorkel and mask.) Be sure to walk the 1.1-mile nature trail along the springs in the woods. This path interprets the life of the aboriginal people who hunted and fished here. The spring itself gushes from an underground river at the rate of 80 million gallons a day, the water eventually winding east to feed the St. Johns River. On cold winter mornings the water, which remains at 72 degrees F year-round, sends steam into the air, enveloping the subtropical palms and cypress trees that grow along the spring's shoreline.

Alexander Springs Recreation Area has an easy 0.9-mile spur bicycle path to the 22-mile Paisley Woods Bicycle Trail, a winding trek through longleaf pines and grassy prairie, home to white-tailed deer and black bear. You can hike a 10.6-mile loop of the Paisley Woods bike path if you don't want to complete the entire route. This trail leads to the Clearwater Lake Recreation Area and campground. NOTE: Although there are water sources at each end of the bike trail, there is no fresh water along the way, so plan to bring your own.

Leaving Alexander Springs, turn right (south) on CR 445. In about half a mile, you can turn left onto unpaved FR 538 and travel half a mile to the designated parking area on the right, which serves the Ocala South unit of Florida's National Scenic Trail. This statewide trail will eventually meet up with the Appalachian Trail. This parking area also serves the Paisley Woods Bike Trail, and is most often used by bicyclists who aren't based at Alexander Springs.

Keep going south on CR 445, and in about 0.4 mile note on the left and right sides of the road a pathway, with signs indicating the Florida National Scenic Trail. In another 0.4 mile the Flatwoods Horse Trail crosses CR 445. You can bring your own horse and enjoy 100 miles of designated horse trails in the Ocala National Forest, or you can reserve excellent steeds, schedule lessons, or enjoy guided trail rides and forest campouts at Fiddler's Green Ranch about 7 miles south of the visitor center at Altoona.

Continue about 4 more miles to the T intersection of CR 445 and SR 19. (If you don't plan to stop at the forest visitor center or Lake Dorr and its campground, you can turn right at this intersection, heading north on SR 19, cutting off half an hour to one and a half hours from the trip.) To continue the drive, turn left at this intersection onto SR 19 and travel 2.3 miles south to the Pittman Visitor Center. This is a small and informative museum that interprets past and present forest life, with exhibits on significant archaeological discoveries and current fire ecology practices.

Opposite SR 19 from the visitor center is the entrance to Lake Dorr Recreation Area. It features one of the forest's largest lakes, with an expansive shore. It has a lovely fishing area, campground, and birding area, and white-tailed deer can sometimes be seen in the vicinity at dawn and dusk. Returning to SR 19 from Lake Dorr Recreation Area, turn right and travel north on a fairly straight path through tracts of planted pine to continue the drive. This stretch of SR 19 is one of the areas where black bears are repeatedly hit by nighttime traffic. There may be only 500 to 1,500 bears left in the entire state, and this forest may support up to 200 of them. Studies are ongoing, and so are projects involving wildlife underpasses, to be installed under roads at locations crossed regularly by bears.

About 2 miles past the T intersection with CR 445, the Flatwoods Horse Trail, which earlier crossed the drive on CR 445, now crosses SR 19. About a quarter of a mile later, the Ocala South portion of the Florida National Scenic Trail also crosses SR 19. In another 2 miles, unpaved FR 535 travels about 2.5 miles in to the Buck Lake primitive campsite. Buck Lake is without electricity or flush toilets, but is well-used because the Florida National Scenic Trail passes through it, and it is on a lake where you can fish and swim, although there is no beach. Continuing north on SR 19, in about 1 mile the Little Lake Sellers site, on the left, offers a boat launch on a small lake, and in about a quarter of a mile on the right, Grasshopper Lake is a larger forest lake with a boat launch. Both launch areas are excellent for nature observation.

In 3.3 miles, SR 19 intersects SR 40, a busy east-west forest corridor. Turn right on SR 40 to finish this drive. In about a quarter of a mile on the right, the wayside stop for Wildcat Lake offers a small, pleasant swimming area and boat launch. Wary nocturnal bobcats aren't as frequently seen in the Ocala National Forest as are deer, but they are considered common residents and are regularly reported by visitors exploring forest roads or paths near dawn, especially in timbered scrub habitat. To finish this drive, continue east on SR 40 about 4 miles, through Astor Park and Astor, returning to Volusia. From here you can take a side trip to Barberville-DeLand; see details below.

Barberville-DeLand side trip

After returning to Volusia, continue east on SR 40 about 8 miles to the Barberville Pioneer Settlement for the Creative Arts, on the right about a quarter of a mile before SR 40 intersects with US 17. Although the farm-style grounds and buildings are a pleasure to visit anytime, they are especially interesting during special events, such as the Country Jamboree, held every November, with barrel making, fabric dyeing, blacksmithing, hay baling, log milling, storytelling, and more. About a quarter of a mile beyond the Settlement, turn right on US 17 to travel to the Lake Woodruff National Wildlife Refuge, an exceptional preserve that attracts flotillas of wintering waterfowl and is also known for its healthy population of federally listed threatened bald eagles. Access is in about 4 miles, on the right. After the refuge, return to US 17 and turn right (south) for any of several other parks and preserves in the DeLand region, including Blue Spring State Park, about 6 miles south of DeLand. This is a natural refuge in winter for manatee, which are easily seen from a boardwalk above the spring run. Downtown DeLand has attractive restored buildings that include charming bookshops, cafes, and antique dealers.

17

The Tomoka Region
Ormond Beach to Flagler Beach

General description: A 22-mile quiet back way from Ormond Beach to Flagler Beach, that travels in the dark cypress swamps and historic live oak forests of Tomoka Basin Geopark, then through Gamble Rogers Memorial State Recreation Area, on the oceanfront at Flagler Beach.

Special features: Tomoka State Park and Bulow Creek State Park with the ancient Ormond/Fairchild Oak, Tomoka River Canoe Trail, North Peninsula State Recreation Area, Gamble Rogers Memorial State Recreation Area at Flagler Beach, wildlife watching, birding, hiking, camping, canoeing, beachcombing, fishing, crabbing.

Travel seasons: Best in fall through spring. Open year-round, but biting bugs, temperatures of 95 degrees and higher, and lightning storms in summer make other times preferable in the Tomoka area. Summer is nesting season for loggerhead turtles. Winter brings the chance to glimpse rare right whales in their seasonal calving grounds.

Location: Florida's east coast.

Drive route numbers: North Beach Street/Old Dixie Highway, Walter Boardman Lane, High Bridge Road, A1A/Ocean Shore Boulevard.

Camping: There is woodland camping in Tomoka Basin Geopark and oceanfront camping at Gamble Rogers Memorial State Recreation Area at Flagler Beach. There are private campgrounds along A1A, in the Ormond Beach area and north of Flagler Pier. There are also numerous private campgrounds in the Ormond/Daytona Beach area on the mainland. NOTE: During racing events at Daytona Beach, area campgrounds fill with motorcyclists and racing enthusiasts.

Services: All services are available in Ormond Beach, with limited services in Flagler Beach.

Nearby points of interest: Bulow Plantation Ruins State Historic Site, Bulow Creek Canoe Trail, Florida National Scenic Trail, Washington Oaks State Gardens, Marineland, and Princess Place Preserve in the Flagler area. In the Ormond/Daytona area: the Casements, the Rockefeller winter home; Ormond Memorial Art Museum/Gardens; Ponce de Leon Inlet Lighthouse; Ponce Preserve, Green Mound Archaeological Site; Daytona Museum of Arts and Sciences; Spruce Creek Preserve and Canoe Trail; Mary McLeod Bethune Home and grave; Harvey Lee Art Gallery at Bethune-Cookman College; Jackie Robinson Ballpark; Halifax Historical Museum; Southeast Museum of Photography at Daytona Beach Community College.

Time zone: Eastern.

Drive 17: The Tomoka Region
Ormond Beach to Flagler Beach

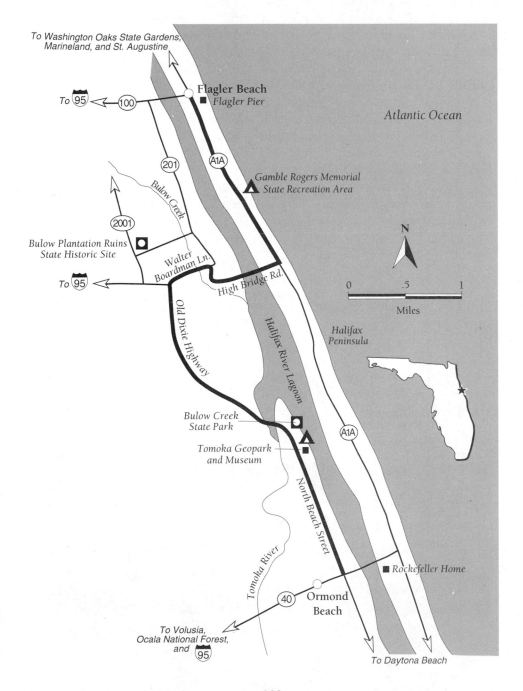

To Washington Oaks State Gardens,
Marineland, and St. Augustine

To 95

100

Flagler Beach
■ *Flagler Pier*

Atlantic Ocean

201

A1A

*Gamble Rogers Memorial
State Recreation Area*

2001

N

Bulow Creek

*Bulow Plantation Ruins
State Historic Site*

*Walter
Boardman Ln.*

To 95

High Bridge Rd.

0   .5   1

Miles

Old Dixie Highway

Halifax River Lagoon

*Halifax
Peninsula*

*Bulow Creek
State Park*

A1A

*Tomoka Geopark
and Museum*

North Beach Street

■ *Rockefeller Home*

Tomoka River

40

*Ormond
Beach*

To Volusia,
Ocala National Forest,
and 95

To Daytona Beach

109

 # The drive

This 22-mile hidden drive just north of Daytona Beach winds on a two-lane road through dark, still cypress swamps. A marsh causeway leading away from the Tomoka Basin Geopark emerges at an undeveloped stretch of coastline. The drive skims the tops of sand dunes along the Atlantic Ocean to end up in the picturesque village of Flagler Beach.

WARNING: Use caution in the low-lying areas of this drive after heavy rains. The coastal section can flood after summer and fall storms. Large recreational vehicles should be aware that Walter Boardman Lane and High Bridge Road, north of Tomoka Geopark, are narrow and without shoulders. Low tree branches limit vehicle height to 8 feet, 6 inches (vehicle height warning signs are posted). Expect also to share the road with a parade of bicycles, as this drive is a popular bike route.

Begin this drive in the downtown district of Ormond Beach, on North Beach Street at its intersection with Granada Bridge. The high bridge is a landmark, taking traffic over the dark Halifax River to the beach. NOTE: The names Ormond Beach and Daytona Beach apply to both the mainland and beach sections of each town.

Tomoka's wide vistas include the panoramic confluence of the Tomoka River and Halifax River Lagoon.

The Halifax River, on the east side of the drive, isn't a true river but a tidal lagoon. Although people fish here, the once-clear waters are now polluted, so it's wise to release your catch. A lovely park under the bridge at the drive's start features boat launching, gazebos, picnic tables, and a small flower garden. Just across the bridge on the Halifax Peninsula sits the Casements, John D. Rockefeller's winter home, which is open to the public.

Travel north on North Beach Street away from the bridge and note, in the first block on the left, the New Britain Historic Residential Area, settled by New Britain, Connecticut, factory workers in 1874. The village became Ormond Beach in 1880, renamed for a British plantation family of the region. In 2.5 miles the road enters an overhead tunnel of live oak tree branches. The trees arch from each side of the road to touch in the middle, forming a leafy green canopy, with gray Spanish moss hanging from their branches. The oak limbs are covered with one of Florida's most stunning plants, the native resurrection fern, so named because it turns from brown to lime green after a rain. Magnolia trees and sturdy cabbage palms, the official state tree, are also found along this route.

The Tomoka Basin Geopark boundary is 3 miles north of Granada Bridge on North Beach, with the main park access a mile farther. At the park's boundary North Beach Street becomes Old Dixie Highway. A visit of at least half a day is recommended. Try the park canoe trail on the Tomoka River. Canoes can be rented in the park. The saltwater marsh is a shallow nursery for shrimp and fish, attracting great blue herons, great egrets, wood storks, and otters, with marsh rabbits feeding along the water's edge. Walk on at least one of the park's hiking trails, including a brief one through a former Timucua village, where a stunning 40-foot-tall painted sculpture by famed artist Fred Dana Marsh offers a fanciful interpretation of the native culture. *Tomoka* is a variation of *Timucua*, the name of the Native American tribe that once inhabited this area. These native families fished and hunted in the tidal salt marshes, cypress swamps, coastal forests, and scrubland, and also farmed. A small but informative park museum interprets the history of the Tomoka region, with aboriginal items dating back as far as the 15th century on display.

Also within park boundaries lie the Addison Blockhouse ruins and Dummett Sugar Mill ruins, from British plantation days. A living history festival the first weekend in February offers reenactments of Native American skills and pioneer pursuits. Check with rangers for best spots to sight wildlife, including the federally listed endangered wood stork. Osprey, brown pelican, and pileated woodpecker are easily spotted. Campers can hear the loud call of tiny screech owls and also the chorus of spring peepers after a rain. Alligators are seen year-round, swimming in tidal creeks and the river, and federally listed endangered manatees return here every winter. White-tailed deer are abundant.

Tomoka's remote palm-fringed creeks once attracted a notable visitor, naturalist John James Audubon.

Leaving the park gate, turn right onto Old Dixie Highway and continue north across a wide marsh before entering another low-lying oak forest, or hammock. In 5 miles turn right onto a small, unpaved road leading to tiny Bulow Creek State Park. Stop at the grassy parking area and walk under the ancient Ormond/Fairchild Oak, with its expansive canopy of branches. At least 300 years ago, this huge tree was a gathering place for Indians, and it shaded settlers and slaves of the Damietta Plantation, one of several 1700s and 1800s plantations in the area. It is probably a unique specimen in today's Florida; most of the state's elder live oaks were cut down long ago for shipbuilding, the wood being more buoyant and durable than other hardwoods.

After returning to Old Dixie Highway, turn right and travel 1 mile. At this point, you can take a side trip to Bulow Plantation Ruins State Historic Site, described at the end of this chapter. To continue the main drive, turn east here onto Walter Boardman Lane, to reach the ocean and Flagler Beach. After 1 mile, take a sharp left (east) on High Bridge Road through a marsh for the most narrow and winding portion of the drive, including two hairpin curves. Occasional pullovers next to the marsh not only allow faster travelers to pass, but also offer the opportunity to see stilt-legged birds and small alligators.

After 1.5 miles, cross High Bridge over the Intracoastal Waterway, to enter a fragile barrier island known as the Halifax Peninsula. After a brief climb over dunes, the route reveals a stunning view of the Atlantic Ocean at its intersection with A1A, called Ocean Shore Boulevard. Turn left on Ocean Shore to ride atop striking, white dunes in the undeveloped North Peninsula State Recreation Area.

WARNING: Deep, soft sand at the road's edge makes pullovers along Ocean Shore dangerous in all but the designated areas.

In the ocean dunes on either side of the road look for spikes of sea oats, prickly pear cactus, and red-and-yellow wildflowers called gaillardia. Look in late summer for loggerhead turtle eggs hatching from nests on the beach. From about December to March, the endangered right whale gives birth offshore here before migrating back to Nova Scotia waters. Brown pelicans are frequently seen, flying at eye level because of the road's position on top of the dunes high above the sloping beach. Out in the ocean, wooden boats with winglike structures on either side are working shrimp boats.

After about 2 miles the drive enters Gamble Rogers Memorial State Recreation Area at Flagler Beach, which stretches from lagoon to ocean. This park is famous for oceanfront campsites, and for pompano, whiting, drum, and bluefish caught by casting into the surf. On its Intracoastal Waterway side the park has a popular boat launch, with a half-mile-long hiking trail into the coastal scrub.

WARNING: In Atlantic surf be alert for occasional opposing tides called rip tides, and for surges of water called runouts, which can sweep even strong swimmers into deep water in seconds.

Beyond here, continue north 3 miles to Flagler Beach, the end of this drive. Enjoy the town's 600-foot ocean pier and the ambience of an unhurried coastal community, with many buildings built on stilts so floodwaters can flow through. The Flagler North side trip departs from this point (see below).

Bulow Plantation Ruins State Historic Site side trip

To reach this site, take a left (west) on Old Dixie Highway at its intersection with Walter Boardman Lane. In a quarter of a mile, turn right on Old Kings Highway and continue about 3 miles until you see the sign for Bulow Plantation. This historic site is sought out by bird watchers, historians, and naturalists. You can walk among plantation ruins made of tabby, a sturdy concrete made of shell. The live oak woods used to harbor native black bear, now gone from this area of Florida. Bulow Creek has a quiet 13-mile canoe trail through salt marshes. A short section of the Florida National Scenic Trail, which will eventually connect to the Appalachian Trail, winds through this preserve in hardwood hammocks of magnolia and live oak.

A couple enjoys the surf at Flagler Beach.

Plantations like this once thrived by shipping timber, indigo dye, sugar, rice, and cotton. Naturalist John James Audubon stayed here in 1831 using the plantation as a base for his hunting trips.

Flagler North side trip

If you continue north on A1A from the end of this drive, two roadside sites await. Washington Oaks State Gardens is about 6 miles north. The green expanse features an unusual coquina "rock" outcropping and stretches from the Matanzas River to the Atlantic Ocean. About 2 miles north of the state gardens, on either side of A1A, is the original Florida Marineland tourist attraction, an architecturally appealing complex on the oceanfront, listed on the National Register of Historic Places.

18

Sea Turtle Shelter at Turtle Mound
New Smyrna Beach to
Canaveral National Seashore

General description: This 14-mile drive bisects a narrow finger of land, bordered on one side by the Atlantic Ocean, and on the other side by the sheltered Mosquito Lagoon marsh and islands. The drive dead-ends at an undeveloped barrier beach historic site, once a federal House of Refuge for shipwreck victims. This drive features abundant marine animals and birds, a walk to a ghost town, and a boardwalk climb up a 50-foot mound left by a Paleo-Indian culture, considered the largest remaining Native American mound in the nation, and among the most ancient.

Special features: Bethune Beach, Canaveral National Seashore, Turtle Mound, Eldora ghost town, Castle Windy Trail, canoe trail, year-round informative ranger talks and guided walks, surf and lagoon fishing, birding, canoeing, kayaking, crabbing (seasonal), beachcombing.

Location: Florida's central east coast.

Drive route numbers: State Road 44 and County Road A1A.

Travel season: October through April, to observe migrating and wintering birds and to avoid summer temperatures of 95 degrees or more, intense lightning storms, and clouds of biting bugs. This is also the best time to surf fish for whiting and bluefish. The beach often fills to capacity on summer weekends. Summer nights offer the opportunity to see loggerhead turtles dig their nests and lay eggs. The drive is open year-round.

Nearby points of interest: Smyrna Dunes Park; Old Fort Mound; New Smyrna Sugar Mill Ruins State Historic Site; Ponce Inlet Lighthouse and fishing village; Green Mound Archaeological Site; Ponce Inlet; Spruce Creek Preserve, Port Orange; Historic DeLand; Lake Woodruff National Wildlife Refuge; Blue Spring State Park, DeLeon Springs State Recreation Area; Daytona Beach Museum of Arts and Science; Mary McLeod Bethune Home at Bethune-Cookman College; Halifax Historical Museum, Daytona Beach.

Camping: Only primitive backcountry camping is allowed at Canaveral National Seashore. Private camping is available in New Smyrna Beach, the Daytona Beach area, and Ormond Beach. A new regional public campground is just north of New Smyrna Beach on US 1 at Rose Bay. Tomoka State Park, north of this drive in Ormond Beach, offers public camping. Blue Spring State Park, along the DeLand side trip, has public camping. At Titusville (south of this drive) a regional public park, Manatee Hammock (on US 1 and the Indian River Lagoon), offers camping, as do many private campgrounds.

Services: All services are available in New Smyrna Beach. There are no food services or concessions at the national seashore. There is fresh water at the visitor center but none at the beach parking areas. Portable toilets, but no showers, are available at beach parking areas.

Time zone: Eastern.

 # The drive

This drive starts in New Smyrna Beach, on the mainland south of Daytona Beach. It crosses the marshy Mosquito Lagoon onto a barrier island that features a national seashore noted for marine, avian, and archaeological features. The drive features an enjoyable portion of undeveloped Florida coastline, and has two recommended side trips.

Begin this drive in downtown New Smyrna Beach, at the intersection of US 1 and SR 44. Turn east on SR 44, traveling over its arched bridge across the northernmost reaches of the Mosquito Lagoon–Indian River Lagoon waterway, descending onto a famous barrier island that includes, farther south, Cape Canaveral.

Native American tribes, with roots going back as far as 6,000 years, still thrived at New Smyrna Beach when the first Europeans arrived in the 1500s. Within the boundaries of Canaveral National Seashore, about 100 Native American sites have been saved, including one on this drive, considered to be the largest remaining Native American mound in the United States.

After about 1 mile on SR 44 the drive curves to the right, where SR 44 becomes CR A1A. Drive south on CR A1A through an area of beach condominiums, shopping complexes, and homes on stilts, some built high enough above ground for storm-driven floodwaters to flow underneath. The Atlantic Ocean is on the left beyond a narrow beach.

In about 6 miles a sign on the right notes Bethune-Volusia Beach. The famous educator Mary McLeod Bethune, who founded a school (now called Bethune-Cookman College) in 1904 in nearby Daytona Beach, once owned land here with other African-American investors. They created a seaside resort area with picnic grounds, bathhouse, and snack bar. This site is on Florida's Black Heritage Trail. The drive continues past resort cottages and local businesses. About 7 miles after SR 44 joins CR A1A, J.B.'s Fishing Camp, on the right, has a boat launch and restaurant featuring fresh seafood and also, alligator. About half a mile farther is the entrance to Canaveral National Seashore, at the end of Pompano Avenue off CR A1A, on the Mosquito Lagoon.

Drive 18: Sea Turtle Shelter at Turtle Mound

New Smyrna Beach to Canaveral National Seashore

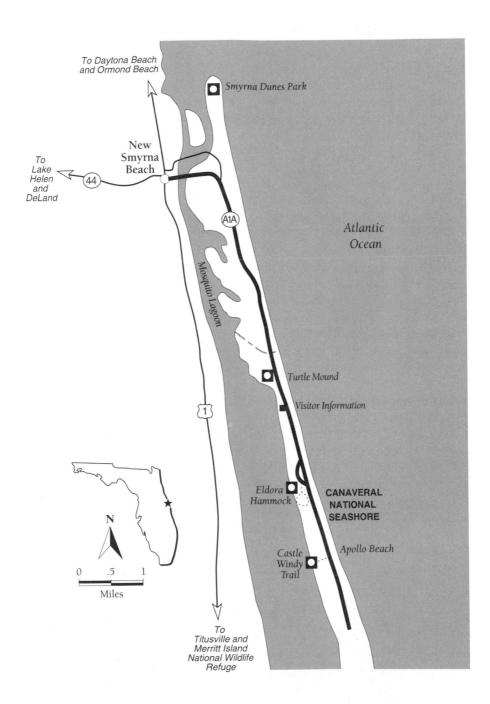

To Daytona Beach
and Ormond Beach

Smyrna Dunes Park

New
Smyrna
Beach

To
Lake
Helen
and
DeLand

44

A1A

Atlantic
Ocean

Mosquito Lagoon

Turtle Mound

Visitor Information

1

Eldora
Hammock

CANAVERAL
NATIONAL
SEASHORE

Castle
Windy
Trail

Apollo Beach

N

0   .5   1

Miles

To
Titusville and
Merritt Island
National Wildlife
Refuge

Canaveral National Seashore preserves the longest stretch of undeveloped coastline (24 miles) on Florida's eastern seaboard. This drive follows a panoramic 6-mile route to historic sites in the northern part of the seashore. There is beach access via boardwalks on top of 20-foot dunes, lagoon access, and opportunity to view abundant wildlife. The ocean is close by on the left, with the lagoon on the right, so at times when the road is on top of high dunes, you can view both shores at the same time. This drive deadends at the point where vehicles are not allowed to continue any farther along the seashore. As you travel, look for gopher tortoises along the roadside, clouds of migrating butterflies, foraging armadillos, pods of porpoises, brown pelicans, ospreys, shorebirds, and alligators sunning in the lagoon. Spring and summer visitors can spot manatees surfacing for air in the lagoon, and summer visitors may see a flock of feeding roseate spoonbills. In summer, there are nighttime, ranger-led beach walks (by reservation only) to see federally listed endangered loggerhead turtles nesting. The rarest marine sighting occurs in late winter to spring—the federally listed endangered right whale, which calves offshore here before returning to Canadian waters for summer.

Immediately on the right inside the seashore boundary, there is a boat launch on Mosquito Lagoon. The lagoon is a nursery for crabs, shrimp, mullet, redfish, oysters, scallops, and a host of other marine creatures; it has provided food for Florida residents from the time of the first natives to the present. A quarter of a mile inside the seashore gate, look on the right for parking and a sign for Turtle Mound. Here a quarter-mile-long shell path and boardwalk, with small interpretive signs along the way, climb Turtle Mound, said to be the largest surviving Native American mound in the nation. It was so high in its original form that it served as a prime navigational aide, sought out by explorers in wooden sailing ships. The mound is a feature on the earliest maps of the peninsula and can be seen from 7 miles out at sea. It covers 2 acres and is about 50 feet high today.

This important mound, called a kitchen midden, grew bit by bit as natives discarded refuse here year after year, beginning as early as 2000 B.C. Kitchen middens like this contain primarily shells of oysters, clams, and coquinas that the natives tossed after meals. The mounds also collected bits of pottery, and deer and alligator bones. In 1924, Turtle Mound was bought for preservation by the Florida Historical Society, and is now listed on the National Register of Historic Places.

From Turtle Mound, continue south on the park road about half a mile to the small visitor center on the right. Here occasional slide talks are given by park rangers, followed by a conducted tour of the mound. Pick up a map of the national seashore and a brochure about Castle Windy Trail, check the monthly schedule of ranger-led events, watch a national seashore orientation video, and get information on the self-guided, 2-mile canoe trail near

Canaveral National Seashore preserves 24 miles of shoreline for the hatching of loggerhead turtles.

Turtle Mound. The picnic area along Mosquito Lagoon, near the visitor center, is a good location to watch wildlife. The visitor center is the only source of fresh water in this part of the national seashore, and there are no food facilities.

Return to the two-lane park road and turn right (south), to notice the thick blanket of protective plants and trees, such as sea oats, prickly pear cactus, sea grape trees, scrub live oak, and palmettoes. These plants help to anchor the extremely fragile and constantly shifting sand dunes. After severe storms, parts of them can drift over the park road.

A mile past the visitor center on the right, look for a one-way park road. This 1-mile loop leads to several sites along Mosquito Lagoon, including the ghost town of Eldora. You can park at several paved parking areas on this loop for views, fishing, and crabbing. Two short walking trails along this loop are recommended. One is the quarter-mile-long path to the site of Eldora, a former 19th-century village on Mosquito Lagoon. Pioneers heading south stopped at this busy waterfront community for supplies, and local residents shipped out lumber, pecans, Spanish moss for furniture stuffing, hearts of palm, figs, guava, salt, and sea turtle meat. The industrious residents also kept bees, tended citrus groves, and collected palmetto berries for the Salmetto tonic, sold in northern states and overseas. The arrival of the mainland railroad diminished Eldora's commerce, and today a lone crumbling building identifies the site of the ghost town. Another quarter-mile farther along the loop, the Eldora Hammock trail departs for its half-mile trek into the coastal forest.

The loop road rejoins the main park road half a mile beyond, near a popular beach access called Parking Area 2. You can visit the beach and dunes here or head south along the main park road to the next beach access, Parking Area 3. Any of four labeled beach parking areas provides access to a beach that is recommended more for beachcombing, birding, or surf casting than for swimming. The steep slope, strong, dangerous currents, and occasional stinging jellyfish can make swimming hazardous. There are no lifeguards. In cool weather, the beach is an alluring hiking area, especially for long-distance trekkers seeking to reach the south unit of the national seashore some 20 miles away. (Register for backcountry camping at the visitor center, and tote adequate supplies including fresh water.) Even a short walk along the beach can reveal piles of empty shell skeletons, which are allowed to be taken.

Parking Area 3 is the trailhead of the Castle Windy Trail, a popular walk to the Mosquito Lagoon. Castle Windy Trail is a 1-mile round-trip path, with 14 numbered points of interest along the way explained in the free trail brochure. Upon reaching the lagoon shore, you can see another Native American shell mound reaching about 17 feet above ground level.

Returning to the main park drive, turn right (south) and continue to the turnaround point, an uninhabited place of grassy dunes offering a sweeping vista of ocean, dunes, and lagoon. Looking south, you can see NASA's Vehicle Assembly Building on the horizon, some 20 miles in the distance on Cape Canaveral. Here in the dunes in 1884 a different sort of building, a federal House of Refuge, rose up, one of ten such lifesaving stations constructed on Florida's east coast by the U.S. government to aid shipwreck victims. These wooden houses were maintained by keepers, similar to lighthouse keepers, who often had a family on site. When wrecks were spotted offshore, the keeper took to the sea in hopes of bringing back survivors. The houses also operated as way stations for stranded travelers who had drifted ashore and then walked along the beaches until they came to a refuge. The old wooden houses, including the one that stood here, succumbed to the tides and storms, except for one still standing and restored, featured on Drive 22. From this turnaround, trace your path back to New Smyrna Beach. At this point, you may want to visit Riverfront Park in New Smyrna Beach or depart from there to DeLand (see details below).

New Smyrna side trip

At the town of New Smyrna Beach, Riverfront Park on the waterfront is a well-maintained park tucked under the SR 44 bridge over the Mosquito Lagoon. The park has a boardwalk, playground, and garden pond. You can walk from the park north a few blocks along Riverside Drive to the nearby Turnbull Ruins, at North Riverside and Julia Street. This was the site of a Native American village discovered by the first Spanish explorers. The area was also the southern terminus of the continent's first road, the King's Highway from St. Augustine, built for Spanish colonists in the 1500s. In 1767 a colony of 2,400 Greeks, Italians, and Minorcans was begun here. After nine years of indentured servitude, 77 survivors fled to northern Florida. The New Smyrna Sugar Mill Ruins State Historic Site, interpreting more area history, is located at West Canal Street and Old Mission Road.

DeLand area side trip

About 28 miles west of New Smyrna Beach on SR 44 is the 1870s village of DeLand. In the DeLand area, visitors can enjoy the attractive downtown district; 19,000-acre Lake Woodruff National Wildlife Refuge, with its large numbers of nesting bald eagles; DeLeon Springs State Recreation Area; and Blue Spring State Park, a noted winter home of the federally listed endangered manatee. This park reaches visitor capacity on many winter weekends when manatees are present; try arriving before noon, or visit on a weekday.

19

Birdland on the Atlantic Coast

*Titusville to Merritt Island National Wildlife Refuge
and Canaveral National Seashore*

General description: This drive midway down Florida's east coast is a 15-mile route through the saltwater lagoon marsh of a federal refuge that shelters thousands of birds in winter. The drive visits towering 30-foot dunes and the Atlantic Ocean beach of Canaveral National Seashore, an undeveloped coastal area that was once the home of the Ais Indians. The two preserves adjoin Kennedy Space Center at its northern boundary.

Special features: Merritt Island National Wildlife Refuge, Black Point Wildlife Drive, Canaveral National Seashore, surf fishing, freshwater fishing, crabbing, beachcombing, birding, wildlife photographing, canoeing, inland and beach hiking, primitive camping.

Location: Florida's central east coast.

Drive route numbers: State Road 406, State Road 402, Black Point Wildlife Drive, State Road 3.

Travel season: October through March for best birding. Summer isn't recommended except for visitors seeking to glimpse federally listed endangered loggerhead turtles nesting at night, roseate spoonbills, or the federally listed endangered manatee. Summer brings temperatures of 95 and higher, humidity, and sudden lightning storms. In November and December duck hunting is allowed in the refuge.

Camping: Primitive camping only is allowed in Canaveral National Seashore, with registration required. An excellent new regional park, Manatee Hammock, offers public campsites in Titusville, and the public Jetty Park in Cape Canaveral also offers public campsites. Private campgrounds are in Titusville, Cape Canaveral, Cocoa, Cocoa Beach, Merritt Island, and the Melbourne area. Sebastian Inlet State Recreation Area, on US A1A at Melbourne Beach, also has campsites.

Nearby points of interest: NASA and Kennedy Space Center; Astronaut Memorial Planetarium and Observatory at Brevard Community College; U.S. Space Camp Florida; Brevard Museum of History and Natural Science and the Windover Story Exhibit; commercial dolphin-watch cruises; U.S. Astronaut Hall of Fame; North Brevard Historical Museum, Titusville; Enchanted Forest Nature Sanctuary; Brevard Zoo; Historic Cocoa Village; Melbourne downtown historic area and Crane Creek manatee-observation boardwalk; Space Coast Science Center at Melbourne; Melbourne

Beach Historic Pier; Audubon Turkey Creek Nature Sanctuary; Sebastian Inlet State Recreation Area; Green Mound Archaeological Site; Ponce Inlet Lighthouse and fishing village.
Time zone: Eastern.

 # The drive

This 15-mile drive is on narrow, paved and unpaved park roads through side-by-side preserves—a federal refuge famed for birding, and a national seashore famed as a nesting ground for the federally listed endangered loggerhead turtle.

Along this drive the Merritt Island National Wildlife Refuge shelters a saltwater marsh that attracts wintering waterfowl and feeding birds. During the fall and winter it is one of the best bird watching areas in the southeastern United States. Canaveral National Seashore protects the longest ribbon of undeveloped Atlantic shore in the state. This drive is busy with avid birders from October through March. In spring and summer manatees can be spotted surfacing for air in the inshore lagoon. A total of 1.2 million visitors see the refuge and seashore each year, making it one of Florida's most popular wildlife-viewing destinations.

Begin this drive in Titusville, on the mainland. While you're here, you may want to visit the Brevard Museum of History and Natural Science (see side trip description below). Titusville also provides a convenient location from which to depart to NASA's Kennedy Space Center.

From the junction of US 1 and SR 406, head east on SR 406 across a 1.3-mile bridge and causeway over the Indian River Lagoon. The lagoon is an estuary, a shallow wetland where freshwater meets saltwater, and it serves as a vital nursery for marine life. The brackish water here is moved more by wind than by daily tides, and thus also provides prime breeding ground for mosquitos. The waterway was in fact once called Mosquito River; the name was banished from this waterway and several area landmarks from the mid-1800s through the early 1900s to encourage settlement. However, one lagoon in the national seashore kept this descriptive name.

At the end of the causeway on SR 406, note the sign announcing the Merritt Island National Wildlife Refuge, a 140,000-acre island preserve next to the estuary. The preserve shelters 310 bird species, 14 federally listed endangered or threatened species, and 700 plant species. Travel 1.5 miles on SR 406 into the refuge through marsh and past ponds to a Y intersection with SR 402. Veer right on SR 402 and travel at the edge of tiny Gator Creek, then through pine uplands that also shelter Florida's state tree, the cabbage palm. In 2.5 miles along SR 402, stop at the roadside visitor center for maps,

Drive 19: Birdland on the Atlantic Coast

Titusville to Merritt Island National Wildlife Refuge and
Canaveral National Seashore

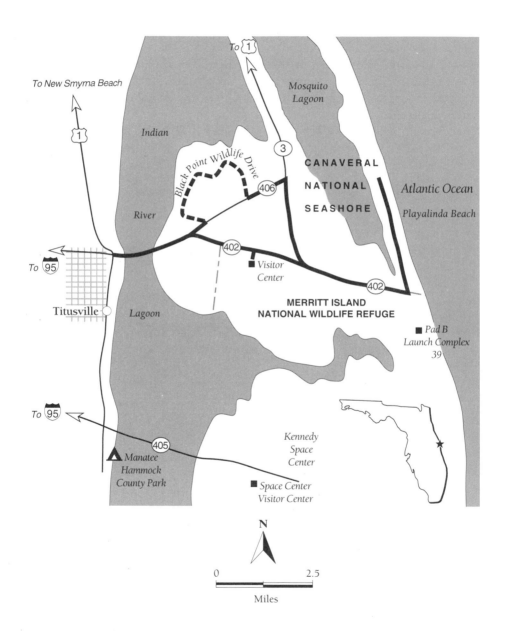

Salt marsh, Merritt Island National Wildlife Refuge (Drive 19).

Top: Kingsley Plantation, Fort George Island (Drive 11).
Bottom: Lake Kissimmee State Park (Drive 21).

Top: Live oaks in a temperate hammock.
Bottom: Alligator, Merritt Island National Wildlife Refuge (Drive 19).

*Top: Beach, Dr. Julian G. Bruce St. George Island State Park (Drive 3).
Bottom: An assortment of shells.*

JAMES VALENTINE

JAMES VALENTINE

Top: Sand dune, Dr. Julian G. Bruce St. George Island State Park (Drive 3).
Bottom: Great blue heron, Everglades National Park (Drives 24, 25, 26).

Pine forest, Blackwater River Region (Drive 1).

Top: Seagrass, Dr. Julian G. St. George Island State Park (Drive 3).
Bottom: Suwannee River State Park (Drive 9).

Blue flag iris and bald cypress.

a schedule of ranger-led programs, and an interpretation of the natural and human history of the refuge. At least seven distinct Indian cultures fished and hunted in these marshes and dunes, including the mound-building Ais Indians who collected sea turtle eggs, caught shrimp and fish, and harvested oysters. You can ask rangers for advice on fishing, hiking trails, canoe trails, and recent sightings of resident bald eagles and of Arctic peregrine falcons, which fly 6,000 miles from the Alaska tundra to Florida each winter. The refuge and seashore also offer a rare chance to spot the occasional right whale, an extremely rare marine mammal that calves offshore during the winter. Porpoises are commonly seen, manatees less often.

The wildlife refuge is a combination of natural lagoon marsh and manmade pond habitat. The significant feature of the refuge's shallow ponds and adjoining uplands is the quantity of migratory and wintering birds that are seen feeding and resting. During the winter season 2,000 raptors, such as American kestrels, are counted, and as many as 100,000 coots swim in the shallow ponds. Alligators are frequently seen swimming in marsh ponds and sunning on muddy banks.

From the visitor center, turn right on SR 402, and in just a quarter of a mile, turn left at a small parking lot accessing two loop trails. (The trails may be under water during the summer rainy season.) Oak Hammock Trail here is a half-mile amble through subtropical forest. The longer hike is Palm

Brown pelican at Canaveral National Seashore.

Hammock Trail, a 2-mile journey that features palms, open marsh, and hardwood trees.

After visiting one or both trails, return to SR 402 and take a right to retrace your path 2.75 miles back to the Y intersection with SR 406, near the refuge entrance. Take a right turn onto SR 406 and travel half a mile. Look on the left for the beginning of Black Point Wildlife Drive, a one-lane unpaved road. This begins a 7-mile causeway drive meandering through one of the South's best birding areas. There are plenty of designated areas to pull off the road and watch flocks feeding on the water. Except in designated areas, refuge staffers recommend visitors stay in the car; the flocks will float away or even fly off at the sound of car doors opening and closing. Some refuge visitors like to walk the Black Point Drive, and a free pamphlet is available from the self-service box at the drive's entrance, interpreting 11 numbered stops along the way.

A short observation tower halfway through the drive is well worth a five-minute walk, for the view and to use the photography blind. If you have time, walk into the marsh along the adjoining 5-mile Cruickshank Trail (named after Allan Cruickshank, the naturalist whose efforts are largely responsible for the conservation of this portion of the Indian River Lagoon region). Some visitors can't get enough of Black Point Drive and at the end, return by taking a right on SR 406, driving about 1.5 miles to re-enter the drive again on the right. To continue route, however, take a left on SR 406, go about 1 mile, and then take a right at the unmarked T intersection with Brevard SR 3.

Travel about 3 miles on SR 3, across an abandoned railroad track, and at the intersection with SR 402 take a left. Rising on the horizon on your right is the Kennedy Space Center's massive Vehicle Assembly Building. Continuing toward the ocean, you will soon cross into the Canaveral National Seashore. The best way to view wildlife here is by using the designated pull-overs next to wetlands.

The national seashore is a combination of natural habitats: rugged, drifting dunes, a steeply sloping beach, and, inland, a labyrinth of mangrove islands (with a stunning canoe trail snaking through) in Mosquito Lagoon. Soon SR 402 brings you right up close to the narrow metal towers that are launch gantries 39 B and A of Kennedy Space Center. This launch site of Apollo 11 is listed on the National Register of Historic Places. You can't legally get any closer to a launch site, except by means of a guided NASA bus tour. This portion of the drive and part of the national seashore are closed to the public during launches and landings. Here, SR 402 ends in sand dunes at Playalinda Beach, an undeveloped area along the Atlantic Ocean. The drive takes a sharp left here, to connect a string of 13 paved parking areas, for close beach access. Each area has boardwalks across the

Canaveral National Seashore is famous for its sea turtles, which visit only once a year.

20-foot dunes, primitive chemical flush toilets without sinks, and no showers. Playalinda Beach is very crowded with families and teenagers in the summer. The northernmost section of the beach is sometimes visited by nudists, so stay at the shore near the parking areas if you want to avoid them. WARNING: Bring all food and water supplies, sunscreen, and insect repellent, as there are no concessions in these two preserves. Afternoon summer thundershowers are predictable, and lightning can be severe. In the winter expect strong, chilly ocean breezes at times.

As in the northern part of the national seashore, this is an undisturbed nighttime beach for sea turtles, including the federally listed endangered loggerhead turtle. About 14,700 loggerhead nests are laid each season within the seashore boundary, though only about one of every 10,000 hatchlings survives to reproduce. Turtle watchers fence off nests that are close to public activities, and help hatchlings into the sea in late summer and early fall. Look for the fences if you arrive at this time. The federally listed endangered green turtle, the rarest of the sea turtles, also nests along this shore, with about 1,100 nests a year.

Depending upon what the waves toss up, this beach can be a beachcomber's delight, with plenty of empty skeletons, including oyster, large pen shell, tiny coquina clam, lightning whelk, calico scallop, great heart cockle, jingle, moon snail, incongruous ark, and southern quahog

127

clam. Swimming can be risky, with rip tides, runouts, and other strong currents, and an occasional stinging jellyfish or Portuguese man-of-war. Look along the shore for brown pelicans diving into schools of fish and for plovers, sandpipers, seagulls, and other shorebirds.

NASA side trip

NASA's Kennedy Space Center's Spaceport USA, via US 1 and SR 405, offers a look at our early space program. Sit in a lunar rover; look inside a shuttle command module; pose next to a living history guide, clad in astronaut suit with functioning airpack, walking around the complex; touch a rocket; remember watching live broadcasts from the cape in the 1960s. Ride the Spaceport USA bus around the complex, and enjoy the sites of our race to space.

Windover People side trip

The Windover Story, at the Brevard Museum of History and Natural Science at Titusville, takes visitors back in time, to at least 8,000 years ago. Windover presents archaeological finds recovered from the Windover Pond near Titusville. These early residents collected freshwater mussels, killed deer, gathered prickly pears and wild blackberries, made fabric and jewelry, and traded with others across the Florida peninsula. The fabric these people made is perhaps the oldest ever recovered intact in the Western Hemisphere. The archaeological discoveries made at Windover Pond are ranked among the greatest finds in the world.

20

Myakka River and Marsh
Sarasota to Myakka River State Park

General description: This 18-mile drive in southwestern Florida takes you into a river marsh system, to oak and palm forests, vast prairie, and two rural lakes within one of Florida's largest state parks, with opportunity to explore a true wilderness on foot and the chance to see abundant birds, alligators, and other wildlife.

Special features: Almost guaranteed viewing of alligator, waterfowl, wading birds, cottontail rabbit, turkey, and deer in Myakka River State Park and Wilderness Preserve; Wild and Scenic Myakka River; visitor center; tram ride; fishing; canoeing; hiking; birding; bicycling; nature trails and boardwalk; Crowley Museum and Nature Center.

Location: Southwest Florida.

Drive route numbers: State Road 72, Park Drive.

Travel season: October through April is the recommended season for birding and to avoid summer temperatures of 95 and higher, humidity, biting bugs, and thunderstorms that leave most nature trails under water. However, the winter dry season is less ideal for canoeing, due to low water. This park attracts crowds on weekends during winter.

Camping: Myakka River State Park has two camping areas, primitive wilderness camping, and five log cabins. Oscar Scherer State Park, in Osprey, south of Sarasota, has two camping areas, and Lake Manatee State Recreation Area, north of Sarasota near Bradenton, has one campground. There are also private campgrounds in the Sarasota area.

Services: All services are available in Sarasota.

Nearby points of interest: Ringling Museum complex, Mote Marine Laboratory, Pelican Man Bird Sanctuary, Marie Selby Botanical Garden, gulf shore beaches on Siesta Key, all in Sarasota; regional fishing guides; Oscar Scherer State Park and Historic Spanish Point, Osprey; Warm Mineral Springs; Lake Manatee State Recreation Area; South Florida Museum and Bishop Planetarium, Bradenton.

Time zone: Eastern.

 # The drive

This drive in southwest Florida takes you into the rural Myakka River basin and cattle country east of Sarasota for a panorama of wide marshes and dense palm forests. The drive, with frequent nature walks and other wildlife viewing opportunities, offers a glimpse into Florida's interior, territory that is fast converting from cattle country to residential development. The drive is primarily within the Myakka River State Park, one of Florida's largest state parks.

Begin this inland drive at the SR 72 interchange, on I-75 at Sarasota. (To explore Sarasota itself, see the side trip at the end of this drive.) Turn east onto SR 72 and in about 1 mile you will pass the Twin Lakes Park complex on the right, with picnic areas scattered among ponds. Continue east 4.5 miles through scattered rural development. You will begin to notice, on each side of the road, turtles and alligators sunning themselves along the banks of water-filled roadside ditches. In another 1.5 miles, SR 72 passes the western boundary of Myakka River State Park. The actual park entrance is 2.3 miles farther, on the left.

Turn left from SR 72 into the park. It is best to plan on spending at least one night here, so that you can enjoy campfire programs in the evening, and rise early to wander the park. (Reservations are advised.) Visitors can instead stay overnight in the Sarasota area and arrive at the park early in the morning, before traffic picks up. Upon entering the park, stop at the office and pick up a weekend schedule of ranger-led programs, such as nature walks, campfire programs, and a beginning birding class. The office also has a bird list; a trails brochure; a wildflower, plant, and tree list; information about recent wildlife sightings; and brochures for the nearby private nature center and wildlife guide services. There are bicycles for rent from the lakeside concession, and canoes for paddling along the 12 miles of river that are within park boundaries. The many nature trails, some of them with interpretive signs along the way, offer a chance to enjoy the lush terrain yet remain close to civilization. There is also a tram ride that offers a rolling orientation to the park.

For backcountry enthusiasts, a 7,500-acre wilderness within the 28,875-acre park boundaries defines the Myakka experience. This hikers' paradise offers the opportunity to live as traveling pioneers did in Florida more than 100 years ago. Wilderness walkers, who must register at the park office, have reported bobcat sightings in the backcountry.

About 700 yards past the park office, turn left into the parking area for the interpretive center. This small museum, housed in a 1936 horse barn, offers a video introduction to the natural features of the region; small exhibits on reptiles, mammals, and birds; and information on human activity in the

Drive 20: Myakka River and Marsh
Sarasota to Myakka River State Park

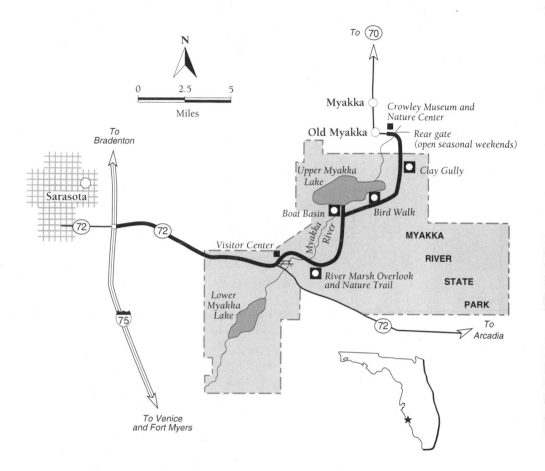

region, dating back at least 10,000 years. Another 1.5 miles on Park Drive brings you to parking for a wayside picnic shelter made of palm tree logs, a building material commonly used by Florida's Native Americans and pioneers, but rarely seen today. (The park's five cabins are also made of palm logs.)

In half a mile, Park Drive crosses the Myakka River, a designated Wild and Scenic River. Park on the right to enjoy this panorama of wide skies and river marsh. Look for basking alligators near the banks, an occasional otter surfacing in the river, feeding herons, and other birds. From the parking

White ibis flutter in the Myakka River basin.

area you can walk the 40-minute William S. Boylston Nature Trail, with opportunity to see deer and turkey.

About 2 miles beyond the bridge is a Y intersection. The left fork takes you about half a mile to a dead end on Upper Myakka Lake and its boat access, canoe rental area, camp store, restrooms, and boat basin (a small marina). Swimming isn't allowed in the lake. Exotic aquatic plants choking the lake make fishing unpredictable. Opposite the camp store on a muddy bank of the boat basin, alligators are commonly seen on sunny days.

From here, return to the Y intersection and take a left to continue on the main park road. In about 1.5 miles, turn into the entrance on the left for the parking area to a boardwalk at Upper Myakka Lake. This boardwalk is the park's famed Bird Walk, so called because of the abundance of waterfowl and other birds from October through April. Look here for coots, white ibis, great and little blue herons, tricolored herons, great and snowy egrets, and limpkins.

Returning to Park Drive, go another 2.5 miles to a parking area on the right for the Clay Gully Trail, a lush picnic area and path to a creek that feeds the Myakka River. When you leave this parking area, a right turn takes you a quarter of a mile to the park's rear entrance, closed except for weekends in winter. If this exit is open, you can leave here to tour the private

This cabin of palm logs at Myakka River State Park reflects the architecture of early pioneers and Native Americans.

Crowley Museum and Nature Center. To visit the center, turn left out of the park onto Myakka Road. Follow this road across Myakka River, past grazing cattle, about 1 mile to the nature center on the right. If you aren't visiting the nature center, take a left from the Clay Gully picnic area back onto the park road, to return to the main park entrance.

To end this drive, turn right from the main park entrance onto SR 72, tracing your path back about 8 miles to I-75 in Sarasota.

Sarasota side trip

Sarasota is a cultural resort, with condominium towers on residential Gulf of Mexico islands, primarily Siesta Key and Longboat Key. The community is known worldwide for its state cultural landmark, the Ringling Museum complex. Sarasota also has an acclaimed aquarium and marine research center, Mote Marine Laboratory. Blankets of orchids and other tropical blooms thrive in the lush Marie Selby Botanical Garden. A fine local museum and archive is housed in the former Sarasota Library on the Tamiami Trail (US 41), near the Van Wezel Performing Arts Hall on the bay.

21

Kissimmee Prairie and Cow Hunters' Camp

Lake Wales to Lake Kissimmee State Park

General description: A 33-mile round-trip through tended pasture, wet prairie, and dry savannah. The region is a former Seminole and Miccosukee Indian stronghold, and the park contains the site of a former U.S. military outpost during the Second Seminole War. The drive ends at 5,030-acre Lake Kissimmee State Park, nearly surrounded by three lakes and famous for its resident bald eagles. It is the only major park to celebrate Florida's cow hunter history and continuing cattle industry.

Special features: Lake Kissimmee State Park, Florida National Scenic Trail, observation tower overlooking Kissimmee Prairie, birding, fishing, boating.

Location: Central Florida.

Drive route numbers: County Road 17A, Old Mammoth Grove Road, Camp Mack Road, Kissimmee Park Road.

Travel season: Open year-round, but in summer expect biting insects and temperatures of 95 degrees and higher.

Camping: Lake Kissimmee State Park has a campground, a youth camping area, and primitive campsites. There are private campgrounds and traditional fish camps along the drive route and also near Lake Wales.

Services: All services, including the old-world–style Chalet Suzanne Inn, a noted restaurant and lodge, are at Lake Wales.

Nearby points of interest: Bok Tower Gardens on Iron Mountain; Pine Ridge Nature Preserve Trail at Lake Wales; Audubon Nature Center, Museum of Fishing, in Winter Haven; Cypress Gardens, about 22 miles northwest of the drive via US 27; horseback riding at area cattle and dude ranches.

Time zone: Eastern.

 The drive

This is a rural route through pine flatlands and wet and dry prairie that shelters abundant wildlife, including federally listed threatened bald eagles.

Drive 21: Kissimmee Prairie and Cow Hunters' Camp

Lake Wales to Lake Kissimmee State Park

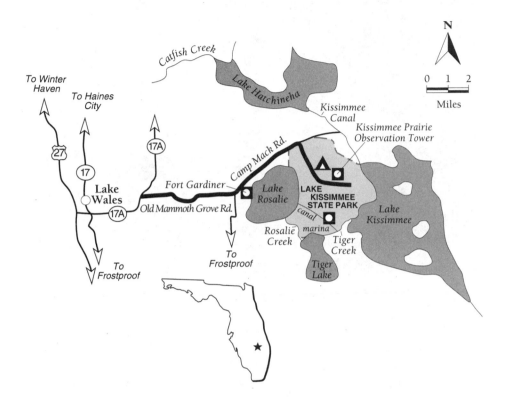

The drive starts about 1 mile northeast of Lake Wales at the intersection of CR 17A and Old Mammoth Grove Road. Turn east onto Old Mammoth Grove Road, where occasional small groves and homes give way to large cattle fields with small ponds, spreading live oak trees, and large clusters of prickly pear cactus. The cactus, native to Florida, is prime food for the endangered Florida gopher tortoise. After about 8.6 miles on Old Mammoth Grove Road, take the angled left turn onto Camp Mack Road.

Soon after this turn, there is a green sign commemorating Fort Gardiner, a U.S. military outpost believed to have been on the shores of Lake Kissimmee during the Second Seminole War in the 1830s. Some of the descendants of these Seminole warriors tend a busy tribal cattle ranch in southern Florida. Continue along Camp Mack Road, watching for sandhill cranes in wet prairie

Florida's cow hunters are remembered at Lake Kissimmee State Park.

and bald eagles soaring in the sky, and in about 8 more miles you will arrive at the park entrance on your right.

This park preserves an area of Florida that is rich in history. Pioneers from the North, arriving by covered wagon and ox cart in the 19th century, lived a life of hardship on this Florida prairie frontier, similar to the rugged experience of settlers in the Old West. As did pioneers in the West, many of Florida's pioneers raised cattle. Florida in fact became home to America's first cattle in 1521, when a few heifers were brought over from Cuba by Juan Ponce de León on his second visit to the peninsula. By 1774, when naturalist William Bartram visited this area, Florida's native tribes were tending large, free-roaming herds.

One hundred thirty years ago, after the last of the Seminole Wars, this area became the third and final homeland of Alabama-born Chipco, a respected and wealthy leader of a group of people known as the Catfish Lake Seminoles. This was Chipco's hunting territory, where his hunters brought in as many as 10 deer and 40 wild turkey in a single day's hunt. His people also farmed and raised horses here. Although he had been a warrior in his younger days, Chipco and his people created friendly relations with settlers after the wars, including some of the early cattle ranchers. His role in peace is honored with a small memorial and park on Lake Hamilton, northwest of here.

Later, when the Indians lost rule over their Florida prairies and pioneers dominated the grazing land, Florida's rugged cattle still roamed over free range, with the Kissimmee Prairie region being prime cattle land. But the cattle also wandered into swampy and inaccessible areas and were prey for wolves and Florida panthers. Cattle rustlers were a threat, as were rattlesnake bites and wild boar attacks. The cow hunters, which is what Florida's version of the cowboy were called, were tormented by mosquitoes and often sank in the marshes as they attempted to herd their cattle. These hardy range riders were visited by the famed artist Frederic Remington, who thought their life was more rugged than that of their contemporaries in the West. He camped with them, painted their portraits, and reported in 1899 that the existence of both cow and cow hunter was miserable. He wrote, ". . . the poor little cattle, no bigger than a donkey, wander half starved and horribly emaciated. . . ." And of the cow hunters he observed, ". . . they steal by wholesale, any cattle hunter will admit. . . ." This colorful heritage is remembered in the park. On weekends and holidays park rangers, dressed

White-tailed deer forage in the woods of Kissimmee Prairie.

as 19th-century Florida cow hunters, inhabit a re-created cattle camp, brewing bitter coffee, cooking hardtack, and spinning tales of Florida frontier life that are worlds apart from the peninsula's image of tropical waters and coconut trees.

Park rangers lead photography walks to help visitors capture the Kissimmee Prairie vistas and wildlife on film. A three-story observation tower provides excellent views of the surrounding landscape. Plan an early morning or late afternoon visit for best wildlife viewing, especially on two park trails. Nesting American bald eagles are year-round residents, easily seen with binoculars from the park's lookout tower and at other locations. Other residents include the distinctive red-capped sandhill cranes, rare kites, burrowing owls, wild turkey, bobwhite, and white-tailed deer. Tracks believed to be those of the nearly extinct Florida panther have been found, though there have not been any verified sightings. Lake Kissimmee, the state's third largest lake, is reached by canoe or motorboat through a lush canal from the small park marina. This park hugging Lake Kissimmee's wild western shore is an unusual path to an overlooked part of Florida's past.

After your visit to the park, trace your route back to the beginning of this drive.

22

Wild River and Wild Ocean
Jupiter to Stuart

General description: This 35-mile inland and coastal drive travels to a national wildlife refuge. It visits a lush state park on the Wild and Scenic Loxahatchee River. And it also takes you to a unique geological feature at the oceanfront, and a historic site associated with an 18th-century shipwreck.

Special features: Hobe Sound National Wildlife Refuge and Hobe Sound Nature Center, Jonathan Dickinson State Park, Loxahatchee River and Canoe Trail, Loxahatchee Queen II river ride to Trapper Nelson Jungle Cabin, Florida National Scenic Trail, Jupiter Island, Jupiter Inlet Lighthouse, Blowing Rocks Preserve, Hutchinson Island, House of Refuge, Elliott Museum, canoeing, biking, birding, hiking, beachcombing.

Location: Southeast coastal Florida.

Drive route numbers: U.S. Highway 1, County Road 707/Alternate A1A, County Road 708/Bridge Road, State Road A1A/MacArthur Boulevard.

Travel season: October through March is best for wildlife viewing and to avoid summer temperatures of 95 and higher, thunderstorms, and biting bugs. Jonathan Dickinson State Park campsites and cabins can fill up on weekends; reservations are recommended.

Camping: Jonathan Dickinson State Park has two campgrounds and simple cabins. Because of their popularity, you may want to secure a campsite before you start the drive at the refuge. There are also private campgrounds in the Jupiter-Stuart area.

Services: All services are available in Jupiter, Stuart, or Hobe Sound.

Nearby points of interest: River Bend County Park; Loxahatchee Historical Society Museum; St. Lucie Inlet State Preserve (boat access only); Marinelife Center of Juno Beach; William T. Kirby Nature Center/John D. MacArthur Beach State Park; Flagler Museum; Norton Gallery; J. W. Corbett Wildlife Management Area/Hungryland Boardwalk and Trail; Florida Oceanographic Society Coastal Science Center; Barley Barber Swamp, Indiantown; Savannas Recreation Area; Environmental Learning Center and Laura Riding Home, Wabasso Island; Fort Pierce Inlet State Recreation Area; Jack Island State Preserve, UDT-SEAL Museum, Harbor Branch Oceanographic Institution and Florida Ranch Tours, all at Fort Pierce; McLarty Treasure Museum and Mel Fisher's Treasure Museum, Sebastian.

Time zone: Eastern.

The drive

This inland and coastal drive begins in a little-known national wildlife refuge in southeastern Florida that has rare sand pine and scrub oak forest along a relatively undeveloped section of US 1. It then travels to an inland river preserve in mangrove wetlands that also spans a rare, dry world called sand scrub habitat. It continues to visit historic sites and parks on two barrier islands, including an 1860 lighthouse, an unusual ocean rock formation, and a restored federal House of Refuge, built in 1875 for shipwreck survivors.

Begin this drive at the mainland entrance of Hobe Sound National Wildlife Refuge on the east side of US 1, about 79 miles south of Fort Pierce and about 4.5 miles north of Jupiter.

This quiet refuge has an ocean tract and this mainland headquarters. Here you can explore a rare sand pine and scrub oak forest in 232 mainland acres. (The refuge's 735 acres of coastal sand dunes and mangrove forest on Jupiter Island are visited later in this drive.) The refuge's abundant wildlife and plant species are the same as those of Jonathan Dickinson State Park, with the addition of an island sand dune habitat that shelters beach-dwelling species and offers productive nesting areas for the federally listed endangered loggerhead turtle. Park in the designated parking for the Elizabeth W. Kirby Interpretive Center (open weekdays), which has a fine small museum and hosts seasonal environmental talks and occasional guided nature hikes. A quarter-mile Sand Pine Scrub Trail begins near the center and is an excellent path from which to observe the federally listed endangered Florida scrub jay. If you are lucky you may find tracks of white-tailed deer and bobcat.

After visiting this excellent small refuge, return to US 1 and turn south, traveling about 1 mile to the Jonathan Dickinson State Park entrance, on the right. The 11,500-acre park was formerly Camp Murphy, a 1944 Army camp that was part of the famed Signal Corps. Today park habitats—from pinewoods and sand pine scrub, to freshwater creeks and cypress and mangrove wetlands—offer a haven to 140 species of birds, including federally listed threatened bald eagles, and sandhill cranes, Florida scrub jays, woodpeckers, tree swallows, warblers, ospreys, great blue herons, little blue herons, great egrets, white ibises, and double-breasted cormorants. The park waters are also home to river otters, alligators, and federally listed endangered manatees. White-tailed deer browse in the uplands, along with gopher tortoises, armadillos, and abundant raccoons.

A unique feature of this park is a guided boat trip to the site of an old 1930s riverfront tourist attraction, Trapper Nelson's Jungle Zoo, now an interpretive site that explains the colorful story of a local eccentric.

Drive 22: Wild River and Wild Ocean
Jupiter to Stuart

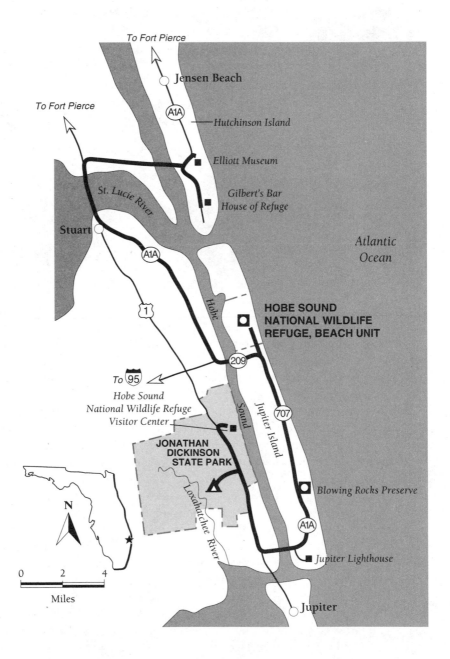

To Fort Pierce

Jensen Beach

To Fort Pierce

A1A

Hutchinson Island

Elliott Museum

Gilbert's Bar
House of Refuge

St. Lucie River

Stuart

A1A

Atlantic
Ocean

1

Hobe

**HOBE SOUND
NATIONAL WILDLIFE
REFUGE, BEACH UNIT**

209

To 95

Hobe Sound
National Wildlife Refuge
Visitor Center

707

Jupiter Island

Sound

**JONATHAN
DICKINSON
STATE PARK**

Loxahatchee River

Blowing Rocks Preserve

N

A1A

Jupiter Lighthouse

0   2   4

Miles

Jupiter

A former House of Refuge for shipwreck survivors on Hutchinson Island.

NOTE: Cabins and campsites in this popular park are booked well in advance.

Near the paved park entrance is a trailhead that accesses a 9.3-mile section of the Florida National Scenic Trail called the East Loop Trail. Along this trail, you can see globally imperiled deer moss, and you might catch a glimpse of the federally listed threatened Florida scrub jay. Past the trailhead, continue on the main park road to a T intersection, just a quarter of a mile beyond the entrance booth. To the left is access to one of two park camp-grounds, a campfire ring, conference center, and bicycle trail. To the right and around the curve, in about a quarter of a mile, is a right turn into a parking area for access to a 20-minute walk at Hobe Mountain. There aren't any mountains in Florida but this path leads to a high sandy promontory and 22-foot-tall observation tower. From here, visitors can see Hobe Sound, an important marine nursery; Jupiter Inlet with its red brick lighthouse; and the state park interior. The name Hobe is from an aboriginal Indian tribe that lived here. Returning to the main park road, take a right to travel the winding route through the park.

In about 4 miles a left turn takes you to the cabin loop access and, beyond that, to a boat launch for the Loxahatchee River, a Wild and Scenic River. A quarter of a mile farther on the main park road is the concession, picnic area, and river landing. Here you can rent a canoe or reserve a seat on a pontoon boat, the Loxahatchee Queen II. If you head to the right on the river, you are going in the direction of the Trapper Nelson cabin. Shoving off to the left takes you in the direction of the canoe trail. The guided Loxahatchee Queen II tour is about two hours long and glides past 100-year-old cypress trees, lush fern, strangler fig, pond apple, and mangroves. Visitors sometimes see federally listed endangered manatee, and almost always see alligators, white ibis, egrets, herons, and anhingas. If you are canoeing the river, plan a trip for early morning or late afternoon to avoid busy river traffic. Near the river landing, there is a self-guided, 4-mile hiking trail that travels through slash pine forest and saw palmetto habitat, past the lush ferns and cypress trees that line Kitching Creek.

The park itself is named for a Quaker, Jonathan Dickinson, who was on board a British ship traveling to Philadelphia from Jamaica in 1696. The ship ran aground, and Dickinson, his wife, and baby were among the 24 survivors. He later published a journal about the group's struggle to make their way to the safety of St. Augustine. Dickinson's volume was a 17th-century bestseller, with at least 16 printings. His observations about the group's fate, the culture of the natives, and the area's plants, trees, and animals are still a source of fascination.

(Dickinson Park managers also oversee the St. Lucie Inlet State Preserve at the northern tip of Jupiter Island, reached only by boat. It offers a 3,300-foot boardwalk through mangrove forest and boardwalks to a barrier island beach. Ask for a brochure at this park.)

After the park visit, return to US 1 and turn right (south), traveling about 3.5 miles to the traffic light at the intersection of US 1 and CR 707. Turn left here, onto CR 707/Alternate A1A/Beach Road, crossing a two-lane drawbridge over Hobe Sound onto exclusive Jupiter Island, a wealthy Atlantic Ocean enclave of tree-hidden estates. Turn right almost immediately into the driveway of the Jupiter Lighthouse, its imposing red brick tower visible from the road. During its early years the lighthouse was a Native American trading site of the late 1880s, where Seminoles who had never signed a peace treaty or accepted relocation in the West began emerging from their isolation in the Everglades to trade. This working lighthouse marks the treacherous waters of Jupiter Inlet.

Returning to CR 707 from the lighthouse, turn right and continue following CR 707 as it sharply curves left to head north, parallel with the Atlantic Ocean. Note secluded driveways that lead to private island retreats. In two miles, on the right, look for the sign indicating Blowing Rocks Preserve, and turn right directly into the small preserve parking area.

Blowing Rocks Preserve extends a little more than 1 mile along Jupiter Island and covers 73 acres, from the Atlantic coast to the shore of Hobe Sound. This is a place to observe shorebirds, such as brown pelicans, and three species of summer-nesting sea turtles: the federally listed endangered loggerhead turtle (the most common), the rare federally listed endangered

Jonathan Dickinson State Park is a riverfront retreat.

green turtle, and the federally listed endangered leatherback turtle. Manatees swim in Hobe Sound in the winter.

During winter storms and extreme high tides the ocean explodes through holes that were carved here over time along the shore's marine sediment cliff. As tons of water gush skyward through these blowholes, spectacular saltwater plumes can be seen and heard, giving the preserve its name. Although open to the public, Blowing Rocks Preserve is private, operated by The Nature Conservancy and purchased by Jupiter Island residents. Fishing, snorkeling, diving, and swimming are allowed, but food and beverages are prohibited.

Returning to CR 707, turn right and continue north for about 5 miles of manicured private enclaves of the wealthy and quietly famous. When you come to the Y intersection, take the right fork, Beach Road. In about 1.3 miles the drive comes to a stop sign at CR 708/Bridge Road. At this intersection, Hobe Sound Beach, a public park with restrooms, picnic area, dune walkovers, and a snack concession, is directly on the right. Continue north on North Beach Road, which ends in about 1.5 miles at the Beach Use area of Hobe Sound National Wildlife Refuge. No picnicking on the beach is allowed, but this is an ideal spot to see osprey, pelicans, and, offshore, bottlenosed dolphins. Weekday visits are best, to avoid crowds. Trace your route back south, to the intersection with Alternate A1A and CR 708 at Hobe

Sound Beach. Turn right on CR 708/Bridge Road, and continue through a tunnel of trees, then onto a drawbridge over Hobe Sound and back to the mainland. In about three-quarters of a mile, after First Avenue, turn right on SR A1A toward Sewall's Point, traveling about 10 miles to its waterfront area, where the St. Lucie River meets the Indian River Lagoon. In Stuart, SR A1A takes a right turn onto Ocean Boulevard, heading east toward the Indian River via a bridge and causeway, to Hutchinson Island, this drive's second barrier island.

In half a mile, take a right turn from SR A1A/Ocean Boulevard onto MacArthur Boulevard for a spur trip on a narrow two-lane beach road that parallels the Atlantic Ocean, visible on the left. After about 1 mile look for the sign for Gilbert's Bar House of Refuge on the left. This oceanfront museum is in a fully restored 1875 federal House of Refuge, one of ten that were built on Florida's east coast. These houses were operated by families who helped rescue shipwreck victims at sea, and helped survivors who washed up on shore. During World War II this refuge house served as a lookout for German submarines lurking offshore. This museum and home contain a model ship collection, maritime artifacts, early lifesaving equipment, a World War II German submarine lookout tower, and exhibits on area history, particularly shipwrecks. In 1715 an armada of 11 Spanish sailing ships, carrying at least $6.5 million worth of silver, gold, and other cargo, was hit by a hurricane, and all but one of the ships sank on an offshore reef near here. One of the ships was rediscovered in 1928, and another in the 1950s.

After visiting the House of Refuge, you can continue south (left) along MacArthur Boulevard. In just under 1 mile the road ends at Bathtub Reef oceanfront park, on the left.

Trace your path on MacArthur Boulevard back to SR A1A, turn right, and continue about 2.5 miles to Elliott Museum. This museum features a collection of Americana, including railroad memorabilia, a watch and clock collection, hunting and fishing tackle, blacksmith forge, dolls, old automobiles, recreated country store, local history room (including a Seminole Indian open-air house called a chickee), and the inventions of Sterling Elliott, who created a unique wood bicycle in 1886 and published *Bicycling World* magazine in the 1880s.

Elliott Museum, the end of this drive, is part of a beachfront public park complex, with picnic area, dune walkovers, snack concession, and a coastal science center.

23

Native American Everglades
Snake Road to the Seminole Tribe

General description: This 45-mile round-trip drive into the middle of Florida's Everglades and Big Cypress Swamp introduces these important Florida ecosystems, as well as the Seminole Tribe, with its indomitable spirit and rich history. The drive includes visits to an outstanding tribal museum and a wildlife park carved from the glades.

Special features: Snake Road; Big Cypress Seminole Indian Reservation; Ah-Tah-Thi-Ki Museum with re-created Seminole chickees and Big Cypress Swamp Boardwalk; Billie Swamp Safari with re-created native camp, storytelling, canoeing, horseback riding, nature paths, birding, and wildlife watching.

Location: South-central Florida.

Drive route numbers: Snake Road/County Road 833, West Boundary Road.

Travel season: November through April is best. In the dry winter, migratory and wintering birds join other species at water holes, creating the best wildlife watching. The summer season (May through October) brings temperatures of 95 degrees and higher, high humidity, intense lightning storms, and the possibility of hurricanes.

Camping: There are no campgrounds along this route.

Services: There is one gas station with some supplies at the start of this drive. At the reservation's Big Cypress community about 15 miles into the drive, roadside vendors offer food and crafts year-round. At the Billie Swamp Safari, there are a gift shop, cafe, restrooms, public telephone, and camp-style lodging. Reservations are recommended.

Nearby points of interest: Big Cypress Hunting Adventures, Big Cypress Rodeo and Entertainment Center (scheduled events only).

Time zone: Eastern.

 The drive

This 45-mile drive winds its way to a remote community isolated in the middle of exceptional natural beauty, where the edges of Florida's Big Cypress Swamp and Everglades meld in stunning panorama.

Begin this drive about 60 miles west of Fort Lauderdale on Interstate 75, at the Indian Reservation exit (Exit 14). Exit 14 leads only one way, onto

Drive 23: Native American Everglades
Snake Road to the Seminole Tribe

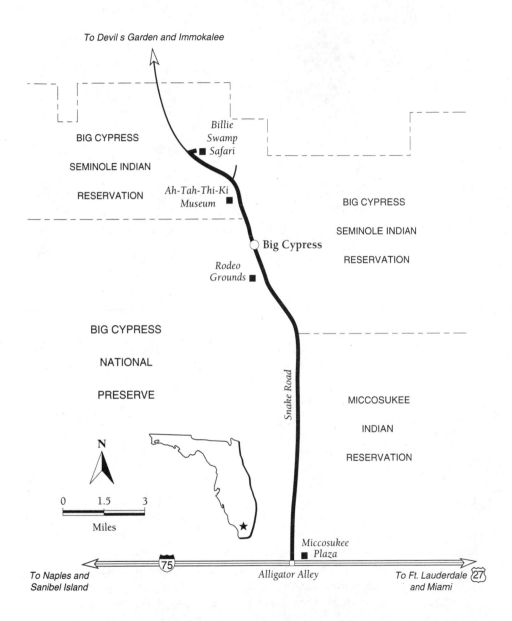

To Devil's Garden and Immokalee

BIG CYPRESS

SEMINOLE INDIAN

RESERVATION

Billie Swamp Safari

Ah-Tah-Thi-Ki Museum

BIG CYPRESS

SEMINOLE INDIAN

RESERVATION

○ **Big Cypress**

Rodeo Grounds

BIG CYPRESS

NATIONAL

PRESERVE

Snake Road

MICCOSUKEE

INDIAN

RESERVATION

N

0   1.5   3

Miles

Miccosukee Plaza

To Naples and Sanibel Island

75

Alligator Alley

To Ft. Lauderdale and Miami

27

When Seminole Indians were forced to leave their log cabins in northern Florida, they eventually fled to the Everglades and developed the palm-thatched chickee.

CR 833 (Snake Road), this round-trip drive's main road.

After exiting I-75, travel north on Snake Road, a narrow, paved, two-lane road that has occasional soft shoulders and no designated pullouts. Along Snake Road look down into the roadside canals for wading birds, such as great blue heron, and for alligators cruising the canal waters. The islands of trees far off in the prairies are cypress domes, sheltering other plants and animals. In dry areas along the grassy roadside shoulder, you can see large yucca plants with 4-foot spikes. The drive rolls past pastures, wide wetlands, and scattered homes and buildings.

This region is the remote world of the Seminole Tribe of Florida, a prosperous and independent entity that operates citrus groves, cattle ranches, and high-stakes bingo halls, among other businesses. Tribal headquarters in urban Hollywood, Florida, features a helipad on top of a modern office tower and a fleet of 4 airplanes. For many years the tribe didn't welcome outsiders on tribal lands, although it operated tourist sites in urban areas. The reservation now invites visitors, but cattle pens, homes, citrus operations, and some other features aren't open to the public. Areas where visitors are welcome are clearly marked, including two sites on this drive.

The first is the Ah-Tah-Thi-Ki Museum (open Tuesday through Sunday), at the intersection of Snake Road and West Boundary Road, about

Palm trees and prairie make up the view along Snake Road on the Big Cypress Seminole Indian Reservation. Jan Godown photo

17 miles into the drive. The introduction to the museum is a short documentary, *We Seminoles*, a compelling film that unfolds across five screens. The film is fast-paced, uplifting, and poignant. The museum, which opened in 1997, offers well-crafted walk-through exhibits introducing late-1800s Seminole economy, culture, and spiritual beliefs. Rare artifacts from the museum's collection of war rifles, beaded bandolier bags, palmetto splint baskets, tools, and other items are sheltered in exhibit cases. Some artifacts are on loan from a museum partner, the Smithsonian Institution's Museum of the American Indian. Just beyond the museum's library and archive area, a 2-mile boardwalk leads into a portion of the Big Cypress Swamp for a close-up look at orchids, air plants, ferns, strangler fig trees, cypress trees, and the birds, insects, reptiles, and mammals that live here. The reservation shelters wild bobcat and also the federally listed endangered Florida panther, on the verge of extinction. The boardwalk leads to re-created ceremonial grounds and to an area of chickees (palm-thatched huts) where crafts are demonstrated.

After leaving the museum grounds, continue west 3.5 miles on West Boundary Road, then turn right into the driveway that goes to the Billie Swamp Safari, the second reservation site on this drive open to the public. An overnight visit is recommended, booked in advance, to best experience this private park. Storytelling, folklore lessons, and music usually unfold at night around a campfire. The evening hours offer an opportunity to see the celestial Everglades and to hear the sounds of nocturnal animals. Overnight accommodations, similar to traditional chickees, are small, screened huts on short stilts, thatched with palm fronds, featuring log-frame beds. As in state and federal park campgrounds, a community bathroom and shower building serve guests. The Swamp Safari displays alligators, crocodiles, fish, turtles, and snakes near its gift shop. A boardwalk through a cypress dome originates near the camping huts. Guided swamp buggy tours take you to other interesting Safari animal exhibits. There are also canoes for rent and horses available, for a quieter tour of Safari grounds. Special events and concerts are held at the Swamp Safari throughout the year.

The Safari is the end of this drive, so from here trace your path back to I-75. If you are going to the Miami area, make a left turn onto I-75 from Snake Road. A right turn sends you toward Florida's Gulf Coast.

24

Beyond the River of Grass to Mangrove Coast

Everglades National Park East Entrance to Flamingo

General description: An 80-mile, paved, round-trip meander within famed Everglades National Park. The drive winds south past pinewoods, sawgrass prairie, and tropical hardwood hammocks, into mangrove swamp and coastal prairie at the park community of Flamingo, perched on stilts at the edge of Florida Bay.

Special features: Everglades National Park, an International Biosphere Reserve; Ernest F. Coe Visitor Center; Royal Palm Visitor Center; canoe trails; tram ride; Flamingo Visitor Center and Lodge; Flamingo interpretive center; scenic overlooks; wildlife watching; fishing; guided boat trips; canoeing; hiking; abundant birding.

Location: Southeastern Florida.

Drive route number: Main park road.

Travel season: November through April for best weather and wildlife views. The park is open year-round, but most services, including lodge and restaurant, close from about May through mid-December, and park staff is reduced. Summer brings increased numbers of biting bugs, temperatures of 95 degrees and higher, humidity, and storms, including occasional hurricanes.

Camping: There are park campgrounds in the woods at Long Pine Key Campground and on the saltwater coast at Flamingo. Campsites may be rented in advance; others are first come, first served. Some backcountry campsites are on solid land or at island beaches, while others are mainly platforms over water; all require permits. About 15 miles north of this drive, the Chekika unit of Everglades National Park, via SR 997 and Richmond Drive, reached by going outside this entrance to the park, offers a small and popular campground. At Florida City, a local public campground on State Road 9336 also operates. At Flamingo, a park concessionaire offers motel rooms and cabins. Reservations are advised.

Services: All services are available in Homestead, about 11 miles north of the park entrance; there are limited services in Florida City, about 9 miles north of the park entrance. At Flamingo, a small marina store offers limited groceries, camping supplies, guidebooks, cold drinks, and marine gasoline. The Flamingo Lodge has a restaurant famous for its view of the bay, fresh seafood, and breakfast buffet.

Nearby points of interest: Fruit and Spice Park, the Original Orchid Jungle, and Biscayne National Underwater Park and Convoy Point Visitor Center in Homestead; Florida City fruit and vegetable stands; Chekika unit of Everglades National Park; Shark Valley unit of Everglades National Park; many Miami attractions, such as Fairchild Tropical Garden, Miami Metrozoo, and the Barnacle State Historic Site; John Pennekamp Coral Reef State Park, Key Largo.

Time zone: Eastern.

The drive

This round-trip drive in southeastern Florida begins in flat pinewoods at the main entrance to Everglades National Park. It continues about 40 miles to the coast on two-lane paved road, with several spurs of 1 mile or less to short boardwalks in the subtropical jungle, or to wayside overlooks for spectacular park views that range from sawgrass prairie to mangrove forest. There is abundant opportunity to see wildlife, especially large birds. This route crosses a part of the country's largest sawgrass prairie, a shallow river of rainwater slowly moving toward Florida Bay and the Gulf of Mexico. Hardwood hammocks form islands in this river of grass. The drive enters mangrove forest near the end of the mainland, finally arriving at a tiny park community called Flamingo, on island-dotted Florida Bay.

NOTE: Although the drive is only 80 miles round-trip, plan on visiting for at least a full day, to enable you to take as many of the spur stops as possible.

To reach the start of the drive, take SR 997/Krome Avenue south from Homestead to its intersection with SR 9336/Tower Road in Florida City, a tiny agricultural and migrant labor community that was historically part of the Everglades. Like much of southern Florida, this area was drained and manicured for farming. Take SR 9336 south, following several sharp turns before it ends at the park entrance.

The first stop is the Ernest F. Coe Visitor Center, just a quarter of a mile inside the entrance, where there are displays, photographs, videos, booklets, guidebooks, and hiking and canoe trail brochures. You can also pick up a national park system newspaper with information about the Gulf Coast, Shark River, and Chekika units of Everglades National Park, and other National Park Service preserves in the region, as well as a schedule of ranger-led events. Well-versed rangers are on hand to explain various natural features of the 1.5-million-acre preserve, which was dedicated in 1947. The visitor center provides the first clues about the abundant life to be found

Drive 24: Beyond the River of Grass to Mangrove Coast

Everglades National Park East Entrance to Flamingo

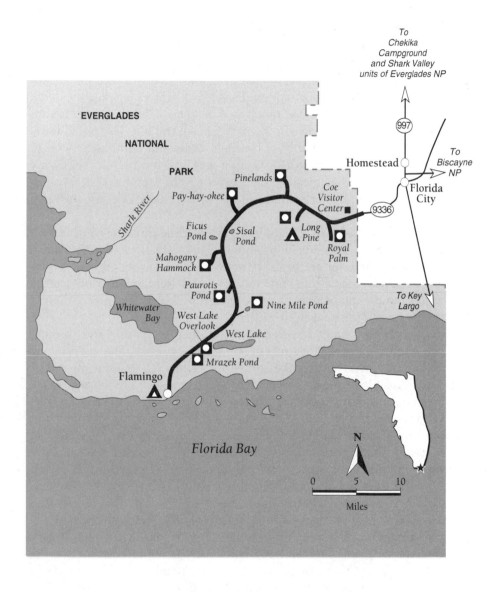

To
Chekika
Campground
and Shark Valley
units of Everglades NP

EVERGLADES

NATIONAL

PARK

Shark River

Pinelands

Pay-hay-okee

Coe
Visitor
Center

Homestead

(997)

To
Biscayne
NP

Florida
City

(9336)

Ficus
Pond

Sisal
Pond

Long
Pine

Royal
Palm

Mahogany
Hammock

Paurotis
Pond

Whitewater
Bay

West Lake
Overlook

Nine Mile Pond

West Lake

To Key
Largo

Mrazek Pond

Flamingo

Florida Bay

N

0   5   10

Miles

here, including some 500 species of fish, 900 species of marine inverte-brates, 350 kinds of birds, 100 kinds of butterflies, 40 types of mammals, 65 types of reptiles and amphibians, 100 types of trees, and 1,000 plant spe-cies. The land is not as flat as it looks; take time both inside and outside the visitor center to learn how to read the land, to see a ridge of elevation here, a limestone depression over there. The Everglades are so different from any-where else in America, and its habitats at first so unrevealing, that learning the language of the place is as important to a fulfilling visit as learning the language is when visiting a foreign country.

After your orientation at the visitor center, return to the main park road and turn south, toward Flamingo. The terrain here, called pine rockland, is the driest part of the park, as much as 6 feet above sea level, and it sup-ports the only pine that grows in the park, the slash pine. The pitted lime-stone rock is composed mainly of crushed shells and coral, deposited in layers eons ago when this part of Florida was covered by sea. The many fissures and holes in the limestone are made by rainwater that collects acids from pine needles and other plant materials, which gradually erode the lime-stone.

NOTE: Although you can glimpse park wildlife from the car, the park offers many other wildlife-viewing opportunities. Plan to visit the short, generally 30-minute, nature trails, to venture out on wooden boardwalks over the wetlands, or to climb observation towers. Rent bicycles and canoes at Flamingo and explore areas that intrigue you. Expect mosquitoes, espe-cially at dawn and dusk, even in winter.

Travel about 2 miles across an edge of sawgrass prairie and through Taylor Slough, a sweeping channel of slow-moving water. The sawgrass on both sides of the road, with spikes sometimes 8 feet tall, is a cutting sedge, not a true grass, growing in inches-deep rainwater. As the sawgrass sedge dies, then decays, it turns into a rich peat, which supports other plant life, such as willows and cypress. Around the underwater stems of sedge and other plants exists a universe of life called periphyton—living yellowish green masses floating on the water. Periphyton is composed of algae, zoo-plankton, and other organisms, and is probably the Everglades' most impor-tant life form, the very bottom of the food chain here. The water that sup-ports life here comes solely from rain; the watershed for the park is way upstream, outside of the park boundaries. An old pattern of diverting water away from the Everglades, including areas far north of the park, has imper-iled the region. Thanks to loud and constant voicing of citizen concern, steps are now being taken by the state of Florida and the U.S. Congress to help restore the natural water flow and diminish the damaging effects.

In a little less than 2 miles, turn left off the main park road onto Royal Palm Road, driving about 1 mile to Royal Palm Visitor Center, taking the

At Flamingo on Florida Bay, the sky is big and the feeling laid-back.

left when the road forks. Royal Palm quickly sends you into the Everglades along two footpaths. One, in wintertime, is usually packed with wildlife, including alligators; the other is a dense, cool jungle island with towering tropical trees.

The visitor center here is small, but notable for its walls, which are covered with the artwork of famed wildlife artist Charles Harper. Just beyond the center the Anhinga Trail is a half-mile loop that takes a boardwalk into a sawgrass prairie at the edge of Taylor Slough.

On this path visitors see an abundance of alligators, great blue herons, snowy egrets, and anhingas, a black diving bird with a long neck. Snakes, turtles, frogs, butterflies, and dragonflies thrive here, too. Anglers may identify largemouth bass, but easier to see are the ancient, spotted, long-nosed fish called gar, a food of alligators but nothing else.

The second path here, Gumbo Limbo Trail, is a dark half-mile walk, with interpretive signs, into a tropical hardwood hammock, a natural garden of old-growth trees and plants. Tropical hardwood hammocks exist only under specific conditions, including a perch on a limestone ridge, an elevation of maybe 1 to 3 feet above the freshwater marl prairie. Look here for wild coffee, for the stately royal palm, and for the gumbo limbo tree, with its distinctive reddish brown peeling bark. Some royal palms here tower 125

A visit to the Everglades may include a glimpse of wood storks and great white herons in majestic flight.

feet tall. Interpretive signs also identify the strangler fig, air plants, and live oak. Carpeting tree limbs are blankets of mosses and ferns, some aerial, such as the resurrection fern. Curled and brown in drought, it uncurls and turns lime green after a rain. If you are lucky, you might see univalve shells moving almost imperceptibly on the limbs of hammock trees. These are the houses of tropical tree snails, nearly wiped out by collectors years ago, and now protected on the federal government's endangered species list.

A third trail here is 11 miles one-way and takes some planning. It begins at the visitor center and follows the Old Ingraham Highway into tree island hammocks, through sawgrass prairie and slash pinewoods.

Tracing your path back to the main park road, if you take the fork you passed up on the way in, this time a left, you reach the Long Pine Key Campground. This also features a picnic area and parking for a connecting network of about 7 miles of long-distance hiking trails through airy, slash pine forest.

Returning to the main park road, turn left and drive about 2.5 miles, then turn right to access the half-mile Pinelands Trail. This trail, with informative signs along the way, explains how the land here, a slight ridge perhaps 5 feet high, was formed when the oceans covered southern Florida. Pinelands is one of the hunting grounds of the federally listed endangered Florida panther. Ten or fewer of these animals still survive in the Everglades, and are monitored by electronic tracking devices. A federal and state panther recovery program is working to improve the odds that Florida panthers will survive in the wild, but the going is tough. The panthers are threatened by reproductive problems brought on by inbreeding, by mercury lurking in the Everglades food chain, and by encroaching development.

Returning to the main park road, turn right and pass out of the pinelands and over Rock Reef Pass, a channel of water about 3 feet above sea level in a freshwater marl prairie. The drive next enters a dwarf cypress forest. On the right in about 6 miles, the next stop is access to a quarter-mile-long boardwalk to reach Pay-hay-okee Overlook, an observation tower at the edge of a tropical hardwood hammock, overlooking one of the Everglades' vast sawgrass prairies. *Pay-hay-okee* is the Seminole Indian name for the Everglades. It means "grassy waters." Look here for great white heron and the federally listed endangered wood stork.

Continuing on the main park road, in 3.5 miles look on the left for Sisal Pond, and, one mile farther on the right, Ficus Pond, both prime bird-watching areas. In about 4 miles, turn off the main park road to the right for a short drive to parking for a short boardwalk leading past a portion of sawgrass prairie into a tropical island called Mahogany Hammock. Most mahogany trees were felled and hauled from southern Florida for lumber, or destroyed by hurricanes or fire. Among the mahogany trees that survive here is one that is 90 feet tall and 12 feet around, the largest in the United States and probably more than 100 years old.

Returning to the main park drive, turn right and continue through the drive's last freshwater prairie. Now you are getting closer to the coast, where freshwater becomes mixed with saltwater. About two-thirds of the park is in coastal brackish or saltwater area. In about 5 miles, look for a parking area on the right, at Paurotis Pond. The trees with exposed roots are mangroves, coastal trees that actually build land as silt and debris get trapped in their tangled roots. The roots also act as a marine nursery, sheltering young fish, shrimp, and other aquatic species. The branches and leaves provide nesting space for large birds, such as pelicans, egrets, and herons.

Turn right, back onto the main park road, and continue through mangrove forest to an access on the left for Nine Mile Pond, a popular picnic area and the first opportunity since the park entrance to put a canoe in the water. The 5.2-mile canoe trail is a loop through shallow marsh and scattered islands, with the chance to see alligators, wading birds, and bald eagles.

From Nine Mile Pond, turn left (south), continuing about 2 miles to the access on the left for the 2-mile Noble Hammock Canoe Trail, named for an early settler. Although you'll likely bang into trees on this twisted, narrow canoe route, some select it for its shorter length and calm water on windy days.

Practically opposite Noble Hammock, across the park road and south about 700 yards, is access for the Hell's Bay Canoe Trail, the first canoe trail that features overnight camping; the sites are platforms over the water. Their use requires a backcountry permit issued by rangers at the visitor centers. This canoe trail is a sheltered, snaking path that is calm on windy days.

Continue along the main park road about 3.5 miles to a left turn into access for West Lake, the park's only lake you can see right from this drive, without a hike. There are restrooms here, and access to a half-mile boardwalk path that tunnels through mangrove forest that can be plagued with biting bugs. Here also is the put-in for a 15-mile round-trip canoe trail through West Lake and a series of other lakes, with camping platforms above water.

West Lake is crocodile habitat. Crocodiles are often confused with alligators, especially in the Everglades, the only place in the world where both can be found in the same waters. Crocodiles are lighter in color, a grayish green, while alligators are black. Crocodile snouts are narrower and more pointed than those of alligators.

To continue the drive, turn left onto the main park road, noticing coastal prairie on the right. Salt-tolerant plants such as railroad vine and some grasses grow in coastal prairie, along with red and black mangroves. In a little under 2 miles, look on the left for the entrance to the 4-mile round-trip Snake Bight Trail. You can walk, ride bicycles, or take a tram ride on this popular path. (The Snake Bight Trail tram ride originates in Flamingo; check at the Flamingo Lodge Gift Shop for times and tickets.) The Snake Bight Trail travels a former roadbed and leads directly to the coast. The Everglades coast and areas slightly inland were occupied mainly by the Calusa and Tequesta tribes. When the first Europeans sailed by in the Everglades coastal waters in the 1500s, Cuban fishermen also lived here. Later, the region sheltered Seminole and Miccosukee Indians. U.S. soldiers manned two stockades west of Flamingo. A commercial fishing company operated at Snake Bight as late as 1940.

From Snake Bight Trail you can connect with the 2.6-mile (one-way) Rowdy Bend Trail, which takes you to the main park road closer to Flamingo. Rowdy Bend is a path on an old roadbed into coastal prairie. Back on the main park road, turn left and in just a few hundred yards beyond Snake Bight Trail, look on the left for Mrazek Pond, named for an early park naturalist. This is a wayside stop where both wading and diving birds feed.

Continuing on the park road, in about 1 mile look on the right for

The Everglades' mangrove coast is a wall of odd tropical trees whose roots curve downward into the water.

Coot Bay Pond, which connects to the interior Coot Bay. The 6.8-mile Mud Lake Canoe Trail starts from Coot Bay Pond. On the main park road in another mile on the left look for the entrance to the 2.6-mile Rowdy Bend Trail, which links up with Snake Bight Trail. Along the main park drive in another 1.8 miles, look on the left, just before the bridge, for the entrance to the Christian Point Trail, a 4-mile round-trip path to a coastal prairie at Snake Bight Bay (not connected to Snake Bight Trail). Buttonwood trees—a tropical mangrove that was once cut and burned to produce charcoal—are common along this path. Raptors, such as osprey and federally listed threatened bald eagles, are seen in skies overhead. After Christian Point Trail the drive climbs a short, humped bridge over the Buttonwood Canal, the terminus of the park's Wilderness Waterway. Only experienced canoeists should tackle the 100 to 120 miles of paddling it takes to complete the trek, in usually no less than eight days. It is a once-in-a-lifetime route. Rentals for this particular canoe journey are only available at the point of origin, Everglades City.

Continue on to Flamingo. Isolated Flamingo, founded in 1893, was once a charcoal-making center, sugar cane–growing community, and fishing village, reachable only by boat. Residents also hunted plume birds, sold alligator and otter hides, and operated secluded stills. The community never had a regular school, local government, or conventional medical care. The community didn't prosper, even after the road was extended here in 1922. Most of its buildings were destroyed in a 1935 hurricane. Today the tiny community is a popular stop for park visitors who eat at the Flamingo Lodge restaurant, and walk the nearby nature trails.

The Flamingo Visitor Center is in the park building that sits between the marina and the lodge, and covers topics on park wildlife and early Indian residents, primarily the Calusa. At the information desk, check the schedule of ranger-led activities, and ask rangers about recent wildlife sightings and details on footpaths and canoe trails.

The Flamingo marina is headquarters for boat rentals, including houseboats, and guided trips into the backcountry and out into Florida Bay. The bay is a vast area of mud flats and shallow water that comprises about one-fourth of the park. Florida Bay is a popular area for anglers, and wildlife watchers can usually spot alligators, and an occasional crocodile or manatee, near the marina. NOTE: If you rent a houseboat, be sure to study the marine charts and get recommendations about places to anchor. Low tides can leave you stranded. Canoeists should be aware that the wind on Florida Bay can be quite stiff. Check conditions with rangers before venturing onto the water.

Birds abound in the Flamingo area, and you can readily see them before you even start down one of the many nature trails. Hunchbacked white ibis feed on insects in the grassy areas next to the parking lots. The pink feeding birds on stilt legs aren't flamingoes but roseate spoonbills; they can be seen, along with stately great white herons, stalking in the waters of Florida Bay.

The most popular footpath at Flamingo, about 1 mile past the visitor center along the main park road, is the boardwalk loop around Eco Pond, a half-mile trip rich in bird life. The 1-mile Guy Bradley footpath, along Florida Bay from the visitor center to the Flamingo Campground, honors an Audubon Society wildlife warden, a Flamingo resident, who was murdered on an island offshore by poachers of plume feathers in 1905. Other trails include the 2-mile Bayshore Loop Trail and the 15-mile round-trip Coastal Prairie Trail, both originating near Camping Loop C of Flamingo Campground, with Bayshore Loop veering left toward the bay. Coastal Prairie Trail takes you to a primitive campsite at the edge of Florida Bay in the park's remote Cape Sable beach region, which requires a ranger-issued backcountry camping permit.

Along Everglades beaches you'll have a chance to see porpoise in offshore waters. The beaked whale and false killer whale also thrive in park waters, as well as federally listed endangered loggerhead turtles and other sea turtles, which come ashore at night to lay their eggs. All live mollusks, both fresh- and saltwater, are strictly protected. Taking dead shells is also limited; check with rangers on restrictions. Indian pottery shards are occasionally seen along the beaches; they are protected by law and must remain behind.

Flamingo is at the end of the drive, so from here retrace your path from Flamingo to the park entrance.

25

Shark Valley Birdland
Tamiami Trail to Miccosukee Cultural Center

General description: A 60-mile round-trip drive straight into the wet sawgrass prairie of the Everglades along the Tamiami Trail/U.S. Highway 41, beginning about 10 miles west of Miami. The drive crosses the famous flat prairie known as the River of Grass and takes you into a winter bird feeding ground at the park's Shark Valley entrance. Nearby, a Native American site open to the public re-creates pre-1930s Miccosukee Indian tribal life.

Special features: The Tamiami Trail; Everglades National Park, Shark Valley unit; Shark Valley tram ride, observation tower, and bike path; hiking paths; Miccosukee Tribal Cultural Center and Village; birding; wildlife viewing.

Location: South-central Florida.

Travel season: The Tamiami Trail is open year-round. The region is excessively hot in summer, with temperatures in the high 90s and higher, and plagued with biting bugs from late spring through early fall. Also, in summer, intense lightning storms occur. November through March is the best time to view migratory birds, winter resident birds, and other wildlife species converging to feed in scarce dry-season wetland ponds.

Drive route number: U.S. Highway 41/Tamiami Trail.

Camping: There is no national park camping at the Shark Valley unit. There is a campground at the park's Chekika unit, about 30 miles southeast of Shark Valley (east along the Tamiami Trail, then south on SR 997). Other public camping is at the Big Cypress National Preserve's Midway site, about 15 miles west of Shark Valley on the Tamiami Trail. Private camping is available along US 41.

Services: Services are available in Sweetwater along US 41. A restaurant and gas station is operated on US 41 by the Miccosukee Tribe opposite the national park's Shark Valley unit entrance, but the facility closes at times, usually when workers attend tribal events.

Nearby points of interest: Big Cypress National Preserve Oasis Visitor Center; Everglades National Park, Chekika unit; Fruit and Spice Park in Homestead, near Miami; Everglades National Park Royal Palm Visitor Center.

Time zone: Eastern.

Drive 25: Shark Valley Birdland
Tamiami Trail to Miccosukee Cultural Center

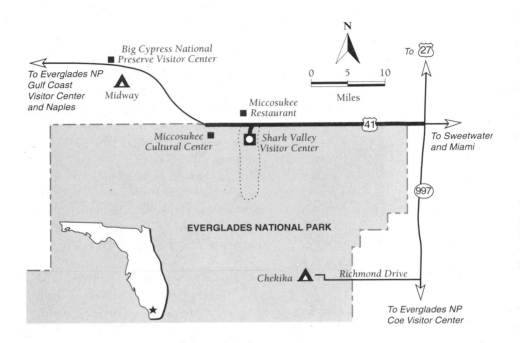

 The drive

This drive starts at the intersection of US 41/Tamiami Trail (locally called, simply, the Trail) and SR 997 at Sweetwater, a small community about 10 miles west of the western edge of metropolitan Miami. The drive quickly enters the wide, wet sawgrass prairie of the Everglades. The Tamiami Trail serves, roughly, as a border of Everglades National Park. Construction of the trail was considered an engineering feat and makes the highway, in itself, a historic site.

This drive is a straight path into the Everglades, which the Seminole and Miccosukee people called *pay-hay-okee,* "grassy waters," and which noted activist Marjory Stoneman Douglas made famous as the River of Grass. This drive takes you to Shark Valley, where, in the dry winter season, wading birds and other birds and animals mass in great concentration to feed—on snails, fish, insects, small reptiles, and amphibians—at scarce water sources.

As you drive along the Tamiami Trail, notice the canal on the right. The canal was first dynamited and then dredged to provide a limestone rock base for the roadbed. Some fish from these waters aren't recommended for consumption due to the high levels of mercury they carry; scientists are studying why some Everglades fish are plagued by mercury poisoning. But as you drive, you will still see residents honoring the area's longtime tradition of perching on camp stools to fish the canal with simple cane poles.

Along the drive look for red-winged blackbirds perched on cattails growing from canal banks. Along utility wires, belted kingfishers perch above the canal as they look down for fish. In the canal and along its banks, turtles and alligators catch sunshine. Black-tipped white wood storks, North America's only stork, fly overhead to nesting grounds.

Narrow, soft shoulders characterize this stretch of highway, so use designated stopping areas only, such as access points near bridges and canals, boat launches, and commercial vendors' places. The land around the trail is dotted with private inholdings, and privacy should be respected. Also, observe Lights on for Safety warning signs along this busy route, which is used by commuters as well as tourists.

For thousands of years, natives of this region crossed the Everglades river along waterways they knew well. Pioneers later followed those same canoe paths, and used them to haul out boatloads of furs, skins, and other items for sale. But when pioneers switched from poled flat-bottomed skiffs to ox carts, and later, automobiles, the desire for a road became apparent. But many doubted that a road could be built, and it took a team of road-boosters and Miccosukee guides pushing and pulling nine Ford Model-T's across the Everglades to convince doubters that autos could cross the River of Grass. For 12 years after their 1923 stunt, this Everglades highway was blasted and dredged from the prairie of the watery Everglades and Big Cypress Swamp, with the help of Miccosukee and Seminole guides. It became the first automobile link between southern Florida's Atlantic Ocean and Gulf of Mexico coasts in 1928.

The road is considered both an engineering feat and a mistake. The road altered crucial water flow of the Everglades' vast drainage system, which extends far north beyond park boundaries. At the time, draining the Everglades was thought to be a good idea, to make it solid land. Along this drive look for a series of water control gates and locks on the north side of the canal, built years after the road was made. These giant water faucets have also altered the Everglades' natural water cycle, while providing water for

Patchwork clothing and sweetgrass baskets are among the items crafted by Miccosukee artists.

southeastern Florida agricultural, commercial, and personal use.

The Tamiami Trail, named for linking Tampa to Miami, opened the Everglades to the new class of automobile tourists. Yet despite developers' sales pitches and visits to Florida by as many as a half-million tourists in the years leading up to the Great Depression, few became residents once they understood the rigors of year-round Everglades existence. Summer temperatures in the high 90s and low 100s, high humidity, lightning storms, swarms of mosquitoes and attacks of other biting bugs, poisonous snakes, and alligators kept new residents away.

But those who hunted and fished delighted in the Trail. It provided new access to the region's big game—panther and bear—and smaller mammals such as deer and otter, and also birds such as turkey. Panthers are now an endangered species, with perhaps 30 to 40 still in existence in the entire state. Black bear hide out in the Big Cypress Swamp and occasionally a portion of Everglades National Park, plus sections of central and northern Florida.

After about 30 miles of sawgrass studded with hardwood and palm tree hammocks—lush elevated islands of trees just above the waterline—this drive approaches the Everglades National Park Shark Valley unit. Look for the brown Shark Valley sign and turn left, on the south side of the Trail. You are now entering Everglades National Park; an entry (or re-entry) fee is required. Ask at the park entrance for a park map and information on ranger-led programs.

As soon as you drive into the parking lot, listen for the calls of hundreds of birds, drawn to the fish, snakes, insects, and other food of sawgrass prairie ponds and wetlands sloughs—channels of slow-moving water in marsh. You will see large birds, such as wood storks and herons, flying overhead. From your vantage point in the parking lot, you will probably see an alligator sunning itself.

Before walking out on the main path, stop at the visitor center for an orientation, and get information on walking and bicycling tips. The main Shark Valley path is paved and flat, but still no easy jaunt. The 15-mile loop is the longest hiking trail in the national park. There is no food or shelter available on the path, but fresh water and a restroom are offered at the midway point. Riding a bike on the path is another option, and bicycles can be rented in the parking lot. No matter how you venture out on the path, you should apply sunscreen, even in winter, as there is little shade.

The most popular way to enter Shark Valley is to take the tram ride down this same 15-mile paved path. The schedule is posted at the tram ticket kiosk at the parking lot, and reservations are recommended. The guided tram ride takes two hours.

Alligators rule in the Everglades' Shark Valley.

Alligators are abundant in the wetlands here. These ancient reptiles will come up onto the paved path, crossing from one wetlands area to another, or for warmth. It is tempting to get close, but keep your distance. About halfway out, the 2-hour tram tour stops at a 50-foot-high observation tower for a 360-degree view of the River of Grass. The path returns on a parallel paved route through the sawgrass back to the parking lot. Occasional sunset and nighttime tram tours are well worth the effort of booking in advance.

If you don't have enough time to take the 15-mile loop, or haven't made tram reservations, you can still experience Shark Valley on two lush short paths. The Bobcat Hammock Boardwalk is a 500-yard visit into a sawgrass prairie. The Otter Cave Trail is a 200-yard loop into a tropical hardwood hammock, an island of curious jungle trees, including the strangler fig and gumbo limbo. Both are reached from the tram path, not far from the visitor center.

Shark Valley is an evocative name that seems to leave a question hanging, without a shark in site or without seeing any feature of this flat landscape, barely above sea level, that looks like a valley. The wetlands of this region, the freshwater Shark River Slough, are a headwaters for the Everglades' Shark River, which flows past Shark River Island into the Gulf of Mexico, a haven for sharks, about 45 miles southwest of here. Don't look for slopes or the shoulders of a valley. It's just one of those names that is more colorful than informative, except for those who know the territory.

After visiting Shark Valley, treat yourself to a meal at the Miccosukee Restaurant. Almost opposite the Shark Valley unit entrance, on the other side of the Trail, is Miccosukee Reservation land, where this special restaurant is located. It offers diner-type fare, as well as fresh catfish and a sweet Indian pumpkin fry bread that you shouldn't leave without sampling. Continue this drive by traveling west on the Trail about a quarter of a mile to the entrance to the Miccosukee Tribal Cultural Center and Village, on the left. Here, meet modern tribal members who will tell you about how their ancestors lived. Wait for a guided tour of the recreated village, or walk around the village on your own. Either way you will see craft areas and cooking and living areas under palm-thatched huts called chickees. The Seminole and Miccosukee tribes, pushed farther and farther south in Florida in the 19th century, eventually settled in the Florida Everglades, and learned to adapt to the vast grassy water. They created a stilt-house, the open-air chickee, to live above the water and to keep cool and dry. They farmed the Everglades muck and lived off fish, fowl, and mammals.

Across from the Miccosukee Cultural Center, airboat tours into wetlands are sold. Airboats, and elevated, large-tired transports called swamp buggies, which vendors also market elsewhere on the Trail, are loud vehicles, intrusive to wildlife and wetlands habitat. Quieter alternatives include canoes, flat-bottomed boats with low-horsepower motors, or flat-bottomed skiffs poled through the water.

To finish this drive, trace your path back to its origin, along Tamiami Trail.

26

Ten Thousand Islands of Everglades National Park

Carnestown to Chokoloskee

General description: A 15-mile round-trip drive through mangrove forest wetlands to Everglades National Park's Gulf Coast unit, which has a small interpretive center and guided boat tours into the park's Ten Thousand Islands. The drive enters two historic fishing villages; one is on an island created by aboriginal Indians who piled up discarded shells. The drive also visits a former 1917 Seminole Indian and pioneer trading post, a national historic site.

Special features: Everglades City; Everglades National Park Gulf Coast Visitor Center; Chokoloskee Island; Smallwood Store and Ole Indian Trading Post Museum; origin of Wilderness Waterway canoe trail; boat tours; guided wildlife trips; canoeing; kayaking; excellent birding, fishing, and beachcombing at park islands; bicycling.

Location: Southwestern edge of Florida.

Drive route number: State Road 29.

Travel season: October through March to see migrating and wintering birds. Summer brings temperatures of 95 and higher, high humidity, tropical storms, biting bugs, and closure of some services.

Camping: There is no campground at this unit of the national park. This unit's campsites are in the backcountry (mainly elevated platforms in remote mangrove forests or on islands). All require reservations and are accessible only by boat. Nearby public campgrounds are located in Collier-Seminole State Park, about 25 miles west of the Carnestown junction on US 41; at the Big Cypress National Preserve's Dona Drive site, 5.5 miles east of the drive at Big Cypress on the south side of US 41; and at the preserve's Monument Lake site at Monroe Station, about 25 miles east of Carnestown on the north side of US 41. Private campgrounds operate in Everglades City, on Chokoloskee Island, and on US 41 about 15 miles west of Carnestown at Port of the Islands.

Services: Excellent fresh seafood is available in Everglades City and on Chokoloskee Island, along with gas and limited supplies; full services and medical care can be found in Naples.

Nearby points of interest: Fakahatchee Strand State Preserve Big Bend Boardwalk; Collier-Seminole State Park; Collier County Museum; Ochopee Post Office, the smallest post office in the United States.; Big Cypress National Preserve Oasis Visitor Center; Florida National Scenic Trail; Big Cypress Gallery.

Time zone: Eastern.

 # The drive

This 15-mile round trip into the fringes of mangrove forest ends on an island at the edge of the remote Ten Thousand Islands. This region of Everglades National Park is a lesser-known territory of the vast delta drainage system and wildlife shelter at the southern tip of Florida. The drive is an introduction to the watery world of mangroves, porpoises, and bird rookeries, easily seen by guided boat tour, or with area wildlife guides via canoe or small boat. The drive also introduces a range of aboriginal, Native American, and pioneer history.

The drive begins about 30 miles southeast of Naples, at the intersection of US 41/Tamiami Trail and SR 29. The drive immediately cuts through the mangrove-fringed western border of Big Cypress National Preserve. The drive enters a riverfront fishing village, visits the national park's Gulf Coast Visitor Center, and then meanders along a windy causeway out to an ancient shell mound island and fishing village.

At this remote intersection, known as the Carnestown junction, the Everglades Area Chamber of Commerce welcome center is a good stop. It offers information on regional seafood and pioneer festivals, fishing, beachcombing, wildlife guides, guided tours, wilderness treks, accommodations, and seafood restaurants; it also has restrooms, souvenirs, and limited supplies. (To see more of the Everglades area, see the side trip description at the end of this drive.) From the welcome center, take SR 29 south about 3 miles on straight, two-lane road. Note the narrow canal hugging the left side of the road, lined with mangrove trees. Their gnarled, water-loving roots curl downward, trapping silt and leaves to form small mangrove islands, where various Everglades wading birds roost. Look above the canal on utility wires for the belted kingfisher, perched to look for fish in the canal. You may also see alligators sunning themselves along the banks.

In 3 miles, the drive bridges the narrow and winding Barron River. It is one of several regional drainage streams that lace the Florida delta here. On the right, shaded by royal palm trees, is the riverfront fishing village of Everglades City, which was incorporated in 1923 as a company town. Here you will see old-style streetlights and old wooden cottages bordering the river. About a mile after the bridge, SR 29 enters a small traffic circle. On the

Drive 26: Ten Thousand Islands of Everglades National Park

Carnestown to Chokoloskee

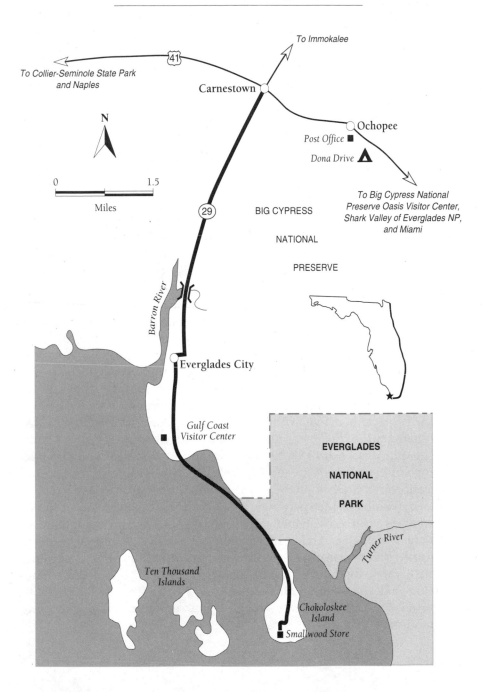

To Collier-Seminole State Park and Naples

To Immokalee

Carnestown

Ochopee

Post Office

Dona Drive

To Big Cypress National Preserve Oasis Visitor Center, Shark Valley of Everglades NP, and Miami

N

0   1.5
Miles

BIG CYPRESS

NATIONAL

PRESERVE

Barron River

Everglades City

Gulf Coast Visitor Center

EVERGLADES

NATIONAL

PARK

Turner River

Ten Thousand Islands

Chokoloskee Island

Smallwood Store

right is an imposing 1923 building with white columns, originally the county courthouse before the county seat was moved to Naples (no tours are offered). It is a good place to stop and stretch your legs, and perhaps meet someone who remembers when freshly caught fish sold in the village for 25 cents a pound (1939), or who recalls the late 1920s, when these steps served as the "pit" for wagered weekend fights between captive rattlesnakes and king snakes.

Everglades City was the base of operations for the building of the Tamiami Trail in the 1920s, but once the road was completed, it went back to being a small commercial fishing community. The population is about 700, which temporarily swells to 11,000 in February during the annual seafood festival. The village is known for a signature seafood, stone crab claws, and for fishing and birding. Owls, pileated woodpeckers, kingfishers, osprey, pelicans, and great white herons are visible as you stroll on village streets. You can see more once you get out onto the Barron River or other area waterways.

Everglades National Park was dedicated here in Everglades City in 1947 by President Harry Truman, who said, "Here are no lofty peaks seeking the sky, no mighty glaciers or rushing streams. Here is land, tranquil in its beauty, serving not as the source of water but as the last receiver of it."

Returning to the traffic circle, you can explore the village by taking Broadway West. Follow the signs about three blocks to the Everglades Rod and Gun Club, once frequented by industrialists and such politicians as Truman and Dwight Eisenhower, or explore any side street, such as Copeland North, which intersects with Camellia Street at the historic Ivy House. In season, from November through April, the Ivy House operates as a ten-room inn and a base for bike and canoe rentals and guided nature trips.

To continue the drive, take Copeland South from the traffic circle to follow SR 29 south, marked with a sign for Everglades National Park. Travel about half a mile to the Everglades National Park Gulf Coast Visitor Center, on the right (west) side of SR 29. It is a waterfront boat basin and marina at the edge of Everglades City and Chokoloskee Bay, with restrooms, a park concessionaire's ticket window, and a gift shop. The second floor offers interpretive exhibits about park wildlife and an informative video. Ask the park rangers at the desk about wildlife sightings of otter, manatee, alligator, manta rays, whales, and other species, and also for backcountry trip advice, fishing tips, and park maps. Ranger-led activities include an occasional guided moonrise canoe tour of the Ten Thousand Islands to observe flocks of birds such as white ibis heading for their roosts. Other events include evening ranger talks in Everglades City, and morning and midday river and canoe explorations.

Ospreys, the "saltwater eagles," fledge young from large nests like this one in an Everglades mangrove.

Boat access is the key to beginning to understand this region. There aren't any footpaths, trails, or boardwalks at this unit's access. Ranger-led events, privately guided trips with local wildlife experts, and the park's excursion boat tours that cast off from the visitor center boat basin offer a chance to visit the Ten Thousand Islands region. There is no vehicle access into this unit of the Everglades. This scenic drive, which continues onto Chokoloskee Island, is the closest you can get by driving.

This is the starting point for the canoe trip on the park's Wilderness Waterway, a 100- to 120-mile trail that eventually winds its way to Flamingo on Florida Bay. Backcountry registration and extensive planning are required. Shorter canoe trips, such as an 8-mile trip on nearby Turner River, with routes recommended by rangers, are better for beginners. The Turner River trip starts at a put-in on the Tamiami Trail, where the road bridges the river near Ochopee, a recommended side trip to this drive. The Turner River canoe trail ends downriver where the river empties into Chokoloskee Bay near Chokoloskee Island. NOTE: Canoeists should expect high winds out on the open bay.

Across SR 29 from the park visitor center, an observation tower offers a stunning view of Chokoloskee Bay with the opportunity to see osprey, federally listed threatened bald eagle, and hosts of wading birds feeding in the water. At low tide the oyster bars are exposed. Next to the tower, canoe and kayak rentals and tours are offered from November through April by world-class canoe and kayak champions. NOTE: Although airboats and swamp buggies are available along the Tamiami Trail, these noisy, invasive vehicles aren't allowed in any unit of the national park, except as needed by rangers and scientists. Canoes, kayaks, and sailboats are less intrusive watercraft; motorized skiffs and pontoons are next best. You may want to rent a bicycle here and pedal the 3.4 miles to Chokoloskee Island.

To continue this drive, either on foot, by bicycle, or by car, head south on SR 29, which leaves the mainland here and becomes a curving, mangrove-bordered causeway and bridge hugging the edge of Chokoloskee Bay. The route was built in wetlands from Everglades City to Chokoloskee Island in 1954-1955, replacing a 20-minute motorboat, or longer rowboat, trip. Stiff winds whip up waves that slap against the low-lying causeway. The bridge and causeway link mainland Florida to an ancient site. The aboriginal Indians who lived in villages here about 3,000 years ago developed a complex cultural life, digging canals, fishing, collecting shellfish, hunting, and building mounds. They had leisure time in which to pursue art in the form of carved, painted wooden sculptures, and to make music. More recently, the Calusa Indians (the Gulf Coast people who met Ponce de León's ships in 1513) inhabited this area and added to Chokoloskee Island, piling up shucked shells and other discards year after year until a giant kitchen midden, or garbage heap, was created. (Some of the shells of oysters, clams, and scallops remain, and you can see the heaps as you meander on the privately owned island's narrow streets.) Later, 19th-century pioneers used the native-built island as a commercial terminus for farm products, such as sweet potatoes and sugar cane syrup; as a security lookout; and as a homesite.

As the causeway passes onto the island, continue straight about half a mile to the stop sign. Leaving SR 29, turn right (west) on Chokoloskee Drive, go less than a quarter of a mile, then take a left at the next stop sign onto Mamie Street. Follow signs along this winding street about a quarter of a mile to a dead end under palm trees in the sandy, waterfront parking area of Smallwood Store and Ole Indian Trading Post Museum (closed Wednesday and Thursday). The store was built by Captain Ted Smallwood and his wife in 1917, and was put up on pilings in 1924 when storm waters flooded it to a depth of four feet. In the early days, it served Seminole Indians, who came to the store landing by poling hand-hewn canoes, and also settlers, arriving by sailboat, rowboat, or motorized skiff. It was run as a store by the family until 1982. Today parts of the trading post appear similar to years ago, with shelves of supplies still intact. Using artifacts from the island's varied inhabitants, the museum relates stories of the rugged Everglades life

Boat tours in the Ten Thousand Islands introduce a watery region of manta rays and porpoises.

that challenged men, women, and children. The trading post is listed on the National Register of Historic Places.

If Chokoloskee Island piques your interest, you may want to read Peter Matthiessen's best-selling meditation on the region, *Killing Mr. Watson,* the story of the death of local legend E. J. Watson, who cultivated sugar cane, potatoes, and tomatoes at a nearby island. Watson, who was linked to seven murders in Western states, was murdered by frightened local residents outside this trading post after the bodies of three of his farmhands were found in the muck of a mangrove forest.

Everglades area side trips

At the Carnestown junction (the beginning of this drive), a right turn on US 41 takes you about 5 miles east of SR 29 to the Ochopee Post Office, a wooden tomato farm shed that is said to be the smallest post office in the United States, a bit of roadside Americana.

Fifteen miles east of the post office on US 41, the Big Cypress National Preserve Oasis Visitor Center offers an excellent video introduction to the wide sawgrass and palm hammocks of the preserve. The center sponsors ranger-led events in the fall and winter months, such as talks on alligator lore, Florida panther recovery efforts, the area's Native Americans, and the history of the Tamiami Trail. Rangers also guide bicycle trips, birding walks, and popular swamp slogs in ankle-deep water. The preserve is a destination of orchid enthusiasts during the summer season. Florida's section of the National Scenic Trail begins here. Hunting is allowed on portions of the preserve, so if you arrive during hunting season for deer and wild hogs, October through December, be aware of hunters when walking on preserve trails.

About half a mile east of the Oasis Visitor Center, on the south side of the Tamiami Trail, the Big Cypress Gallery offers a lush nature walk in the former gardens of an attraction called Orchid Isle, with outstanding black-and-white photography and artwork of the region's special habitats.

Back at the Carnestown junction, if you take a left, travel about 7 miles on US 41 and look on the north side of the road for a sign that indicates the entrance to Fakahatchee Strand State Preserve. Here begins a 1.2-mile walk, 860 feet on land and 2,300 over water, known as the Big Cypress Bend Boardwalk. It ends in a dense swamp that resembles a tropical jungle. Look for feathery air plants, orchids, strangler fig trees, climbing vines, cruising alligators, otter, swimming snakes, tropical spiders, and the signature tree, the bald cypress. Bald cypress is an impressive native species that can grow 120 feet tall, with reddish brown feathery leaves in the fall and new lime green ones in the spring. It is known for its stumps of wood, called knees, that surface in the water alongside it.

Farther west on the Tamiami Trail, directly on US 41, Collier-Seminole State Park offers a recreated Seminole War blockhouse, an interpretive center, a preserve of native royal palms, a canoe trail through mangrove forest, a section of the Florida National Scenic Trail, and one of the dredges used to make the Tamiami Trail.

The Tamiami Trail story is also interpreted at the excellent Collier County Museum, a 5-acre historical park with orchid house, at the Collier County Government Center, directly on the Tamiami Trail in Naples, about 17 miles west of Collier-Seminole State Park.

27

The Shell Islands of Stilt Birds and Tarpon

Punta Rassa to Captiva Island

General description: A 32-mile round-trip drive through the mangrove forest islands of Sanibel and Captiva in the Gulf of Mexico to a national refuge world-famous for sheltering large wading birds.

Special features: Sanibel Island Causeway Park, Sanibel Island lighthouse and pier, Sanibel Historical Village and Museum, Sanibel-Captiva Nature Conservation Foundation, J. N. "Ding" Darling National Wildlife Refuge, Bailey-Matthews Shell Museum, birding, beachcombing, hiking, biking, fishing, crabbing, canoeing, swimming, snorkeling.

Location: Southwest Florida.

Drive route numbers: SR 867/McGregor Boulevard, Sanibel Island Bridge and Causeway, Periwinkle Way, Palm Ridge Road, Sanibel-Captiva Road, Wildlife Drive, Captiva Drive.

Travel season: Open all year. November to April is recommended, but this is the high season, with heavy traffic in areas. Tarpon season is from about May through September. Sea turtles nest in spring and early summer, with hatching late summer and early fall.

Camping: There is one private campground on Sanibel Island. Public primitive camping, at Cayo Costa Island State Park, is accessible by boat from Sanibel-Captiva and Lee County mainland marinas and boat launches. On the mainland, there is camping at Koreshan State Historic Site at Bonita Springs, and at private campgrounds at Fort Myers Beach and vicinity.

Services: Services are available at Sanibel Island, Punta Rassa, and Fort Myers Beach; there are some services on Captiva.

Nearby points of interest: Cabbage Key; Useppa Island; Avenue of Palms/McGregor Boulevard; Fort Myers Historical Museum; Burroughs Home; Edison Winter Home; Ford Winter Home; Calusa Nature Center and Planetarium; Manatee Park; Six Mile Cypress Slough Preserve; Imaginarium; Seminole Gulf Railway; Fort Myers Beach public fishing pier at Lynn Hall Memorial Park; Carl E. Johnson Park and Lover's Key State Recreation Area; Mound Key State Park (by boat only) in Estero Bay; Ostego Bay Foundation Marine Science Center at Fort Myers Beach; Koreshan State Historic Site and Audubon Society Corkscrew Swamp Sanctuary at Bonita Springs; Children's Science Center; Cape Coral; Museum of the Islands at Pine Island.

Time zone: Eastern.

Drive 27: The Shell Islands of Stilt Birds and Tarpon
Punta Rassa to Captiva Island

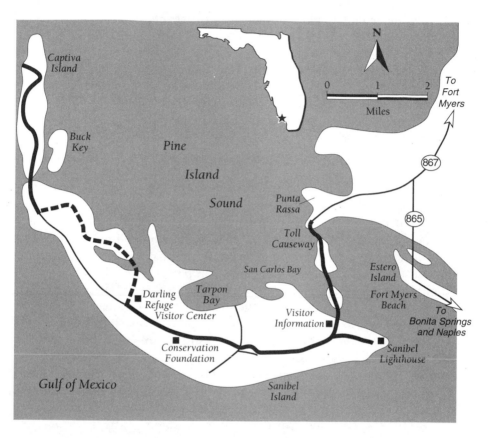

 The drive

This sea-level drive takes you over aqua waters and through two lush subtropical islands. White sand beaches on the gulf side of the islands are shaded by fringed palm trees and exotic pines. Native sea grape bushes, sea oat spikes, and prickly pear cactus anchor the sand. Mangrove forests along the opposite bay shore shelter wading birds and invite canoe travel.

Most of the drive is paved, but expect shell and sand roads in the refuge and at beach parking areas. Heed warning signs and don't drive on beaches. The Captiva part of the ride is narrow, twisting, and not recommended for recreational vehicles. Parking is tight for large RVs at some places on Sanibel. Expect temporary flooding after heavy summer rains. Watch for alligators basking on narrow road shoulders or crossing the road in wetlands.

Begin the drive at Punta Rassa, a flat point of land where the Caloosahatchee River meets San Carlos Bay. About 15 miles southeast of Fort Myers, Punta Rassa is a former Calusa Indian village and Cuban fishery site. Still later, southern Florida's cowpokes drove scrawny, open-range cattle here and shipped them to Key West and Cuba in the mid-1800s. The tired cow hunters slept and ate here in wooden barracks before returning to their wild interior range. Punta Rassa became a tarpon-fishing mecca in 1885, when Henry Ford and Thomas Edison had winter homes here. Today the historic point has a resort and popular public boat launch.

After paying the toll to enter the Punta Rassa bridge and causeway, the drive sweeps across San Carlos Bay, named for the mighty Calusa Indian king. NOTE: During the peak season, January through March, the bridge and causeway, which are the only road to the islands, can have very heavy traffic, and long waits should be expected. A weekday visit, or a visit in late October, early November, or late April, will not be as crowded. You can also consider booking a room off the island. For example, at nearby Estero Island at Fort Myers Beach, there are cottages and condominiums for rent, a beautiful beach, and unique preserves; you can visit a nonprofit aquarium and see commercial fishing docks with shrimp boats and other fishing rigs. From Estero Island, rise at dawn and motor across the quiet Sanibel bridge and causeway to spend the day on the shell islands. A summer visit is likely to be less crowded, too, but you'll have to contend with biting bugs, temperatures of 95 degrees and higher, humidity, intense lightning, and monsoonlike afternoon storms. Early summer attracts anglers to fish for giant silver tarpon flashing in the nearby Boca Grande Pass "Tarpon Bowl."

Parks along the causeway provide fishing spots, picnicking, and a first look at the area's extensive wildlife. Porpoise churn the water here, eating schools of fish, especially near the swift dark waters of the first causeway bridge by Punta Rassa.

In about 2.5 miles you enter Sanibel Island. It's a good idea to stop at the wayside information center immediately on the right, and mandatory if you don't have reservations. Many people try to make the islands a day trip on a drive from the Everglades north to Tampa, but that is a mistake. You'll need at least an overnight stay in the area to explore the wildlife habitats. This also allows time to try the local seafood, such as fresh gulf peel-and-eat shrimp, smoked mullet dipped in lemon butter, and mangrove snapper, all rich regional delicacies. A few hundred feet past the information center, along Causeway Boulevard, is the intersection with Periwinkle Way. The drive turns left here and ends in about a mile, at the Sanibel lighthouse. Its park, beaches, and pier at Point Ybel offer a scenic waterfront view. The

The Sanibel lighthouse in the Shell Islands.

island's first known European visitor anchored off this point for nine days in 1513. Ponce de León's men were attacked by King Carlos's men in canoes and the explorer withdrew to Puerto Rico, calling the island *Matanzas*, meaning "massacre."

Trace your path back to the causeway intersection and cross it to continue on Periwinkle Way. Soon the drive is under a tunnel of arching Australian pine tree branches. In about 2 miles jog right onto Palm Ridge Road, which curves through a small business district, to connect with Sanibel-Captiva Road at a stop sign. Continue straight ahead on Sanibel-Captiva Road. In 1 mile look for the left turn from Sanibel-Captiva Road into the outstanding Sanibel-Captiva Nature Conservation Foundation. It has 4.5 miles of lush trails and 1,100 interior acres including portions of the Sanibel River, guided tours, an observation tower, and interpretive exhibits. It is a peaceful and less-known preserve than the nearby J. N. "Ding" Darling National Wildlife Refuge.

Returning to Sanibel-Captiva Road, turn left. In another mile on the right, look for the well-marked entrance to the main unit of J. N. "Ding" Darling National Wildlife Refuge. This is access for the visitor center and the refuge's 5-mile Wildlife Drive. Wildlife Drive is closed Fridays, but is open sunrise to sunset every other day. The visitor center interprets the story of the refuge's 5,000 acres that fan out on the islands. Study the maps there, select some trails to hike, and consider renting canoes for the two outstanding waterway trails. The best time to see park wildlife is in the early morning and late afternoon, and at low tides. Among those feeding here are 290 species of birds, 50 species of reptiles and amphibians, and 30 small mammal species that migrate through or live here. From the visitor center, follow the signs to the Wildlife Drive entrance gate, just beyond the parking lot on the right. Pick up an illustrated Wildlife Drive interpretive booklet at the self-service donation box. Wildlife Drive separates fresh- and saltwater ponds fringed with mangrove trees. Plan to drive slowly and stop at the frequent pullouts to get better views. The observation tower, boardwalk, and side trails, such as the 2-mile Indigo Trail at the entrance, increase your chances of seeing and hearing wildlife in their natural homes. Wading flocks of roseate spoonbill, white ibis, and wood stork feed in the mud flats, along with hosts of herons and egrets. Dive-feeders, such as brown pelicans and black anhingas, are equally mesmerizing.

Among birds of prey that fly alone here look for osprey and the red-shouldered hawk. In the spring painted buntings and red-eyed vireos are among the migratory songbirds feeding here. Horseshoe crabs and blue crabs are common in the shallows. Almost every visitor spots at least one alligator, usually on the left side of the drive. Alligators are valued by wading birds, which roost above them in mangrove trees to keep safe from predators

Tropical roseate spoonbills find shelter at J. N. "Ding" Darling National Wildlife Refuge.

such as raccoons and snakes. Three separate species of mangrove trees grow on the islands, including the red mangrove, with its exposed, twisting roots plunging into shallow water. The roots trap sand, leaves, and sediment to build the islands you see along Florida's subtropical coasts. Look for small oysters growing on these roots.

Upland near the end of Wildlife Drive, the 0.33-mile Shell Mound Trail in mangrove forest provides a quiet visit to an ancient Native American mound. Native Calusa Indians, who predated the contemporary Seminoles and Miccosukees, carved out towns and canals and built mounds here. About 5,000 to 10,000 natives lived in the southwest Florida region in a political and ceremonial temple mound civilization more than 2,000 years ago. At the end of the refuge drive, follow signs back to Sanibel-Captiva Road. A right (west) turn on Sanibel-Captiva Road continues the Shell Islands drive.

In about 1.5 miles enter the historic Wulfert community at the end of Sanibel, host to restaurants and cottages perched on stilts. If you can find parking (easier before 9 A.M.) visit the beaches on each side of Blind Pass to hunt shell skeletons. Shells can be found on the gulf side beaches, especially after storms and in winter. Some of the 200 species of shells that can be found here wash up only in certain seasons. Experts say this is the world's third best beachcombing region. A shell fair the first weekend in March attracts thousands. The Bailey Mathews Shell Museum on Sanibel is said to be the best in the world devoted just to shells. Shells can be found at almost any beach access here, but some of the best beachcombing is at more remote nearby gulf beaches, reached only by boat. Consider hiring a seasoned beach-combing guide at a marina. WARNING: Shell collecting is prohibited on the bay side of the islands. No shells can be taken in any part of the national whildlife refuge. No live shells can be taken on Sanibel, Cayo Costa, or state-owned portions of North Captiva Island. On Captiva, the legal limit on live specimens is two per person (including sand dollars, sea urchins, and sea stars), but you may not want to take any live ones at all. As local guide Captain Mike Fuery says in his excellent *Florida Shelling Guide:* "Those of us who truly love shelling can't tolerate the killing of live shells."

If you don't find shells, the compensation is still great. Focus on watching abundant wildlife, and soaking up the waterfront views and gentle sea air. At night walk barefoot along the warm gulf sand to look for scurrying crabs at the shoreline and surprise flashes of neon green in the dark water, the phosphorescence of photoplankton.

Continuing on Sanibel-Captiva Road, cross tiny Blind Pass Bridge to enter exclusive Captiva Island, where Charles and Anne Lindbergh once vacationed. The Buck Key tract of the Darling refuge, featuring the canoe trail mentioned above, is just off Captiva on the bay side, reached by canoe or boat. After a twisting 3 miles, sometimes at the edge of the gulf, the narrow drive dead-ends at a tiny beach parking lot. The beach is a lovely perch to watch for porpoise and pelicans feeding in the gulf waters.

To finish the drive trace your route back. With flocks of island-bound tourists, limited parking, stunning gulf and bay vistas, and twisting narrow roads, patience is a requirement. But if you rise early or venture out late, and get away from the main road, you will be captivated by this pair of islands, and the lure of the midnight, phosphorescent sea.

Appendix A
Sources of More Information

Drive 1

Blackwater River State Forest
11650 Munson Highway
Milton, FL 32570
(850) 957-4201

Blackwater River State Park
Route 1, Box 57-C
Holt, FL 32564
(850) 623-2363
www.dep.state.fl.us/parks

Blackwater Canoe Rental and Outpost
1-800-967-6789
(850) 623-0235
(850) 623-3973 fax

Action Canoe Rental
P.O. Box 283
Baker, FL 32531
(850) 537-2997

Drive 2

Grayton Beach State Recreation Area
Route 2, Box 6600
Santa Rosa Island, FL 32459
(850) 231-4210
www.dep.state.fl.us/parks

Seaside
P.O. Box 4730
Seaside, FL 32459
(850) 277-8696

Eden State Gardens/Wesley Mansion
P.O. Box 26
Point Washington, FL 32454
(850) 231-4214
www.dep.state.fl.us/parks

South Walton County Tourism
P.O. Box 1248
Santa Rosa Island, FL 32459
(850) 267-1216
(800) 822-6877
www.beaches of south walton.com

The Welcome Center
66 East Nelson Avenue
DeFuniak Springs, FL 32433
(850) 892-5583

Drive 3

Apalachicola Chamber of Commerce
99 Market Street
Apalachicola, FL 32320
(850) 653-9419
(850) 653-8219 fax
www.homtown.com/apalachicola

Apalachicola Maritime Museum
The Governor Stone
P.O. Box 625
Apalachicola, FL 32329-0625
(850) 653-8700

Julian G. Bruce St. George Island State
    Park
HCR Box 62
St. George Island, FL 32328
(850) 927-2111
www.dep.state.fl.us/parks

St. Vincent National Wildlife Refuge
P.O. Box 447
Apalachicola, FL 32329
(850) 653-8808

Apalachicola National Estuarine
    Research Reserve
261 Seventh Street
Apalachicola, FL 32320
(850) 653-8063, (850) 653-2297 fax

T. H. Stone Memorial St. Joseph
  Peninsula State Park
Star Route 1, Box 200
Port St. Joe, FL 32456
(850) 227-1327
www.dep.state.fl.us/parks

Drive 4

Apalachicola National Forest
Apalachicola Ranger District
P.O. Box 579, Highway 20
Bristol, FL 32321
(850) 643-2282

Fort Gadsden Historic Site
P.O. Box 157
Sumatra, FL 32335
(850) 670-8988

Torreya State Park
Route 2, Box 70
Bristol, FL 32321
(850) 643-2674
www.dep.state.fl.us/parks

Apalachicola Bluffs and Ravines Preserve
The Nature Conservancy
P.O. Box 393
Bristol, FL 32321
(850) 643-2756

Carrabelle Area
  Chamber of Commerce
P.O. Drawer DD
Carrabelle, FL 32322
(850) 697-2585

Drive 5

Edward Ball Wakulla Springs State Park
1 Spring Drive
Wakulla Springs, FL 32305
(850) 224-5950
www.dep.state.fl.us/parks

Tallahassee–St. Marks Historic Railroad
  State Trail
102 De Soto Park Drive
Tallahassee, FL 32301
(850) 922-6007

St. Marks National Wildlife Refuge
P.O. Box 68
St. Marks, FL 32355
(850) 925-6121
www.fws.gov/~r4eao

San Marcos de Apalache State Historic
  Site and Natural Bridge State Historic
  Site
P.O. Box 27
St. Marks, FL 32355
(850) 925-6216
www.dep.state.fl.us/parks

Gulf Specimen Marine Laboratories
  Aquarium
P.O. Box 237
300 Clark Drive
Panacea, FL 32346
(850) 984-5297

Wakulla County Tourism
P.O. Box 598
Crawfordville, FL 32326-0598
(888) 925-8552
(850) 926-1848

Drive 6

Havana
Gadsden County Chamber of
  Commerce
P.O. Box 609
Quincy, FL 32353
(850) 627-9231 or (800) 267-3182
(850) 875-3299 fax

Birdsong Nature Center
2106 Meridian Road
Thomasville, GA 31792
(912) 377-4408

Susina Plantation
Route 3, Box 1010
Thomasville, GA 31792
(912) 377-9644

Pebble Hill
P.O. Box 830
Thomasville, GA 31799
www.web-vista.com/tlh/sghtsee/pebble/index.html

Destination Thomasville
 Welcome Center
135 North Broad Street
Thomasville, GA 31792
(800) 704-2350
(912) 225-3919
www.thomasvillega.com

Alfred B. Maclay State Gardens
3540 Thomasville Road
Tallahassee, FL 32308
(850) 487-4556
www.dep.state.fl.us/parks

Tallahassee Area Chamber of Commerce
P.O. Box 1639
Tallahassee, FL 32302
(850) 224-8116 or (800) 628-2866
(850) 561-3860 fax
www.co.leon.fl.us/cvb/homepage.html

Drive 7

Pisgah United Methodist Church
Pisgah Church Road
Tallahassee, FL 32308
(850) 668-4777

Bradley's Country Store
Route 3, Box 610
Centerville Road
Tallahassee, FL 32308
(850) 893-1647
(850) 893-4742

Reeve's Fish Camp
Reeves Landing Road
Lake Miccosukee
Tallahassee, FL 32308
(850) 893-9940

Miccosukee Boat Landing
Reeves Landing Road
Tallahassee, FL 32308
(850) 893-8513

Red Hills Conservation Association
State Road 12
Tallahassee, FL 32312
(850) 893-4153

Monticello-Jefferson County
 Chamber of Commerce
420 West Washington Street
Monticello, FL 32344
(850) 997-5552
(850) 997-1020 fax

Drive 8

Taylor County Coastal Association
P.O. Box 789
Steinhatchee, FL 32359
(352) 498-3513

Perry-Taylor County Chamber of
 Commerce
428 North Jefferson Street
P.O. Box 892
Perry, FL 32348
1-800-257-8881
(850) 584-8030 fax
e-mail: tacocmbr@perry.gulfnet.com
www.askam.com/chamber

Hagen's Cove
Big Bend Wildlife Management Area
Florida Game and Fresh Water Fish
 Commission
620 South Meridian Street
Tallahassee, FL 32399-1600
(850) 488-4676
www.state.fl.us/gfc

Steinhatchee Landing
P.O. Box 789
Steinhatchee, FL 32359
(800) 584-1709
(352) 498-2346 fax

Forest Capital State Museum and Cracker
    Homestead
204 Forest Park Drive
Perry, FL 32347
(850) 584-3227
www.dep.state.fl.us/parks

Drive 9

Suwannee County Tourist Development
    Council
P.O. Drawer C
Live Oak, FL 32060
(904) 362-3071

Hamilton County Chamber of Commerce
P.O. Box 312
Jasper, FL 32052
(904) 792-1300

Stephen Foster State Folk Culture Center
P.O Drawer G
White Springs, FL 32096
(904) 397-2733
www.dep.state.fl.us/parks

Suwannee River State Park
Route 8, Box 297
Live Oak, FL 32060
(904) 362-2746
www.dep.state.fl.us/parks

Original Florida
P.O. Box 1300
Lake City, FL 32056-1300
(904) 758-1555
(904) 758-1311 fax

Drive 10

Osceola National Forest
U.S. Highway 90
P.O. Box 70
Olustee, FL 32072
(904) 752-2577

Olustee Battlefield State Historic Site
P.O. Box 2
Olustee, FL 32072
(904) 752-3866
www.dep.state.fl.us/parks

Blue/Grey Army
P.O. Box 2224
Lake City, FL 32056
(904) 757-1368

Drive 11

Kingsley Plantation
National Park Service
11676 Palmetto Avenue
Jacksonville, FL 32226
(904) 251-3537
www.nps.gov/crweb1/nr/21.htm

Talbot Islands Geopark
11435 Fort George Road East
Fort George, FL 32226
(904) 251-2320
www.dep.state.fl.us/parks

Huguenot Memorial Park
10980 Heckscher Drive
Jacksonville, FL 32226
(904) 251-3335

Sea Horse Stables
(904) 261-4878

Amelia Island Tourist Development
    Council
102 Centre Street
Fernandina Beach, FL 32034
(904) 277-0717
(800) 226-3542

The Fairbanks House
227 South Seventh Street
Amelia Island, FL 32034
(904) 277-0500
(800) 261-4838

1857 Florida House Inn
22 South Third Street
Amelia Island, FL 32034
(904) 261-3300
(800) 258-3301

Timucuan Ecological and Historic
  Preserve
13165 Mount Pleasant Road
Jacksonville, FL 32225
(904) 221-5568
www.nps.gov/timu

Fort Caroline National Memorial
12713 Fort Caroline Road
Jacksonville, FL 32225
(904) 641-7111

Jacksonville Visitors Bureau
3 Independent Drive
Jacksonville, FL 32202
(904) 798-9148
(800) 733-2668

Drive 12

Guana River State Park
2690 South Ponte Vedra Boulevard
Ponte Vedra Beach, FL 32082
(904) 825-5071
www.dep.state.fl.us/parks

Castillo de San Marcos National
  Monument
1 Castillo Drive
St. Augustine, FL 32084
(904) 829-6506

St. Augustine Tourism
1 Riberia Street
St. Augustine, FL 32084
(904) 829-5681
(800) 653-2489
www.oldcity.com/vcb

Anastasia State Recreation Area
1340-C A1A South
St. Augustine, FL 32084
(904) 461-2033

Lighthouse Museum of St. Augustine
81 Lighthouse Avenue
St. Augustine, FL 32084
(904) 829-0745

Faver-Dykes State Park
1000 Faver Dykes Road
St. Augustine, FL 32086
(904) 794-0997
www.dep.state.fl.us/parks

Fort Matanzas National Monument
(904) 471-0116

Drive 13

Devil's Millhopper State Geological Site
  and San Felasco Hammock State
  Preserve
4732 Millhopper Road
Gainesville, FL 32606
(352) 336-2008
www.dep.state.fl.us/parks

Gainesville Area Chamber of Commerce
P.O. Box 1187
Gainesville, FL 32602-1187
(352) 334-7100
(352) 334-7141 fax
www.afn.org/~acvacb

City of Alachua Chamber of Commerce
P.O. Box 1239
Alachua, FL 32615
(352) 462-3333

High Springs Area Chamber of
  Commerce
P.O. Box 863
High Springs, FL 32643
(352) 454-3120

Alachua County Visitors Bureau
30 East University Avenue
Gainesville, FL 32601
(352) 374-5231
www.afn.org/~acvacb

O'Leno State Park
Route 2, Box 1010
High Springs, FL 32643
(342) 454-1853
www.dep.state.fl.us/parks

Camp Kulaqua
Route 2, Box 244K
High Springs, FL 32643
(342) 454-1351

Ichetucknee Springs State Park
Route 2, Box 103
Fort White, FL 32038
(342) 497-2511
www.dep.state.fl.us/parks

Drive 14

Marjorie Kinnan Rawlings State
   Historic Site
Route 3, Box 92
Hawthorne, FL 32640
(352) 466-3672
www.dep.state.fl.us/parks

Paynes Prairie State Preserve
Route 2, Box 41
Micanopy, FL 32667
(352) 466-3397
www.dep.state.fl.us/parks

Gainesville Area Chamber of Commerce
P.O. Box 1187
Gainesville, FL 32602-1187
(352) 334-7100
(352) 334-7141 fax
www.afn.org/~acvacb

Alachua County Visitors Bureau
30 East University Avenue
Gainesville, FL 32601
(352) 374-5231
www.afn.org/~acvacb

High Springs Area Chamber of
   Commerce
P.O. Box 863
High Springs, FL 32643
(352) 454-3120

Drive 15

Greater Cedar Key Chamber of
   Commerce
P.O. Box 610
Cedar Key, FL 32625
(352) 543-5600

Cedar Key State Museum
1710 Museum Drive
Cedar Key, FL 32625
(352) 543-5350
www.dep.state.fl.us/parks

Lower Suwannee National Wildlife
   Refuge
Cedar Key National Wildlife Refuge
16450 Northwest 31st Place
Route 1, Box 1193
Chiefland, FL 32626
(352) 493-0238
www.fws.gov/~r4eao/nwrswe.html

Shell Mound Park
(342) 543-6153

Manatee Springs State Park
Route 2, Box 617
Chiefland, FL 32626
(342) 493-6072
www.dep.state.fl.us/parks

Drive 16

Ocala National Forest
Pittman Visitor Center
45621 State Highway 19
Altoona, FL 32702
(352) 669-7495

Alexander Springs
(352) 669-3522

DeLand Area Chamber of Commerce
336 North Woodland Boulevard
DeLand, FL 32721
(904) 734-4331
(800) 749-4350

Ocala-Marion County Chamber of
Commerce
110 East Silver Springs Boulevard
Ocala, FL 34470
(352) 629-8051
(352) 629-7651 fax
www.ocalacc.com

Lake Woodruff National Wildlife Refuge
P.O. Box 488
DeLeon Springs, FL 32130
(904) 985-4673
www.fws.gov/~r4eao/nwrlwd.html

Fiddler's Green Ranch
P.O. Box 70
Altoona, FL 32702-0070
(800) 947-2624

Blue Spring State Park
2100 West French Avenue
Orange City, FL 32763
(904) 775-3663
www.dep.state.fl.us/parks

DeLeon Springs State Recreation Area
P.O. Box 1338
DeLeon Springs, FL 32130
(904) 985-4212
www.dep.state.fl.us/parks

Drive 17

Tomoka Basin Geopark
2009 North Beach Street
Ormond Beach, FL 32174
(904) 676-4050
Museum: (904) 676-4045
www.dep.state.fl.us/parks

Bulow Plantation Ruins State Historic
Site
P.O. Box 655
Bunnell, FL 32010
(904) 439-2219
www.dep.state.fl.us/parks

Gamble Rogers Memorial State
Recreation Area at Flagler Beach
3100 South A1A
Flagler Beach, FL 32136
(904) 439-2474
www.dep.state.fl.us/parks

Flagler Beach Chamber of Commerce
400 South Highway A1A
Flagler Beach, FL 32136
(904) 439-0995
(800) 881-1022

Ormond Beach Chamber of Commerce
165 West Granada Avenue
Ormond Beach, FL 32174
(904) 677-3454

Daytona Beach and Halifax Area
Chamber of Commerce
126 Orange Avenue, City Island
Daytona Beach, FL 32114
(904) 255-0981
(800) 854-1234
www.daytonabeach_tourism.com

Drive 18

Canaveral National Seashore
7611 South Atlantic Avenue
New Smyrna Beach, FL 32169
(904) 428-3384

Friends of Canaveral
P.O. Box 1526
New Smyrna Beach, FL 32170-1526

New Smyrna Beach Chamber of
Commerce
115 Canal Street
New Smyrna Beach, FL 32168
(904) 428-2449
(800) 541-9621

Drive 19

Canaveral National Seashore
2532 Garden Street
Titusville, FL 32796
(407) 267-1110

Merritt Island National Wildlife Refuge
P.O. Box 6504
Titusville, FL 32780
(407) 861-0667
www.fws.gov/~r4eao/nwrmrt.html

Titusville Area Chamber of Commerce
2000 South Washington Avenue
Titusville, FL 32780
(407) 267-3036

Florida Space Coast Tourism
8810 Astronaut Boulevard, Suite 201
Cape Canaveral, FL 32920
(800) 936-2326
www.space-coast.com/florida

NASA (recorded visitor and launch
    information)
(407) 867-4636
(800) KSC-INFO in Florida

Jetty Park Campground
400 East Jetty Road
Cape Canaveral, FL 32920
(407) 868-1108

Manatee Hammock Campground
7275 South U.S. Highway 1
Titusville, FL 32780
(407) 264-5083
(407) 264-6468 fax

Drive 20

Myakka River State Park
13207 State Road 72
Sarasota, FL 34241-9542
(941) 361-6511
www.dep.state.fl.us/parks

Crowley Museum and Nature Center
16405 Myakka Road
Sarasota, FL 34240
(941) 322-1000

Oscar Scherer State Park
1843 South Tamiami Trail
Osprey, FL 34229
(941) 483-5956
www.dep.state.fl.us/parks

Sarasota Convention and Visitors Bureau
655 North Tamiami Trail
Sarasota, FL 34236
(941) 957-1877
(800) 522-9799
www.cvb.sarasota.fl.us

Drive 21

Lake Kissimmee State Park
14248 Camp Mack Road
Lake Wales, FL 33853
(941) 696-1112
www.dep.state.fl.us/parks

Lake Wales Chamber of Commerce
340 West Central Avenue
Lake Wales, FL 33853
(941) 676-3445

Drive 22

Jonathan Dickinson State Park
16450 Southeast Federal Highway
Hobe Sound, FL 33455
(407) 546-2771
(800) 746-1466 (boat tours)
www.dep.state.fl.us/parks

Hobe Sound National Wildlife Refuge
P.O. Box 645
Hobe Sound, FL 33475-0645
(407) 546-6141
www.fws.gov/~r4eao/nwrhbs.html

Blowing Rocks Preserve
P.O. Box 3796
Tequesta, FL 33469
(407) 575-2297

Gilbert's Bar House of Refuge
301 Southeast MacArthur Boulevard
Hutchinson Island
Stuart, FL 34996
(407) 225-1875

Elliott Museum
825 Northeast Ocean Boulevard
Hutchinson Island
Stuart, FL 34996-1696
(407) 225-1961

Hobe Sound Chamber of Commerce
P.O. Box 1507
Hobe Sound, FL 33475
(407) 546-4724

Jupiter-Tequesta Chamber of Commerce
800 North U.S. Highway 1
Jupiter, FL 33477
(407) 746-7111
(407) 746-7715 fax

Florida Ranch Tours
P.O. Box 12912
Fort Pierce, FL 34979
(407) 467-2001
e-mail: Ranchtours@aol.com

Stuart/Martin County Tourism
1650 South Kanner Highway
Stuart, FL 34994
(800) 524-9705

Drive 23

Seminole Tribal Tourism
12261 Southwest 251st Street
Miami, FL 33032
(305) 257-3737
(800) 683-7800
(305) 257-2137 fax
www.gate.net/~semtribe.com
www.seminoletribe.com

Ah-Tah-Thi-Ki Museum
HC-61, Box 21-A
Clewiston, FL 33440
(954) 792-0745
e-mail: museum@semtribe.com
www.seminoletribe.com

Kissimmee Billie Swamp Safari
c/o 12261 Southwest 251 Street
Miami, FL 33032 (for reservations)
(305) 257-2134
(305) 257-2137 (fax)

Drive 24

Everglades National Park
40001 State Road 9336
Homestead, FL 33034-6733
(305) 242-7700
(800) 365-CAMP (for campground
    reservations)
www.nps.gov/ever

Everglades National Park-Flamingo
(305) 253-2241

Flamingo Lodge and Marina
Flamingo, FL 33030
(941) 695-3101
(800) 600-3813

Drive 25

Shark Valley/Everglades National Park
P.O. Box 279
Homestead, FL 33030
(305) 242-7700
www.nps.gov/ever

Shark Valley Tram Tours
P.O. Box 1729
Tamiami Station
Miami, FL 33144-1729
(305) 221-8455

Miccosukee Tribal Cultural Center
P.O. Box 440021
Miami, FL 33144
(305) 223-8380, ext. 346
www.miccosukee.com

Drive 26

Gulf Coast Visitor Center
Everglades National Park
P.O. Box 120
Everglades City, FL 33929
(941) 695-3311
(941) 695-2591
www.nps.gov/ever

Everglades National Park Boat Tours
P.O. Box 119
Everglades City, FL 33929
(800) 445-7724 in Florida
(800) 233-1821 out of state

Everglades Area Chamber of Commerce
32016 East Tamiami Trail
Everglades City, FL 33929
(941) 695-3941
(941) 695-3172 fax

Huron Kayak and Canoe
P.O. Box 367
Everglades City, FL 33929
(941) 695-3666

Ivy House Bed/Breakfast and Canoe
   Adventures
107 Camellia Street
Everglades City, FL 33929
(941) 695-3299
(941) 695-4155 fax

Visit Naples
1400 Gulf Shore Boulevard #218
Naples, FL 34102
(800) 605-7878
www.bestof.net/naples

Smallwood Store and
   Ole Indian Trading Post Museum
P.O. Box 367
Chokoloskee, FL 33925
(941) 695-2989
(941) 695-4454 fax

Big Cypress National Preserve
Box 110, Satinwood Drive
Ochopee, FL 33943
(941) 695-4111

Collier-Seminole State Park
Route 4, Box 848
Naples, FL 33961
(941) 394-0375
www.dep.state.fl.us/parks

Drive 27

Sanibel-Captiva Islands
Chamber of Commerce
1159 Causeway Road
Sanibel, FL 33957
(941) 472-1080
www.sanibel–captiva.org

J. N. "Ding" Darling National Wildlife
   Refuge
1 Wildlife Drive
Sanibel, FL 33957
(941) 472-1100
www.fws.gov/~r4eao/nwrjnd.html

Sanibel-Captiva Nature Conservation
   Foundation
3335 Sanibel-Captiva Road
Sanibel, FL 33957
(941) 472-2329

Capt. Mike Fuery's Shelling
www.sanibel–online.com/guides/fuery.htm

Lee County Visitor and Convention
   Bureau
2180 West First Street, Suite 100
Fort Myers, FL 33901
(800) 533-4753, ext. 499
www.leeislandcoast.com
e-mail: lic@cyberstreet.com

Fort Myers Beach Chamber of Commerce
17200 San Carlos Boulevard
Fort Myers Beach, FL 33931
(941) 454-7500
www.coconet.com/fmbeach/info.html

Appendix B
Agencies and Organizations
These are some public agencies and private organizations
interested in natural and historic Florida.

AGENCIES

Florida Parks/Information
3900 Commonwealth Boulevard
Mail Station 535
Tallahassee, FL 32399-3000
(850) 488-9872
www.dep.state.fl.us/parks

Florida Marine Patrol
Boating accident and manatee
    harassment reports (800) DIAL-FMP
(800) 324-5367
Boating Education
(800) 336-BOAT

Florida Game and Fresh Water Fish
    Commission
620 South Meridian Street
Tallahassee, FL 32399-1600
(850) 488-4676
www.state.fl.us/gfc

Wildlife Law Violations HOTLINE
Northwest (800) 324-1676
Northeast (800) 342-8105
Central (800) 342-9620
South (800) 282-8002
Everglades (800) 432-2046
Cellular *GFC (in most areas)

Fresh Water Fishing Information
Florida Game and Fresh Water Fish
    Commission
620 South Meridian Street
Tallahassee, FL 32399-1600
(850) 488-2975

Saltwater Fishing Information
Department of Environmental Protection
Fisheries Management
Mail Station 240
3900 Commonwealth Boulevard
Tallahassee, FL 32399-3000
(850) 488-7326

Florida Tourism Marketing Corp.
Visitor Information
P.O. Box 1100
Tallahassee, FL 32302-1100
(850) 488-5607
(888) 735-2872
www.flausa.com

State Forests in Florida
3125 Conner Boulevard
Tallahassee, FL 32399-1650
(850) 488-6612
(850) 488-6000

National Forests in Florida
325 John Knox Road, Suite F-100
Tallahassee, FL 32303
(850) 942-9300

National Park Service
Southeastern Region
75 Spring Street Southwest
Atlanta, GA 30303
(404) 331-4998

National Wildlife Refuges/Florida
U.S. Fish and Wildlife Service
75 Spring Street Southwest
Atlanta, GA 30303
(404) 331-0830

State Bicycle Program
Department of Transportation
605 Suwannee Street
Tallahassee, FL 32304
(850) 488-4640

Florida Historic Sites Information
Department of State
R.A. Gray Building
500 South Bronough Street
Tallahassee, FL 32301
(850) 487-2333
(800) 847-PAST
www.dos.state.fl.us

Florida Bureau of Archeological Research
R.A. Gray Building
500 South Bronough Street
Tallahassee, FL 32301
(850) 487-2299
(850) 488-3353 fax
www.dos.state.fl.us

ORGANIZATIONS

Florida Trail Association
P.O. Box 13708
Gainesville, FL 32604
(850) 378-8823
(800) 343-1882 in Florida

Florida Association of Canoe Liveries
Box 1764
Arcadia, FL 33821
(941) 494-1215

Florida Wildlife Federation
P.O. Box 6870
Tallahassee, FL 32314-6870
(850) 656-7113
www.arch.usf.edu/ficus/

Florida Audubon Society
460 Highway 4, Suite 200
Casselberry, FL 32707
(850) 260-8300

Florida Sierra Club
462 Fernwood Road
Key Biscayne, FL 33149

Florida Native Plant Society
P.O. Box 680008
Orlando, FL 32868

Florida Defenders of the Environment
2606 Northwest Sixth Street
Gainesville, FL 32609
(850) 372-6965

1000 Friends of Florida
P.O. Box 5948
Tallahassee, FL 32314-5948
(850) 222-6277
www.1000fos.usf.edu/

Florida Conservation Foundation
1191 Orange Avenue
Winter Park, FL 32789
(407) 644-5377

Save the Manatee Club
500 North Maitland Avenue
Maitland, FL 32751
(407) 539-0990
(800) 432-JOIN
www.objectlinks.com/manatee

Florida Historical Society
1320 Highland Avenue
Melbourne, FL 32935
(407) 259-0511
(407) 259-0649 fax

Florida Folklore Society
c/o David Reddy
Florida Humanities Council
1514¹/₂ East Eighth Avenue
Tampa, FL 33605-3708
(813) 272-3473

Florida Archaeological Society
P.O. Box A2255
Tampa, FL 33682

Friends of Florida State Parks/M5535
c/o 3900 Commonwealth Boulevard
Tallahassee, FL 32399

Florida Oceanographic Society
890 NE Ocean Boulevard
Stuart, FL 34996
(407) 225-0505

Additional Reading

Austin, Elizabeth S., ed. *Frank M. Chapman in Florida*. Gainesville, Fla.: University of Florida Press, 1967.

Bartram, William. *Travels Through North & South Carolina, Georgia, East & West Florida*. New York, N.Y.: Dover, 1928 (originally published 1791).

Bell, C. Ritchie, and Bryan J. Taylor. *Florida Wild Flowers and Roadside Plants*. Chapel Hill, N.C.: Laurel Hill Press, 1982.

Bickel, Karl A. *The Mangrove Coast*. New York, N.Y.: Coward-McCann, 1942.

Burgess, Robert F. *The Cave Divers*. New York, N.Y.: Dodd, Mead & Co., 1976.

Cerulean, Susan, and Ann Morrow. *Florida Wildlife Viewing Guide*. Helena, Mont.: Falcon Publishing, Inc., 1998.

Colburn, David R., and Jane L. Landers. *The African American Heritage of Florida*. Gainesville, Fla.: University Press of Florida, 1995.

Dickinson, Jonathan. *God's Protecting Providence*. New Haven, Conn.: Yale University Press, 1945 (originally published 1699).

Douglas, Marjory Stoneman. *The Everglades: River of Grass*. New York, N.Y.: Rinehart, 1947.

Douglas, Marjory Stoneman. *Florida: The Long Frontier*. New York, N.Y.: Harper & Row, 1967.

Downs, Dorothy. *Art of the Florida Seminole and Miccosukee Indians*. Gainesville, Fla.: University Press of Florida, 1995.

Fernald, Ed, and Elizabeth D. Purdum, eds. *Atlas of Florida*. Gainesville, Fla.: University Press of Florida, 1997.

Fuery, Mike. *Capt. Mike Fuery's New Florida Shelling Guide*. Sanibel Island, Fla.: Privately published, 1992.

Gannon, Michael. *The Cross in the Sand*. Gainesville, Fla.: University of Florida Press, 1965.

Gannon, Michael, ed. *The New History of Florida*. Gainesville, Fla.: University Press of Florida, 1996.

Godown, Marian, and Alberta Rawchuck. *Yesterday's Fort Myers*. Miami, Fla.: E. A. Seeman Publishing, 1975.

Grow, Gerald. *Florida Parks*. Tallahassee, Fla.: Longleaf Publications, 1997.

Housewright, Wiley L. *A History of Music and Dance in Florida 1565-1865*. Tuscaloosa, Ala.: University of Alabama Press, 1991.

Hurston, Zora Neale. *Dust Tracks on a Road*. Philadelphia, Penn.: J. B. Lippincott, 1942 (subsequently reprinted).

Jumper, Betty Mae. *Legends of the Seminoles*. Sarasota, Fla.: Pineapple Press, 1994.

Kendrick, Baynard. *Florida Trails to Turnpikes 1914-1964*. Gainesville, Fla.: University of Florida Press, 1964.

Lantz, Peggy Sias, and Wendy A. Hale. *The Young Naturalist's Guide to Florida*. Sarasota, Fla.: Pineapple Press, 1994.

McCarthy, Kevin M. *The Book Lover's Guide to Florida*. Sarasota, Fla.: Pineapple Press, 1992.

Nolan, David. *Fifty Feet in Paradise: The Booming of Florida*. New York, N.Y.: Harcourt Brace Jovanovich, 1984.

O'Keefe, Timothy. *The Hiker's Guide to Florida*. Helena, Mont: Falcon Press Publishing, 1993.

Proby, Kathryn Hall. *Audubon in Florida*. Coral Gables, Fla.: University of Miami Press, 1974.

Purdy, Barbara A. *Indian Art of Ancient Florida*. Gainesville, Fla.: University Press of Florida, 1996.

Rinhart, Floyd, and Marion Rinhart. *Victorian Florida*. Atlanta, Ga.: Peachtree Publishers, 1986.

Sanger, Marjory Bartlett. *Billy Bartram and His Green World*. New York, N.Y.: Farrar, Straus & Giroux, 1972.

Strickland, Alice. *The Valiant Pioneers*. Astor, Fla.: Privately published, 1963.

Wickman, Patricia R. *Osceola's Legacy*. Tuscaloosa, Ala.: University of Alabama Press, 1991.

Index

Dr. Julian G. Bruce St. George Island State Park 13, 14, 18–19
Douglas, Marjory Stoneman 164
Dudley Farm State Historic Site 79
Dummett Sugar Mill ruins 111

E

East Bay 18
East Slough 19
Eastpoint 18, 21, 22–23, 26
Eco Pond 160
Eden State Gardens 6, 12
Edison, Thomas 180
Edison Winter Home 178, 180
Edward Ball Wakulla Springs State Park 27, 28–31
Edward Ball Wakulla Springs State Park Lodge 28
Eisenhower, Dwight D. 39, 172
Eldora 115, 120
Elizabeth W. Kirby Interpretive Center 140
Elliott Museum 139, 145
Elliott, Sterling 145
Emerald Coast Parkway 8
Enchanted Forest Nature Sanctuary 122
Environmental Learning Center 139
Estero Bay 178
Estero Island 180
Euchee Indians 8
Everglades xii, xvi, 146, 150, 156. See also Everglades National Park
Everglades City 159, 169, 170–172, 174
Everglades National Park 151, 152–159, 159, 162, 163–168, 170–176, 173
  Chekika 152, 162
  Gulf Coast 169, 170–176
  Shark Valley 152, 162, 164, 166–168, 167
  Ten Thousand Islands xi, xii, 169, 170, 172–174, 175
Everglades Rod and Gun Club 172
Evinston 88–90

F

Fairbanks House 71
Fairchild Oak 108
Fairchild Tropical Garden 152
Fakahatchee Strand State Preserve 170, 176
Falling Waters State Recreation Area 2
Falmouth Springs 56
Fernandina 67
Fernandina Beach 66, 70, 71–72
Fernandina Beach Historic District 66, 71
Ficus Pond 157
Fiddler's Green Ranch 106
Flagler Beach 108, 110, 112–113, 114
Flagler Museum 139
Flamingo 151, 152, 155, 160, 174

Flamingo Lodge 151, 160
Flamingo Visitor Center 160
Flatwoods Horse Trail 101, 106
Flipper, Henry O. 41
Florida A&M Black Archives 37
Florida Bay 151, 155, 160
Florida Caverns State Park 2
Florida City 152
Florida Cracker Homestead Park 54–55
Florida Game and Fresh Water Fish Commission 45
Florida Marineland 114
Florida Museum of Natural History 79, 83
Florida National Scenic Trail 27, 56, 58, 60, 61, 63, 101, 105, 106, 108, 113, 134, 139, 142, 170, 176, 177
Florida Oceanographic Society Coastal Science Center 139
Florida Ranch Tours 139
Florida Sports Hall of Fame 61
Florida State University Fine Arts Gallery 37
Ford, Henry 180
Ford Winter Home 178, 180
Forest Capital State Museum 49, 54–55
Fort Caroline xv
Fort Caroline National Memorial 66, 72
Fort Clinch State Park 66, 71
Fort Frank Brooke 54
Fort Gadsden Historic Site 21, 24–25
Fort Gardiner 135
Fort George Island 67–69
Fort George Island State Cultural Site 66, 67
Fort George River 67, 69
Fort Matanzas National Monument 75
Fort Mose 74, 78
Fort Myers Beach 178, 180
Fort Myers Historical Museum 178
Fort Pierce 139
Fort Pierce Inlet State Recreation Area 139
Fort Scott, Georgia 25
Fort Walton Beach 6
Fort White 83
Fowler's Bluff 92, 99
Fred Bear Museum 79, 84
Frost, Robert xii, 88
Fruit and Spice Park 152, 162

G

Gadsden, Lieutenant James 23, 25
Gainesville 79, 80, 81, 83–84, 85, 88
Gainesville Historic District 79, 84
Gainesville-Hawthorne State Rail Trail 79, 85
Gainesville's Boulware Springs Park 85
Gamble Rogers Memorial State Recreation Area 108, 113
Gap Point 19
Gator Creek 123
George II (King of England) 71
Gibson Hotel 17
Gilbert's Bar House of Refuge 139, 140, 145

N

O

P

R

About the Author

Jan Godown's newspaper assignments have taken her by helicopter to count coastal northern Florida eagle nests and by horseback past hissing alligators to see bison near Gainesville. Her articles have appeared in major Florida newspapers and others, including the *Chicago Tribune* and *Philadelphia Inquirer,* the Seminole tribal newspaper, and Costa Rica's *Tico Times.* The Florida Outdoor Writers Association and the Florida Trust for Historic Preservation have honored her work. She is a former director of The Florida Historical Society and Florida Folklore Society and is an editorial page editor with the *Tallahassee Democrat.* She moved to Sarasota County, Florida, in 1966 from Hunterdon County, New Jersey.

FALCONGUIDES® are available for where-to-go hiking, mountain biking, rock climbing, walking, scenic driving, fishing, rockhounding, paddling, birding, wildlife viewing, and camping. We also have FalconGuides on essential outdoor skills and subjects and field identification. The following titles are currently available, but this list grows every year. For a free catalog with a complete list of titles, call FALCON toll-free at 1-800-582-2665.

SCENIC DRIVING GUIDES

Scenic Driving Alaska and the Yukon
Scenic Driving Arizona
Scenic Driving the Beartooth Highway
Scenic Driving California
Scenic Driving Colorado
Scenic Driving Florida
Scenic Driving Georgia
Scenic Driving Hawaii
Scenic Driving Idaho
Scenic Driving Michigan
Scenic Driving Minnesota
Scenic Driving Montana
Scenic Driving New England
Scenic Driving New Mexico
Scenic Driving North Carolina
Scenic Driving Oregon
Scenic Driving the Ozarks including the
   Ouchita Mountains
Scenic Driving Texas
Scenic Driving Utah
Scenic Driving Washington
Scenic Driving Wisconsin
Scenic Driving Wyoming
Back Country Byways
National Forest Scenic Byways
National Forest Scenic Byways II

HISTORIC TRAIL GUIDES

Traveling California's Gold Rush Country
Traveler's Guide to the Lewis & Clark Trail
Traveling the Oregon Trail
Traveler's Guide to the Pony Express Trail

WILDLIFE VIEWING GUIDES

Alaska Wildlife Viewing Guide
Arizona Wildlife Viewing Guide
California Wildlife Viewing Guide
Colorado Wildlife Viewing Guide
Florida Wildlife Viewing Guide
Idaho Wildlife Viewing Guide
Indiana Wildlife Vewing Guide
Iowa Wildlife Viewing Guide
Kentucky Wildlife Viewing Guide
Massachusetts Wildlife Viewing Guide
Montana Wildlife Viewing Guide
Nebraska Wildlife Viewing Guide
Nevada Wildlife Viewing Guide
New Hampshire Wildlife Viewing Guide
New Jersey Wildlife Viewing Guide
New Mexico Wildlife Viewing Guide
New York Wildlife Viewing Guide
North Carolina Wildlife Viewing Guide
North Dakota Wildlife Viewing Guide
Ohio Wildlife Viewing Guide
Oregon Wildlife Viewing Guide
Tennessee Wildlife Viewing Guide
Texas Wildlife Viewing Guide
Utah Wildlife Viewing Guide
Vermont Wildlife Viewing Guide
Virginia Wildlife Viewing Guide
Washington Wildlife Viewing Guide
West Virginia Wildlife Viewing Guide
Wisconsin Wildlife Viewing Guide

HIKING GUIDES

Hiking Alaska
Hiking Alberta
Hiking Arizona
Hiking Arizona's Cactus Country
Hiking the Beartooths
Hiking Big Bend National Park
Hiking Bob Marshall Country
Hiking California
Hiking California's Desert Parks
Hiking Carlsbad Caverns
 and Guadalupe Mtns. National Parks
Hiking Colorado
Hiking the Columbia River Gorge
Hiking Florida
Hiking Georgia
Hiking Glacier & Waterton Lakes National Parks
Hiking Grand Canyon National Park
Hiking Great Basin National Park
Hiking Hot Springs
 in the Pacific Northwest
Hiking Idaho
Hiking Maine
Hiking Michigan
Hiking Minnesota
Hiking Montana
Hiker's Guide to Nevada
Hiking New Hampshire
Hiking New Mexico
Hiking New York
Hiking North Cascades

Hiking North Carolina
Hiking Northern Arizona
Hiking Olympic National Park
Hiking Oregon
Hiking Oregon's Eagle Cap Wilderness
Hiking Oregon's Three Sisters Country
Hiking Pennsylvania
Hiking South Carolina
Hiking South Dakota's Black Hills Country
Hiking Southern New England
Hiking Tennessee
Hiking Texas
Hiking Utah
Hiking Utha's Summits
Hiking Vermont
Hiking Virginia
Hiking Washington
Hiking Wyoming
Hiking Wyoming's Wind River Range
Hiking Yellowstone National Park
Hiking Zion & Bryce Canyon National Parks
The Trail Guide to Bob Marshall Country

BEST EASY DAY HIKES

Beartooths
Canyonlands & Arches
Best Hikes on the Continental Divide
Glacier & Wateron Lakes
GLen Canyon
North Cascades
Yellowstone

FALCON®

■ *To order any of these books, check with your local bookseller*
or call FALCON ® at 1-800-582-2665.
Visit us on the world wide web at:
www.falconguide.com

get
FALCON GUIDED

MOUNTAIN BIKING GUIDES

Mountain Biking Arizona
Mountain Biking Colorado
Mountain Biking New Mexico
Mountain Biking New York
Mountain Biking Northern New England
Mountain Biking Southern New England
Mountain Biking Utah

Local Cycling Series

Fat Trax Bozeman
Fat Trax Colorado Springs
Mountain Biking Bend
Mountain Biking Boise
Mountain Biking Chequamegon
Mountain Biking Denver/Boulder
Mountain Biking Durango
Mountain Biking Helena
Mountain Biking Moab

FALCON®

■ *To order any of these books, check with your local bookseller*
*or call FALCON® at **1-800-582-2665**.*
Visit us on the world wide web at:
www.falconguide.com

get FALCON GUIDED

BIRDING GUIDES
Birding Arizona
Birding Minnesota
Birder's Guide to Montana
Birding Texas
Birding Utah

FIELD GUIDES
Bitterroot: Montana State Flower
Canyon Country Wildflowers
Great Lakes Berry Book
New England Berry Book
Plants of Arizona
Rare Plants of Colorado
Rocky Mountain Berry Book
Southern Rocky Mtn. Wildflowers
Tallgrass Prairie Wildflowers
Western Tree
Wildflowers of Southwestern Utah
Willow Bark and Rosehips

FISHING GUIDES
Fishing Alaska
Fishing the Beartooths
Fishing Florida
Fishing Maine
Fishing Michigan
Fishing Montana

PADDLING GUIDES
Floater's Guide to Colorado
Paddling Montana
Paddling Oregon

HOW-TO GUIDES
Bear Aware
Leave No Trace
Mountain Lion Alert
Wilderness First Aid
Wilderness Survival

ROCK CLIMBING GUIDES
Rock Climbing Colorado
Rock Climbing Montana
Rock Climbing New Mexico
 & Texas
Rock Climbing Utah

ROCKHOUNDING GUIDES
Rockhounding Arizona
Rockhound's Guide to California
Rockhound's Guide to Colorado
Rockhounding Montana
Rockhounding Nevada
Rockhound's Guide to New Mexico
Rockhounding Texas
Rockhounding Utah
Rockhounding Wyoming

WALKING
Walking Colorado Springs
Walking Portland
Walking St. Louis

MORE GUIDEBOOKS
Backcountry Horseman's
 Guide to Washington
Camping California's
 National Forests
Exploring Canyonlands &
 Arches National Parks
Exploring Mount Helena
Recreation Guide to WA
 National Forests
Touring California & Nevada
 Hot Springs
Trail Riding Western
 Montana
Wild Country Companion
Wild Montana
Wild Utah

FALCON®

■ *To order any of these books, check with your local bookseller*
*or call FALCON® at **1-800-582-2665**.*
Visit us on the world wide web at:
www.falconguide.com

WILDERNESS FIRST AID

By Dr. Gilbert Preston M.D.
Enjoy the outdoors and face the inherent risks with confidence. By reading this easy-to-follow first-aid text, all outdoor enthusiasts can pack a little extra peace of mind on their next adventure. *Wilderness First Aid* offers expert medical advice for dealing with outdoor emergencies beyond the reach of 911. It easily fits in most backcountry first-aid kits.

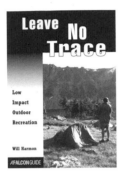

LEAVE NO TRACE

By Will Harmon
The concept of "leave no trace" seems simple, but it actually gets fairly complicated. This handy quick-reference guidebook includes all the newest information on this growing and all-important subject. This book is written to help the outdoor enthusiast make the hundreds of decisions necessary to protect the natural landscape and still have an enjoyable wilderness experience. Part of the proceeds from the sale of this book go to continue leave-no-trace education efforts. The Official Manual of American Hiking Society.

BEAR AWARE

By Bill Schneider
Hiking in bear country can be very safe if hikers follow the guidelines summarized in this small, "packable" book. Extensively reviewed by bear experts, the book contains the latest information on the intriguing science of bear-human interactions. *Bear Aware* can not only make your hike safer, but it can help you avoid the fear of bears that can take the edge off your trip.

MOUNTAIN LION ALERT

By Steve Torres
Recent mountain lion attacks have received national attention. Although infrequent, lion attacks raise concern for public safety. *Mountain Lion Alert* contains helpful advice for mountain bikers, trail runners, horse riders, pet owners, and suburban landowners on how to reduce the chances of mountain lion-human conflicts.

To order these titles or to find out more about this new series of books, call FALCON® at **1-800-582-2665.**